To Steve

see you at ...

Hope it carries on for many years

Graham

Into the Unknown

By Graham Walters

First published in Great Britain 2015
by Thurmaston Publishing

ISBN: 978-0-9935618-0-1

Printed by: Thurmaston Print Shop, 814 Melton Road,
Thurmaston, Leicester LE4 8BE
Telephone: 0116 269 5327 · email: tps@thurmaston.com

Introduction

Eighteen years should seem along time but its passing has gone with the expression, 'in a blink of an eye', but that's how long it is since I rowed the first race across The Atlantic and just six months later I had finished writing this account of this book.

Margaret, my wife sat diligently typing and correcting all my grammatical mistakes, the finished product would mean to me an everlasting memory.

That was it until 2014 when I met a young lad called Fred Walker through work and conversation turned to Atlantic rowing and the fact that I'd written about the first race. Fred asked if he could look at my writing project concerning the race and about a week later we met again and Fred asked if I had any ideas about turning it into a book. My reply probably sounded unenthusiastic. Undeterred, Fred expressed his opinion that it was well worth the effort, could he attempt to turn my amateur blog into a more easily readable narrative, having a degree in creative writing from Cambridge, he seemed ideally suited to the project and promised not to change any of my style of writing.

Dedication

To the memory of Margaret Walters sitting day after day typing and correcting without a single complaint, who lost the battle with cancer on the 10th October 2013.

I must also mention in this dedication Brett Mason who helped me construct the George Geary, without his help and encouragement the Atlantic Rows would not have been possible. Brett also died of cancer.

ACKNOWLEDGEMENTS

Many thanks to all the people who made my first row possible. I apologise if I've missed anyone out.

Firstly of course, Margaret Walters who helped and encouraged me. Keith Skidmore, my partner in the race who acquired some of the vital equipment for the boat.

Brett Mason who gave me unstinting help throughout the preparation in England, Rob Harrison who helped me with the boat, welding the makeshift trailer and then accompanying me to Tenerife where he worked every day with me preparing the boat.

Bob and Jenny Angell who sewed and made all the comfortable bedding, also sending out brochures for sponsors. Paul Blastock who edited the brochure, Jez Midmore for helping with the photographs. Pete and Liz Fleming who helped with the painting.

There are many more who helped with the first row including all the companies who sponsored items.

Thank you to you all.

Graham

PREFACE

Many people live a life of extreme adventure, whether sailing, climbing or venturing to distant parts of our world. I lived a life dictated by hard work and financial security. Like most adventurers, my youth was punctuated by what I like to refer to as "DIY adventure", that's, fishing, sailing, diving and anything you can do relatively cheap that poses minimal threat to your health. However it was only after marrying a very understanding wife I realised adventure was becoming hard work, financial security was becoming DIY and my chance to be the one climbing, sailing or venturing to the distant parts of our world was slipping away. So like any true adventurer I entered into the first Atlantic Rowing Race inexperienced and unprepared. At first and to no surprise, "it's only three thousand miles from Los Gigantes in Tenerife to Barbados" didn't bode too well with the wife, however, without her support and endless affection I embarked on my biggest challenge to date. The event was to be organized by Chay Blyth and his company, The Challenge Business. It would take place on 12th October 1997. My only previous experience of the Atlantic was four years prior when I crewed a delivery trip from Antigua to Falmouth, England. Little did I know I was to experience a tropical revolving storm with winds gusting up to 70mph in which, two boats were lost.

When I learned my application to join the Atlantic Rowing Race had been successful back in June 1995 I had no idea it would take over a year before I managed to find my rowing partner, Keith Skidmore. At the beginning he had high hopes of obtaining sponsorship through his many contacts in youth development, however by the time the 21st July 1997 came around I realised that with only two weeks holiday to the beginning of October and only two and a half months until the race, not only did I have to find the time to build the boat; I also had to find the finance to buy the materials to build it myself. Unless of course the minimum projected cost printed in Paul Blastock's three-page brochure of £30,000 was far too generous and the £220 I had raised in sponsorship could get us across the Atlantic. I was sure at that time I wanted to name the boat after my grandfather, George Geary, who is the only one of us to obtain any sort of fame. He was a well-known cricketer who had played for Leicestershire County Cricket Club and England for many years. To me, it seemed only right that I should honour him and name the boat after him.

With a month and a half to the race I had to make a decision, as it was obvious that the necessary sponsorship was not going to be forthcoming. My hopes of repaying the money already spent to keep our challenge on course, some ten thousand pounds part loan, part savings would have to be forgotten. I would have to borrow another ten thousand pounds or our hopes of entering the Atlantic Rowing Race were gone.

It was unstinting hard work and single mindedness that finally brought us to that position. It was the 11th October 1997, around 1.30pm. We stood looking out at sea thinking that in 20 hours 30 minutes the first Atlantic Rowing Race was to start. That thought may have been more daunting if it wasn't for the many jobs that still had to be completed before our Certificate of Entrance could be issued. I remember we were the last of the thirty boats that were taking part to be certified. We hadn't even been in the water to see if we'd sink or float. The first trip of our boat's life I looked forward to with interest. I was not worried by the fact that a larger number of our competitors had been practicing on river and sea for over a year. I knew their pedigree was not to be taken lightly. They came from Germany, America, France, Norway, Ireland and included British and New Zealand rowers.

As the race progressed I realised that in the rush to prepare I had not considered the long hours of physical and mental struggle whilst rowing, and alternatively, the hours off watch which I spent recuperating. A CD or cassette player might have been a grand idea. Luckily a few paperbacks had been thrown into my bag along with a thick scrapbook, this was to become my saviour. Slowly I slipped into a rowing routine and it was then I realised the need for mental exercise. Having turned fifty years of age it seemed a fitting time to look back over my life. So utilizing a good part of the three-hours I spent at the oars I tracked back through my memory. I would then write these thoughts down in the subsequent daylight hours when off watch. This was the exercise I set myself until the end of the crossing and by good fortune I found myself on the last page of the scrapbook with a mere 50 miles to go.

This is my adventure.

CONSTRUCTION BEGINS

21st July 1997

The only thing keeping my mind from the problems associated with building a twenty-four foot boat and rowing across the Atlantic is the low clattering sound of a diesel engine. 5.45am is too early for anyone's mind to wander - any insightful decisions are at least made after breakfast. Still, Wimborne's not too far - just a few more miles down the M1. The sun's beginning to poke it's head through the light grey clouds. I just hope the 'boat kit' from Laser Profiles fits onto the back of this two-ton Bedford pick-up I have borrowed.

The A31 into Wimborne – Uddens Trading Estate can't be that hard to find, can it? For anyone who wants to know, it's the first left, second right then the first right after you turn off for Ferndown. It's not easy to find, especially on an empty stomach at 6.00am but I'm here now and I don't know if I'm nervous or excited. I do wonder why I'm doing this. Maybe it's because of the large article published in the Daily Telegraph a few weeks ago: "BLYTH SETS OCEAN CHALLENGE TO RIVAL EVEREST." I mean, Chay Bylth and David Jackson have just rowed a new prototype boat under Tower Bridge and are now competing in the first Atlantic Boat Race. I've read their book about their Atlantic row and to experience what they experienced would, if nothing else, be a true adventure.

"Here's the appropriate paperwork Sir," said the seated figure behind the small front desk of Laser Profiles.

I'm now standing outside a large pair of steel doors. Curiosity has already gotten the better of me and I've peered through the gap. A large machine was slowly rising and falling over various materials sending sparks into the air. Partially obscured by the smoke was a large forklift truck carrying what looked like twenty sheets of plywood wrapped in polythene. The doors open.

"Your boat kit, Sir" said a voice I could not locate. Right, now my mind wanders, I better start the truck and let the low clattering sound of it's diesel engine drown out any doubts I have about the flat packed boat kit I've eagerly awaited.

Back on the road and my next port of call is Poole. I'm going to pick up all the epoxy material I need from the Glass-fibre Centre. Why so far from Leicester? Surely it would be easier to buy it closer to home. Unfortunately I am one of those people who don't make plans and it often leads me to make rash decisions. Luckily I have a head start as my good friend Bob has given me a half litre pack of slow hardener, one litre of fast, two litres of resin and a large plastic bag of sawdust to take the place of low density micro-balloons and micro-spheres. I guess with a head start it'd be ok if I stopped for breakfast. I could just drive down to Poole town quay, park in a suitable place and casually walk into the café I used to go to when my old east coast smack *Albion* was moored here.

Here I am, before what can only be described as a gastronomic expedition into the world of high cholesterol adventure. I cut a large slice of fried bread and poke it half-heartedly into the runny yoke of a fried egg. Now I'm eating I think it's fit to consider the enormous task that lies before me, but not for long. I need to walk this off, I'm 50 now. The town hasn't changed much and I don't know if it ever will. I like it here as it reminds me of the great storm of 1987.

Walking just past the Harbour Master's office, lo and behold I come across a large steel structure moored to the quay side. I've seen it before, I'm sure I have. It's the 65-ton monster pictured in the Daily Telegraph. The owner and creator of this artificial whale is none other than Tom McLean, the somewhat renowned Atlantic rower who has rowed twice from St John's, Canada to Ireland. I can't pass up an opportunity to climb aboard, even if I have to be somewhere shortly. It's still early – there's plenty of time.

"50 pence please," said a voice when I touch the deck.

"By all means," I say and without hesitation a large man with thick-rimmed glasses starts a guided tour. He explains the construction and layout of the whale, which was designed not only to spout water every few minutes but also to replicate the beautiful and somewhat sombre sounds of whale song.

I'm now standing in the Poole glass-fibre centre just having given a very vague and somewhat disjointed explanation of the size and make of the boat I'm about to build. I really hope it doesn't manifest itself into a problem a bit later; I have enough problems. I guess, you live and learn, don't you? Even if that expression is costly, it seems to alleviate a lot of hopeless situations. I wonder if have everything I need. Brushes, mixing pots, polythene gloves, epoxy resin, diluent, acetone, rolls of glass-fibre tape, colloidal silica…hand cleaner, I need hand cleaner.

"Excuse me, do you have any hand cleaner?" I say whilst holding the very large box of materials.

"Of course Sir, this way."

Everything I aimed to do today is done, perhaps not on time, but it's done nonetheless, so I can relax. Wareham isn't far and it's always been one of my favourite places. To me it's one of those unlucky places, but for some reason I feel at home there. Crossing the bridge next to the town's quay I realise the town is rammed with summer visitors. I pull into Arne car park and get out and walk briskly toward the dropping sun. Stopping at Shipstal Point I sit down and unload my flask, sandwiches and a slightly squashed piece of chocolate cake from my rucksack. After a short period of time my mind wanders. Outer, inner, jib, foresail, upper, main, stay-sail, course top gallant, royals, main sails, mizon, jigger, gaff and spanker all stretched taught, then, as if by command, the wind disappears leaving the sails of the boat I'm fixated by lifeless and impotent. Ouch, I've spilt coffee on my leg – what a lovely way to be brought back to your senses. Thinking about it, I probably should have put some onion in this sandwich rather than overcompensating with cheese, all that seems to be happening is big shards of hard cheddar are landing at my feet. Maybe I should put it down and allow a last memory to make me shudder.

It was October 1979 and having read the reports in the paper of horrendous damage along the south coast I was spun into action. Before I'd even had time to think about what to take with me, I was sitting behind the wheel of a large red Land Rover heading for Poole. I was dreading that first look across harbour to see if my boat, the

'Albion', was still above water. When I arrived boats of all descriptions lay high and dry, their masts broken. Ugly great scars opened their sides strewing wreckage all over the beach. Driving round that long curved road from Parkstone to Sandbanks was hard for me. I passed many unfortunate people that looked to their boats with sheer disbelief. The thought of my old sailing smack, one hundred years of sailing history lying on a muddy seabed terrified me. Eventually I pulled up on the side of the road and began to scan the main channel for it. There it was, still attached to a mooring buoy. From where I was standing the damage looked minimal, however I'd need a closer look. I quickly pumped up and launched an inflatable dinghy into the waves however I soon became aware that in my state of anticipation, I'd forgotten to fit the outboard engine or bring the oars - a mistake that cost me two very wet trouser legs. After a frantic episode of outboard fitting I motored up to the 'Albion' and to my amazement I noticed the boat was riding about twenty metres away from the mooring buoy. This seemed strange until I reached the low side of the boat. There, I realised the wind had pulled out the deck cleat that the anchor chain was attached to. It had also ripped out the hooded capping of the spurling pipe taking with it the slotted cover that traps the anchor chain. The wind was so strong that week that it had put so much pressure on the side of the boat that it drew a half- inch bolt and square washer through nine inches of Australian oak belonging to the stem head. The bow chain roller was no more.

22nd July, 1997

It's 7.30am and I'm in my front garden in Thurmaston, Leicester. I've just eaten two pieces of toast, drank two cups of tea and had a quick look at the paper. Looking around, I'm amazed to discover that there are far more things to move than I first thought. Making a space to build this boat is not going to be easy. Where's Brett Mason? He said he was going to help. He knows way more about epoxy than I do. I've only used it a couple of times to fill holes.

Now he's here I can reverse the pick-up into the garage, with his guidance of course. "Back a bit, back a bit, left hand down, steady, steady, watch it, right a bit more, stop…go forward, no steady." I said, "Stop!"

Bang!

"Ok, well I'm sure it won't take long to put those coping stones back." I said. At least the pick-up is in position now even if I have to rebuild a small wall. In no time the garage is covered in fifty to one hundred pieces of ply, all shapes and sizes and the driveway is waist high in off cuts. A few sandwiches, two fresh cups of tea and we are off again. By 4.30pm the last sheet of ply comes off the back of the pick-up and I manage to drive out of the front garden without knocking any more of the wall down.

23rd July 1997

The first half of the morning is spent arranging an array of milk-crates, bricks, and blocks of timber. Most of which pass through a rickety Work-Mate, which over the years has lost a few necessary support screws. As my spirit level has been working over time I think it's fair that me and Brett take a seat in my, not so comfortable, garden chairs and admire our work.

"Right, I'm going to the Golf course Graham." said Brett.

"Oh…" I say, unable to complain as his assistance has been, and will always remain unpaid.

The rest of the afternoon is spent on my own. I pull out various pieces of scaffolding from the rotting rack behind the shed. It's needed as it's going to become the front wall of the temporary boathouse. I don't know how my wife, Margaret will feel, but I'm planning to attach the makeshift shed to the front of our bungalow so it can act as a back wall. Obviously it'll need to be sheltered from the rain. I'm sure I have some tarpaulin somewhere...

24th July 1997

It's 8.00am and Brett seems refreshed - perhaps it's the golf. After a cup of strong tea we find a large piece of tarpaulin I knew I had and pull it over the scaffolding. The sun's shining today - it'd be a shame to work in the shade. I guess I could make the covering tarpaulin removable. But how can I do that? Maybe if I fit eyes all along the fascia board just below the gutter I can feed some ropes through them, although I'd need to fix the ropes to something.

"Any ideas Brett?"

Two cups of tea later there are four-inch nails banged in the under side of all the windowsills, which incidentally need painting.

"Let's crack on then." I said quietly so as not to alert the wife.

25th July 1997

"Right Brett, let's stick the first section together."

By that I mean, teach me how to mix epoxy. I won't be admitting that. We start mixing small amounts of various epoxy materials all of which are rather alien to me. Using the off cuts of ply, we make about ten 'T' shaped test pieces by sticking one to the other. Slowly we work in the newly mixed epoxy to form different sized fillets, about half an inch in depth.

By 12.30pm we have six 'T' shaped pieces of ply that are about twelve inches square that have low-density fillets. These range from about a quarter of an inch to three quarters of an inch. We've also got six with high-density fillets. The high-density fillets will have micro-fibres mixed in as a filler to strengthen the joint whereas the low ones will be mixed with sawdust. It's a bit radical but sawdust is cheap. With the way the sponsorship is looking I'm going to need to save every penny I can. So if all goes according to plan when these fillets cure and we break them up we'll find broken ply and not epoxy.

26th July 1997
7.30am is not the best time to discover you have two very large droops in your tarpaulin. It must have rained heavily last night. Standing on our new work- table and acting like a telescopic flagpole I'm able to force the water off the tarpaulin and onto the ground. There's not much else I can do before the fillets are ready to break this afternoon so it'll be an early lunch.

After a healthy salad sandwich and yogurt, it's destruction time. I put on my steel toe-capped boots and begin to stamp on the test pieces. I can see Brett trying to look away. He's laughing at me. After five minutes of the energetic war dance it's time to inspect the shattered pieces. It's looking good…really good actually. Only the very thin fillets have broken on the joint, the rest have broken the ply, which gives us an indication of the size of fillets required. It's time to start filleting the pieces we've put together. I am still not used to mixing the right quantities of epoxy. This becomes obvious when, after ten minutes, I'm left holding a smoking plastic cup, which is now red-hot. Like an idiot I accidentally brush a small amount over my leg which sends me into a different kind of dance.

"I'll never know where you get all your energy from at this time of day," is Brett's only comment but before I have time to answer a call for coffee comes from inside the bungalow.

27th July 1997

I knew that was too much marmalade. Who'd have thought marmalade would be so hard to wipe off. Right, that'll have to do - I need to get to get to rugby. We've got a 'friendly' today.

Aylestone St James Rugby Ground isn't half as glorious as it might sound. In fact, it's probably in worse condition than my front garden. Apparently we're short of players today - which I suppose is to be expected at a pre-season friendly. I have heard there are some players coming from Westleigh Rugby Club though. That gives me time to go to the bar.

A few short introductions, a quick change into my rugby kit and that familiar smell of Deep Heat and Vaseline. Now comes the unenthusiastic 'warm up'. Perhaps I shouldn't have had that pint of beer. Although it has meant I've ended up in the Rugby shirt no one wants and it's full of holes, which will provide minor ventilation on such a hot day. Before long the game gets off to a quick start and I find myself looking up from between our prop and hooker at the opposing team, is he smiling? The opposing hooker usually grimaces. "Graham!" What am I doing? I've lost concentration.

After a refreshing bath I find myself at the bar with Keith – 'the smiler' (sic).

"Yeah, a couple of my friends have entered the race." he said.

"The main problem is finding a partner. I mean, my friend Brett is helping me build the boat but I don't think he's up to the challenge. I'm at the point now where I don't know where else to look. I've asked almost everyone I know." I said.

"Well, it's something I'd certainly consider doing."

I wonder if Keith was serious or if it was the beer talking. We did get through quite a few. He seems like a nice guy though. Time's running out and I can't do this alone. He said he'd give it some thought. I guess all I can do is wait.

28th July 1997

It's finally time to fit the 18 planks of various sizes and make this boat more recognisable as something that one day, might actually be buoyant.

Walking around the bare boned construction forcing hot toast into my mouth I can only admire our handy work. The time seems to have flown by. We've already mixed the quantity of epoxy I assumed would complete the entire boat and we're only about half way. I do wonder what else I might have underestimated. Still, Brett's here now and we've got dry fitting to do. Dry fitting for those who don't know isn't as technical as you might assume it's just holding a piece of wood where it will be fitted and marking where it needs to be sawn off to fit properly. I must confess I've not given much thought to how this will go; it can't go wrong, can it? Yep, plank 'BP2' doesn't fit and now I'm scratching my head. I'm sure if I had a beard, I'd be scratching that too.

'What have we done wrong Brett?" I said checking the other planks, but they're the same. We can't have miscalculated. "Right, I'm going to ring Matt."

"Ok", Matt said, "due to 'changes', it's an unavoidable problem", so that's helpful! This isn't something I needed to hear right now as I was starting to worry.

"So what are we going to do?" said Brett.

"Cut off the tabs and hold the plank in place with cramps and pins."

"Cramps and pins?"

"Yeah, G gramps, sash cramps."

"Well today's going to be..."

"Long."

29th July 1997

As I prepare to do my usual early morning inspection round the boat, the phone rings. I've been dreading this call all week - problem time at work. Up until now my two week holiday had been free from disruptions. I pick up the phone to a rather muffled voice that said, "We've ran out of bricks Graham."

For bricklayers there aren't many bigger problems and as I'm paying them by the day I respond despondently with, "I'll sort it out."

Leaving Brett a note, off I went to fix the problem, yet "Sorry, no chance of a delivery today sir" was the depressing reply from behind the desk of the Builders Merchant. "Why?" I say, hoping it's something I can help with.

"Wheel's gone and come off."

"What?"

"Yeah, off the trailer mate, so can't deliver them today."

"Well do you have the bricks?"

"Yeah we have the bricks."

There is an awkward pause whilst the man looks at me through glazed eyes.

There's not many faster ways to decrease the value of your car than cramming the boot full of bricks and a piling bags of cement and breeze blocks on the other four seats.

Slowly driving out of the Builders Merchants I have a daunting sense of déjà vu. A few years ago I was standing across the road trying to explain to a police officer why I had four-hundredweight bags of cement on my car bonnet. I tried to explain it was counter balancing the six hundredweight bags of building sand I had in the boot but I still got the three points and a £40 fine, the charge being 'unsecured load' as there was nowhere to lash the cement.

30th July 1997

I am surprised my wife's 'boat building blues' hadn't come sooner. She can no longer gaze out of the window and admire the flower arrangements in our front garden due to the large tent like construction spread along the front of the bungalow.

"It looks like a desert encampment Graham." she said and as much as I want to tell her how the view from the front window is now very educational in terms of modern boat building techniques, I don't think she'd appreciate it. Maybe I should get out of the house.

Would it be too soon to call Keith? Surely he's made a decision by now.

"Keith." I say, shocked that he's picked up the phone so quickly.

"Graham, how are you?"

"I'm good thanks mate, I was just wondering if you've had time to think it all through?"

"Well yeah, like I said before, I'm really interested."

"I hate to pressure you it's I just need to write to the Challenge Business in the next few days and give them the name and address of my partner or I won't be allowed to enter."

"Then do it."

"What?"

"Give them my name and address."

31st July 1997

It's not Saturday yet but I can already tell it's going to be a day of Saturday food. Perhaps it's because I'm grateful that I've found my rowing partner but I'm sitting in front of bacon, eggs, black pudding, sausages, beans, tomatoes, mushrooms and a very questionable piece of fried bread. Brett's not coming today, I think he needs a day free of stress. However due to the concerns voiced by my wife yesterday I've asked Alan, an old diving buddy, and Rob another close friend of mine to come along instead.

Both Alan and Rob are picking up the technique of mixing and applying epoxy quite quickly, certainty a lot quicker than I did. Between us, we've planed the last bevels off the boat. Today's one of those days I've had the tarpaulin off. The sun's been beating down all day and as it is now four o'clock a unanimous decision has been made by the garden chairs: it's time for a few cans of ice-cold beer.

4th August 1997
The last few days have been sensible - toast in the morning, a bowl of quiet Corn Flakes in the afternoon and steady progress has been made but today I have to go back to work. The bricklayers have finished which means it's time for me to get up on the roof. I ring Brett and tell him I'll leave him the keys and I'll aim to be back at the boat by four.

It is a long day and when I eventually get to the gym I fall asleep on the weight-lifting machine. A loud voice wakes me up eventually, "Come on it's time to go or you'll be left in here all night."

5th August 1997
Up at 5.30am, I'm determined to get back to the boat earlier. After a gruelling seven hours I'm back at the boat by 2.15pm. I've explained the situation to the people I'm working for and they seem to be OK with it. Brett has done an amazing job considering he's been on his own which makes me feel guilty.

"Get to the golf-course Brett."

6th August 1997
Getting out of bed at 6.30am I know it is just me today, there's no pressure from outside. I fit the last plank to the hull then start to plane the angles for the shape. I begin with my bull-nose plane (short then long), rebate, jack and try plane. This is not the time to re-kindle old trade skills that have been long forgotten. Time is the God of modern day construction, electricity - the driving force...I do like seeing all these shiny

planes though. I'm even tempted to take down some of the wooden planes that are in our living room and use them but I'm sure that Margaret wouldn't share my enthusiasm. She never allows me to forget she must follow me around with dustpan and brush. However recently her domain excludes the front garden. It's now ankle deep in wood shavings.

7th August 1997

It's 5.15am or so the clock said. I'm sure it lies sometimes. Sleep is not possible now. My mind races through all problems that might occur as today's the day we're going to flip the boat over. I've asked two friends Gaz and Pete, who are working in Coventry at the moment, to come and give me a hand first thing in the morning before they set off.

Standing around the boat we look at each other before I ask, "Are you all ready?"

"Wait, how are we going to do this?' said Gaz.

To which I reply "I'm not entirely sure."

"What do you mean you're not sure?' said Pete.

"Let's just give it a go."

Ten minutes later the boat has been flipped. I'm sure Laurel and Hardy would have begged us to film it if they were still alive. Today Brett prepares to finish the upper bulkhead. All I can do is promise to be back as soon as possible to help. I thank the team and get to work because although I've fixed the roof it's time to lath and felt it. I'm thinking if I miss my lunch break and any other break I'd usually take I might be able to get it done by 3.00pm.

8th August 1997

A banging on the door wakes me. It can't be 7.30am, can it? Yes... The alarm I set for 6.00am didn't wake me up. Now there's no time for toast, or even a cup of tea. Dashing outside, I see Brett, but there's barely time to speak. As I drive out of the driveway there's a horrendous crashing noise. Oh, that's not what I think it is, is it? One of the ropes attached to the tarpaulin had become tangled in the luggage rack on my car. Reluctantly I look out of the driver's window and...Oh my God. Half of the temporary boathouse is now a tangled mess on the ground, and, as if this was not bad enough, a ghostly apparition starts rising from under the white tarpaulin. "Brett, are you ok?" Brett grunts. "Right, I'll ring and tell them I'm going to be late today."

9th August 1997

I'm up early this Saturday. I need to make up for the damage done yesterday.

There's smoke rising from the frying pan before anyone else on the street is up. The only noise that disturbs my culinary arts is the clatter of the letterbox. Not more bills...although it could be another letter from the Challenge Business. I still remember the day I received the letter stating that my application to join the race had been accepted. It also informed me of an opportunity to attend a sponsorship seminar at the Southampton Boat Show where there would be a chance to see the prototype boat that was being constructed.

I thought the seminar was a great success. It gave me a chance to meet the project co-ordinator, Matthew Ratsey, and, of course, the man himself, Chay Blyth, who was the speaker.

First there was a video covering his and John Ridgeway's Atlantic crossing, then, as always, question time. After, there was a chance to see a completed boat, which stood outside. The only regret I had of the day was not studying the construction of the prototype boat enough, which should have been a top priority. The bacons burning! Right, that's enough daydreaming there's work to be done.

10th August 1997

It is time to start taping inside the hull. As it is awkward, smaller amounts of epoxy are mixed. I decide to tape the bulkheads first, concentrating on the area where they meet the planks. Rob helps me for a couple of hours in the morning while Margaret keeps us supplied with strong coffee. I work until about 3.00pm then it's off to the gym before it closes at 4.00pm.

11th August 1997

Monday seems to have come around so quickly. Brett is full of enthusiasm today and as usual he quickly inspects the work I've done over the weekend. This is usually accompanied by the verbal probe, "Everything okay, no problems?" I answer him as concisely as possible before leaving him with a string of excuses and head back to work.

Back at work, it's time to start putting the tiles on the roof. Dave has already loaded the scaffold with tiles, much to my delight. It's a gruelling process and allows me too much time to think and at present all I can think about is the mounting problems we face when building the boat. Before long I'm on the roof doing what I have to do to get home in time.

4.00pm approaches as I drive under the tarpaulin and come to a stop just short of the bending figure who informs me that he can't get up until all the epoxy has been used up.

12th August 1997

I slam the front door, put the key under a brick on the boat and rush off. The PVC patio doors and windows are ready to pick up. Normally the window company would deliver them but they're short of drivers so they are going to lend me their van. Everything seems to be against me actually working on the boat. At first I consider leaving the job about 3.00pm but after a while a better idea comes to mind. Why don't I carry on until about 6.00pm then have the day off tomorrow and work on the boat? I'll pick Dave up in the morning and he can finish off the tiling. Seems like a good idea.

13th August 1997

After dropping off Dave I arrive back home just as Brett pulls up. "How long can I expect to have your personal touch today?" he said.

"All day today." I reply.

"Really?"

"Yeah I worked late last night, didn't you notice?"

"And there was me thinking you were going to leave the rest to me."

"I couldn't do that. I intend to float, not sink."

The morning is spent on the lateral joints in the planks, filling and taping, mainly to the inside hull. It's very windy today; so windy in fact, I should probably tighten the tarpaulin ropes. As the wind picks up, conversation becomes almost impossible. The tarpaulin flaps erratically and then, crash! I look at Brett, our eyes wide, both of us hoping that on the other side of the white sheet there's not another unexpected job requiring our attention. Hesitantly I make my way over to the entrance of the boathouse and to my horror the cover, plus the timbers under it have blown off the top of my sailing dinghy, the only object outside our temporary boathouse. I agree to replace the dinghy covers as Brett carries on with the taping.

Looking at the open dinghy now laid bare, showing all it's broken and splintered plywood hull, a sense of guilt came over me.

Ten months ago I hadn't sailed in almost a year. At last, an opportunity had appeared in the shape of a return to the island where my wife's parents, both now deceased, were born. For my wife, Margaret it was to be sentimental journey and for me a chance for some exciting sailing. The island is Barra in the Outer Hebrides of Scotland, lying between South Uist and Vatersay. It protects the north west coast of Scotland from the fury of the Atlantic Ocean. Unfortunately, as with most great holiday plans, the weather was awful. The first day we ventured out from the small stone house belonging to Margaret's cousin Sarah, a strong northwesterly wind was blowing. Walking down the narrow road from Eoligarry to where the North Atlantic meets the white sandy beach, a picture of nature's relentless power burst into view. Great white and blue rollers broke with incredible force as the endless roaring noise deafened us. As for me, in any other circumstances, I would be in awe of the spectacle, but as I intended to sail, it was rather daunting. Not wanting to spoil the first day of our holiday I proposed a long walk to give us a hearty appetite and I assured Margaret, things would be okay for a sail tomorrow.

The next morning I felt slightly optimistic, although the wind was still blowing it had dropped slightly. Before I had time to change my mind, the dinghy was driven down to the beach, rigged and launched. After a quick sail up and down the Sound of Fuday, we stopped at Fuday Island for lunch, so far so good. The dinghy seemed to be sailing quite well under reefed main sail and small jib so I figured it would be alright if I took it for a more broad reaching sail, almost due south towards the Sound of Hellisay. Soon out of the shelter of the land I discovered what the weather conditions were truly like. Great gusts of wind laid the boat over on it's side, desperately I tried to spill wind from it's sails.

After reaching the small island of Greenamul I changed tack onto a broad reach heading for the headland of Rubha Fada then back to a run in sheltered water. Feeling confident I started steering northeast towards the small island of Sgeiran Mora. Knowing that the tide was running through the Sound of Fuday towards me, I should have been more alert. As I'd gone through the motions of tacking and jibing earlier on I was quite confident of my ability to sail the boat where I wanted, not really considering the fact that I had practiced all these manoeuvres in sheltered water. I was going to leave these small islands starboard but before long I encountered another problem - it was only about one and a half hours to high water. As I cleared the islands I saw white water and seaweed ahead so I began to tack immediately through the wind. I tried again and failed, finally jibing. Bang! Suddenly I was thrown against the sails, down went the mast throwing me over the side. On my knees I grabbed for the jib sheet as the dinghy was pounded against the rocks but it wouldn't come up. All I could do then was to try to drag the boat south over the reef but it wouldn't move. At last the boat was freed and just in time I jumped aboard as it tore down wind. Eventually I managed to bring the boat under control. I sailed back the way I came reaching the small outer islands of the headland. There, I began to tack back and forth which quickly brought me into Northbay. Another hour saw me tacking by the slip to the fish factory at Ardveenish. There was a large stone slip by the side of the road and sailed as near as I could. Jumping out in shallow water I tied a line to an old and weathered fishing boat. Darkness fell and after a long day's sailing and some near disasters, the only damage I could see were the many gouges in the paintwork.

14th August 1997

The boat is now at the stage where it needs to be water tested. There are two ways we can do this. Either, we carry the boat down to the river, which could present a few problems or we leave it where it is and fill it full of water. The big advantage of filling it full of water is that all the separate compartments can be tested for leaks individually. As there are eighteen compartments it's probably best if this is how it's tested. Still that'll have to wait until tomorrow, Brett's playing golf (again) and there's still work to be done on the roof.

I'm nervous today. Potentially there may be a lot more work to do than we previously thought. More post? I could oil the letterbox, although hearing the post arrive recently provides momentary release from my anxiety. What's come through the letterbox today is a large brown envelope from the Challenge Business. 'URGENT'. That's one way to get my attention. It's from Meridian Broadcasting, asking if we want to install video cameras on our boat for a two-part documentary. It does sound interesting but they are asking for financial help towards the cost of setting up the cameras. If we had any money to spare, we wouldn't be using sawdust to replace mandatory parts of the boats workings. The letter then goes to inform us of the tracking beacon that we will have to carry. Apparently after doing some research they have decided on the Argos beacon, which can also act as a safety device as it has it's own power pack with a 'distress' button that can be activated in an emergency. The letter also informs us of a medical kit for sale from a company called BCB but before I can read any further a voice said, "This is no time to correspond Graham, we've got a boat to fill with water." As I was immersed in the letter I hadn't heard Brett pull up.

"Right, where are we starting?" said Brett holding a hosepipe.

"Anywhere. The bow? I mean if we fill all the compartments that are separated from each other we'll be able to see if it's leaking internally."

Brett now begins to fill the bow with the hose. After a few compartments are full it's time for a check. The good news is that there are no leaks externally, but there are a few leaks between compartments, mainly just under the deck support. That's better that expected. 'Right Brett, put a mark on that leak.' I say whilst marking the one closest to me. The idea is that when Rob arrives we'll be able to move the water from one compartment to another.

Rob's finally here and as promised he's brought his submersible pump from the concrete plant. This combined with the bilge pump I have from the *Albion*, should make light work of transferring the water...we'll see.

15th August 1997

Yesterday went well considering our lack of experience. I mean, we had to nail some of the planks in - not the most professional way of doing things especially when building something to get you across the Atlantic, but still, there were no leaks (externally). I'd love to stay and give Brett a hand but there's a lot of skirting board and a few hanging doors that require my attention. Sorry Brett, it's down to you again today. At least it's Friday...

16th August 1997

Today we're fitting the floors in the boat. We're going to put foam under them before we seal them shut. I think making them removable would only mean more work during the race. Also, if we get a hole in one of the foam filled compartments it won't allow the seawater to enter. That's the plan anyway. I guess if we got a large hole the seawater could affect the buoyancy but fingers crossed.

I start with the first floorboard, spraying the foam in large layers. It begins to expand immediately but not at the rate I was hoping for. At this rate I'm going to need at least three cans just to fill this one space and I only picked up four for the whole boat. Right, that's it. In future I'm going to make sure I overcompensate for everything. I don't have time to keep running around.

Time is running out. Brett has brought with him some large sheets of polystyrene, which we cut into small shapes and fit them under the floor. The last can of foam goes around the polystyrene and no more discussions are necessary. Brett had the bright idea of weighing it all down with blue house bricks until the foam has set. The weight from the bricks should mean it's airtight. It appears to be working.

By the end of the day all the floorboards are fitted and cleaned. The other six are planed and ready to fit. Today has been one of those hot sunny days. In the morning I untied the tarpaulin. (Still can't get over how much of a great idea that was). By five o'clock we've cleared up and we're sitting down, hands around two ice-cold beers. They taste so good that we have to have two more, and then two more. Before long I'm on a frantic search for long forgotten bottles of beer. I could swear we had more in the fridge. There must be some around here somewhere. Bingo, we're in luck! 'Mort Sabit' or in English: certain death. Perhaps a fitting name for the thick drizzle that is, Belgian beer. I think the only exercise I'll manage today is collecting the empty bottles.

17th August

Today didn't start with my usual inspection, tea in hand. Rather, it was a slow stroll holding a glass of water in one hand and a small bottle of Paracetamol in the other. But hey, self-indulgence never got in the way of great work, so I'm trying to make some progress with the floors. After a well earned sit down the phone rings. It's Keith, my rowing partner. He explains that Andy Baker, a photographer from The Leicester Mercury (our local evening paper), will be calling here tomorrow. He said he's already given a brief outline to the columnist but we'll see about that.

18th August 1997

It is time for the fore deck and bow stem to be filled with foam and polystyrene. Once that's done we'll put in epoxy fillets all round to strengthen it. By the time Keith turns up most of the donkeywork has been done and I've completely forgotten about the photographer.

The photographer arrives and immediately starts taking photographs of us, in and out of the boat - much to the amusement of Brett and Rob. I'm trying very hard to look natural but I don't really know what to do with my hands. Is this an appropriate pose - hand on the chin? No that's far too pretentious. I could put them in my pockets – although I'm sitting down, that'll probably look weirder. This is harder than fitting the floor. Still, it'll be over soon.

19th August 1997

I dropped Dave off at 7.30am to carry on with the roof, which means I'm back home just in time for the post. Today brings another letter from the Challenge Business. It's a notice from Doctor Campbell MacKenzie. MacKenzie is the Medical Officer for both the British Steel and the British Telecom yacht races. So I'm eager to read what he has to say. Fitness training, food and water intake, calorie content, multi-vitamins…I've not even thought about eating during the race, still, I don't have time for that today. I continue reading and I get to the heading 'AS THEY SAY IN AUSTRALIA' This is intriguing, especially as it follows a very technical example fitness plan. 'SLEEP before you are tired, DRINK before you are thirsty, EAT before you are hungry, COVER UP before you are cold or burnt and keep your urine clear, your bowels open and your breath fresh.' A slight contrast there – still, better press on.

23rd August 1997

It's Saturday again - a relaxing breakfast reading the morning paper before Alan comes over to help. The past few days have been spent finishing the keel. If I'm honest I'm quite surprised how well things are going and although there's still a lot to be done, the boat is really starting to come to life. The hull is now constructed, all the panels are in place.

Alan has agreed to help me this morning. All goes well as we work on the second panel to the aft cabin. Alan leaves and Rob arrives to carry on with the upper section.

24th August 1997

There's nothing more exciting than when a rear cabin comes together. It's almost complete! Surely we'll be able to finish it in good time. All of the side panels are in place now, which means that tomorrow we can fit the roof.

26th August 1997

Good progress is made today; the bull-works are planed, tested and finally fitted. Although the boat is looking good, I'm nervous about the coming week. My business partner, Gary, is getting married on Saturday - obviously that's not the problem, I quite like his wife – the problem is that he's taking two weeks off to go on their honeymoon. He's leaving, not one, but two jobs, both of which are incomplete. That means the two considerably large roof conversions in Coventry are now my problem. Oh, and if that wasn't bad enough, the extension I've been working on in Leicester still needs finishing. Sorry Brett...

27th August 1997

Another envelope from the Challenge Business pokes through the letterbox. Point 8.4 of the Class Rules...what does that mean? It must be about the height of the rudder. I thought they'd relax about this. No less than eight inches or more than fourteen inches is far too specific. The letter also requests a marine surveyor's report which will give us permission to take our boat out to sea. They'll also need a copy of our personal insurance certificates - I've not even thought about that. Well, at least I'm getting their letters now. After I entered the race I received no correspondence for five months. In hindsight my nerves could have been cooled if I had decided to contact them sooner. A couple of days after my call I finally received photocopies of all of my missing post accompanied by a very sincere letter of apology. For a brief moment I felt a great weight lift from me, but then I read on. I'd missed an opportunity to go to St Katherine's Race Weekend. There, I could have met some of the other rowers entering the race. Not only that, I could have looked over their boats. Still, can't dwell on that, time to get back to the boat.

28th August 1997

My early morning inspection leads me to the conclusion that I should probably cut part of the bulwarks away from around the seat. I may as well make the row as pleasant as possible. Just as I clear the tools away Gary calls to say he won't be working at Coventry tomorrow as he has last minute wedding arrangements to make. I'd better ring Brett and let him know the score. Hopefully Rob will be able to come give him a hand.

29th August 1997

One of the biggest jobs left is filling and sanding. Today I have no option but to leave Brett and Rob to it. As for me it's off at 7.00am to pick up our new overenthusiastic labourer, Will. I'm not certain he knows what he's doing, and he's not very good at pretending he knows what he's doing either. Still, there's plenty of time to drop some subtle hints if I take a steady drive to Coventry.

30th August 1997
I spend the morning sanding the far side of the rear cabin. This will make it ready to fitting the deck boards. Would it be wrong to not shower before a wedding? That way I could get more done, although I'm not sure if Margaret would appreciate that. I better stop soon…

We join Rob and his wife Jan in the local pub not far from the Church. Let's just hope they don't realise I've not had a shower. After this beer we're going to make our way to the church. Rob said Gary's going to be wearing a top hat and tails - I'm not sure if I'll be able to keep a straight face.

31st August 1997
"She's dead." screams Margaret, which is one way to get any man out of bed regardless of how hung-over they may be.

Who's dead?' I say rushing into the sitting room.

"Diana."

"What?"

"Princess Diana is dead." Margaret said.

"What?"

What tragic news. The early start I wanted now becomes a late one. I'm glued to the television, completely baffled by the breaking news. Eventually I drag myself away and begin fitting the aft decks, marking the area below them so that at a later date I can cut out all of the openings for the individual compartments.

1st September 1997

It's up and out today - not forgetting to leave the keys for Brett. His plan is to fit the starboard rowing deck and mine is to start cutting out the floor hatches in the aft cabin when I return home at four o'clock. Everything goes roughly according to plan. I arrive home from the gym at ten o'clock. As I've been up since six o'clock this morning I'm pretty sure I'll be asleep before my head touches the pillow.

3rd September 1997

Yesterday Brett fixed the port rowing deck. I'm in another rush to leave the house today but before I can, the phone rings.

"Hi Graham it's Steve."

"Who?"

"Steve - the plumber - Gary gave me your number."

"Oh, hi mate, are you alright?"

"Listen, I can't fix the pipes until the floor's laid."

That's not what I needed to hear today. Right, I better get to Coventry.

After a couple of hours of hard work there's a ring at the door. Will quickly jumps to his feet and goes to answer it.

"Hi Mate." said a familiar voice.

It's Brett. What's he doing in Coventry when he should be working on the Boat?

Then it dawns on me, I forgot to leave him the keys.

4th September 1997

Today brings good news for us. The people who own the house we've been working on have decided to go on holiday tomorrow and want us to down tools until they return. At last, something is going our way.

6th September 1997

Not much work was done in the last two days, still, we now have two glorious days to work on the boat. Just as I begin to cut the last hatches out in the rear, Alan arrives. I set him to work gluing O rings around the outside of the hatches and then out of nowhere…bacon and egg sandwiches. What a lovely wife I have.

7th September 1997

The rain wakes me. I look at the clock 5.55am. The rain's so heavy I'd better check the tarpaulin. Today is one of those grey, dark mornings. As I open the front door there is a loud ripping noise and before I can do anything the tarpaulin pulls free and the makeshift shed collapses on Margaret's car. I guess the silver lining is that I was in need of a pressure wash. Also, there's now no trapped water lying directly above the boat. But before I sort that out maybe I should get the morning paper. In fact, it'd be rude not to. At least that's what I'll tell myself.

Once the boat shed has been sorted I start filling the hull to get a final shape. Rob arrives and begins sanding. The end is sight…although it still needs painting.

8th September 1997

Because today I'm working virtually around the corner, I decide to spend the morning working on the boat, that is, after I've dropped off Will. I return just as Brett pulls up. This is our first early meeting since I started working in Coventry and today there's a lot to discuss. One of the main topics of conversation is the open deck hatches. The ones suggested by the Challenge Business: the Lewmar Ocean sixty, forty and thirty seem ideal. Also, we need to consider the rowing deck, although we've decided to use the ply hatches supplied under the seats, the area each side was a different matter.

There are still a few things we need: E bolts, U bolts, rudder attachments, electrical items etc. I think a large spending spree is necessary. The day before I noticed an advert for the Southampton Boat Show next week, which no doubt will have every conceivable item connected with boating on display. I'm sure there are bargains to be had.

After starting work on the boat a car pulls up, the owner gets out and introduces himself. "Stuart Ashby." he said. Keith had already told me about Stuart. He's kindly offered to supply all of the anti-fouling necessary for the boat - a gesture we could not refuse. He explains it's a reasonably new product called Halcyon 5000. After unloading the paint Stuart spends quite some time going over the boat. He gives us some useful advice, explaining the paint mixtures and curing times. The timing couldn't be better. We're painting tomorrow. But now I need to check on Will. He's probably wandering around the property looking confused.

9th September 1997

"There must be some paint brushes around here somewhere."

"You don't have paintbrushes Graham?" said Brett.

"I do, I just can't find them…Aha!"

"What's that?"

"It's a paintbrush…I think."

"Do you not think we should get some new ones?"

"It's fine, just need to blow the sawdust off. Look…"

Stuart walks in carrying in the Halcyon 5000 data sheet.

"What's that?" said Stuart.

"It's a paint brush" I said.

His eyes widen.

As I leave Brett to get on with the painting I remember a phone call I should have made. I needed to sort out the passage for the boat to Tenerife. Yanking the gearstick into reverse the worn brakes squeal. In the time it takes to say, "I'm not stopping Brett, carry on with the painting," I am discussing shipment with Steve Richardson of Interglobal. He informs me that most of the remaining boats are being shipped on the 25th September from Felixstowe. Let's hope those forms arrive soon.

10th September 1997

I can't sleep. Horrific visions of an unfinished boat being thrown about by enormous waves plague my mind. I think today's going to be one of those days where I panic. We've got loads left to do, we've got things we need to buy - wait, what are we going to lie on when we sleep? Gulping down a scorching hot cup of tea, I grab a tape measure, pencil and sheet of paper and walk out into the crisp, early morning air. Ok, Graham, time to draw.

"Are you drawing?" said Brett when he finally arrives.

"I'm thinking we make six foam filled cushions of varying sizes covered in waterproof fabric, plus two extra for the seats." I say in my panicked state.

"What are you talking about?"

"What are we going to sleep on?"

"Do you mean what are *you* going to sleep on?"

"Seriously. Right, you carry on painting I need to ring some foam suppliers."

After I had called the suppliers regarding the foam, I join Brett, painting. A van then pulls up. On the side in big red letters is written Carlines Motor Factors and out comes a familiar figure. It's Dick, my rugby and sailing buddy. True to his word, he's brought two new large batteries suitable to provide us with enough power for our trip.

Another van pulls up, the back doors swing open and there, to my amazement, stand sixty, five litre containers of Buxton spring water. Now I think back, Keith said Buxton would be supplying the entire amount necessary. After stacking all of the water in the garage it was Brett's turn to amaze me. He arrives with eighty, five litre plastic containers with separate tops for carrying water. More unloading. I am starting to wonder – is the boat going to take all of this?

11th September 1997

Brett's still painting. To be honest I'm surprised he's doing such a good job. Who would have thought a pattern maker would be so dexterous with a brush?

"Do you know where the last piece of the rudder is Brett?" Brett shot me a look of amazement before pointing to the maze of materials, now pushed into a haphazard heap at the back of the garage. At last I find it high up in the timber rack. Frustration takes over as I pull and twist this stubborn piece of ply from the rack. Crack, a piece breaks off and comes flying off along with most of the contents of the rack. I look on helplessly as a domino effect has started on the rack above. Small pieces of skirting, architrave, boarding and oddly shaped pieces of timber now cascade about my head. Thud! Two large lengths of wood connect with bone and brain bowling me over backwards. As the dust settles Brett said loudly, "You okay in there?"

"Yes." I reply, "no broken bones."

"You worried me, don't think I'm going to take your place rowing."

Slowly getting to my feet I look down at the offending items. Two halves of a hollow mast, about 20' long.

12th September 1997
When I came round yesterday I almost managed to put the rudder together. Think I'm going to need to ask Alan for some help, he's always saying how good he is at puzzles. In fact I'm sure I've heard him boast about it. Today, Brett starts applying an undercoat while I nip off to work on the extension until after lunch. When I get back I meet a rather grey coloured Brett and he tells me that automatic pilot systems are still banned after much discussion. This doesn't really bother me as they are out of our price range anyway, as are water makers and wind generators. We do, however, require a sunshade cover, not just for the sun but we're thinking it'll keep the rain and seawater away from the cooking area.

4th September 1997
After my early morning inspection I decide to read the Class Rules of the race in more detail…over breakfast, of course. 'IN THE EVENT THAT THE BOAT AND IT'S EQUIPMENT HAS TO BE DESTROYED, NO LIABILITY SHALL BE ACCEPTED BY THE RACE ORGANISER.' That's really not a friendly sentence. I wonder if I can unread that. Nope. I guess that

means if we're not close to land and we have to give up the boat will be sunk. Lovely. Right, that's enough of that, better crack on.

15th September 1997

I spend the morning away from the boat. Brett tells me today he's going to apply the anti-fouling (under strict orders). As taking into consideration the ultra violet sunlight at the surface, I thought it best to ask Brett to apply the anti-fouling six inches above the waterline. We have enough paint, so it's best to play it safe. After that I think he's going to see an old friend, as he might be able to help us out with some proper paint for the boat. Reading the Class Rules yesterday means the only colour I could possibly chose is orange. It's bright and means it'd be easier to see us at sea. I really shouldn't be being paid right now, I'm spending more time thinking about all of the things we need as we are going to the Boat Show tomorrow.

16th September 1997

It's just getting light as we drive down the M1. I like the motorway at this time of morning it's quiet, well, Brett's car is purring away. We're heading to the Southampton Boat Show. Tucked away in my pocket is the show guide and list of things we need. The plan is to be as quick as possible yet I'm sure this won't be the case. A combination of the warm air and early start sends me in a dreamy recollection of last year's boat show.

I was invited to a buffet lunch on the Saturday along with a chance to meet the other competitors of the Challenge Rowing Race. I had planned to drive from Brighton, where I had been diving for two days. The last dive on the Friday, the day before the boat show sticks out in my mind. We were heading for the wreck of the RMS Moldavia 28 miles out in the channel. It was described as one of the most exciting dives in the UK. It was the first of the famous P&O 'M' Series passenger liners, 520' long, weighing 9,505 tons. Driven by 12,000 horse power, it was an absolute beast. Commandeered by the Navy in 1915 as a troop carrier it left Halifax, Nova Scotia on the 11th May 1918 packed with American troops. Everything was fine until it passed the Owers Lightship. Waiting patiently was Ober-Leutant Johann Lohs in U boat UB57. One torpedo in her port side amidships was all it took. Steaming on for 15 minutes as if nothing had happened she slowly began to settle at the head. Kicking up her stern she finally sank below the surface.

There was an air of business like activity as most of the divers sorted out their kit. Alan and I were the only antiquated divers on board, still breathing that old-fashioned stuff - compressed air. We accepted the fact that our time on the bottom would be much shorter. For us it didn't matter. Then, within what seemed like minutes the skipper of the boat, 'Sparticus', shouted, "Time to kit up." We pulled on our well-worn diving suits and waited. The skipper shouted to 'Steve' and 'Paul' giving them instructions to drop the shot line which connected us to the wreck. We were not aware at this time he was talking to us. Alan's dry suit had 'Steve' and mine had 'Paul' written in big letters on the front. The people we had to thank for that misunderstanding are those who have their diving suits made to measure before having their name embroidered across the front. This may be a good idea at the time, but when it comes to selling their old suits to diving scrooges like us, the confusion starts. Dropping the shot line I stood back as one hundred metres of rope flies out over the side. Before long I was pulling myself down the shot line, hand over hand. The tide was still running slightly, which was a good thing as it meant we were just coming to slack water which gave us plenty of time before it started to run again. After what seemed like an eternity, a large dark shape broke through the green/brown light. We flicked our torches on, adjusted our buoyancy, tightened our weight belts and headed towards the middle of the ship. I couldn't see much - no further than three metres. The water was so murky. As I passed one of the 'Moldavia's six-inch guns I looked towards the surface and could just about make out the line of the gun. We swam deeper before we got to where the torpedo hit the ship. It was then our curiosity got the better of us. We delved deeper into her black interior. There, the visibility was much worse. My torch was struggling to break the dark. Looking around all I could make out was a faint sparkle below me. Intrigued I swam towards the tangled mess of lacerated machinery but then, bang! My lump hammer and chisel I carry for easing off small objects had come out of their pocket. They were still attached to me by a thin line that had ravelled round part of the wreckage. Shining my torch, which was slowly fading I tried to free myself, yet the water was so murky I could barely make out my hands. As I'm extremely organised my other side pocket held a small backup torch ready for this very situation, were it not for a slight bout of forgetfulness. I had removed the old batteries but I'd not replaced them. With the dim light of my torch it was almost impossible to find my tools. I had to decide on a plan of action. Drawing my large knife, which is sometimes used in desperation as a hammer, I began tapping my cylinder hoping to attract Alan's attention. He must have been too far away. I had no choice but to cut myself free. As I held the knife to the line Alan came into view. The bright beam of his torch pierced the cloudy water and he was quickly able to locate my tools. As he began to untangle me I used what was left of the dim torchlight to see my diving computer. Twelve minutes had gone by already and at this depth of 45 metres, decompression time was starting to add up. Gesturing to Alan to hurry up, I was starting to panic; soon we'd need to ascend, 14 minutes went by before I was freed. I looked at Alan and I started filling the surface marker with air. I let go of the lever that released the line attached to the surface buoy. The buoy shot up and headed for the surface but the line jammed as it came off the reel. This resulted in me being jerked off the wreck. Before I could gather speed Alan made a dive for my ankles. Holding on like a limpet, we both began dumping the air in our suits and stab jackets. Racing toward the surface I knew we still had about eighteen minutes of decompression to do - blasting up to the surface like that could have quite easily killed us or, at least, confined us to a wheelchair for life. Fortunately we were reasonably heavy and came to a stop as the buoy hit the surface leaving us dangling about eighteen metres under the sea.

"Graham M27 - west or east?"
"What?"
"M27 - west or east?" said Brett again.
"Sorry Brett, east."

Today will, no doubt, be a long day. Our list of items to pick up is endless...

17th September 1997
Gary's back from his honeymoon today so I'm planning to relinquish command of our business to him. We still don't have a name for the boat. I was hoping that perhaps we'd be able to get a sponsor to take over with suitable financial input and name the boat after their company but I don't think that's going to happen. I guess it's up to me. I've had quite a few suggestions: 'No Problem', 'Submerge', 'Death Wish', but I don't think they're serious enough. As I walk into the lounge, the answer is staring me in the face. Mounted on the dresser

stands an ageing photograph of a cricketer shaking hands with the then King of England. The cricketer was my grandfather, George Geary. He played for Leicestershire for 26 years, whacking three centuries and coming second in the batting order in his last year. At the age of 47, he'd played 14 test matches for England. On one test tour in Melbourne he performed a remarkable feat of endurance due to an injury to Larwood - 81 overs, 36 maidens, 105 runs and five wickets all in Australia's first innings, which is still a world record today. I still remember reading that article, written by Terry Wright for the Wisden Cricket Monthly in July 1993. *'Geary the cricketer was resolute, sturdy and zestful. Geary was a personification of cheerfulness, good humour and loyalty. An engaging raconteur, he was held in tremendous warmth and regard.*

Maybe it's time to apologise for carelessly and quickly emptying his flat following his transfer to a nursing home. I still have haunting visions of me dropping his possessions amongst my rusting kit, littered in the back of an old van. The fact that I've never been able to find out anything about the photograph from my parents or knowledgeable cricketers seemed, in some way, retribution. To name the boat in his honour and memory can't change how careless I was at the time, but I feel I owe it to him to name my boat *George Geary*.

19th September 1997

I was working on the main rear cabin hatch but I've just remembered I've forgotten the marine survey the Challenge Business wanted. Better ring my old friend Tony Matts. He owns and runs Foxton Boat Yard, I hope he can help us because we're running out of time, fast. If he can't help, I'm going to have to manipulate him…While I make the call Brett and Rob continue where I left off yesterday. We've decided to make the trailer rather than borrow Bob's. Only because the shipping costs to bring it back is £180.00.

By the time Tony arrives with camera and tape measure Rob's finished the trailer. After a quick inspection Tony asks me to climb aboard and hold the tape measure for the last time. As I pull myself up there is a mighty creek and the boat slowly slides off the timber blocks holding it. I can see the look of horror on Brett's face.

20th September 1997
Although it scared us at the time, the only damage done yesterday was to the paintwork. As Brett has become most dexterous with a brush I think it's best if I make the teas.

Steve arrived to fit the electric about 15 minutes ago. Currently, I think he's wiring up the navigation but he doesn't seem to be moving much.

"Search lights and interiors fitted Graham." he said.

21st September 1997
It's 7.30am and I've already dismantled the tarpaulin, scaffolding and all the other things covering the boat. Rob has gone to fetch the truck with the lifting gear.

The plan is to lift the boat out of the front garden and onto the new trailer. But something tells me it's not going to be that simple. Still, better carry on.

Just as I thought – there's a problem with the truck's hydraulic system - although maybe it's a blessing in disguise. It gives us more time to make sure the boat is extra comfy in the trailer. I'm sure Margaret won't mind if I take a couple of metres off this roll of carpet - surely they give you that much in excess. There, that should do it.

"Right Brett, this needs to go on the supports."

"Carpet?" said Brett.

"Yeah and by the time we've done it the hydraulics might be working."

Slower...slower...careful.

"Is this stressing you out too?" I say to Brett.

"It's a machine."

"'I know, but..."

The boat hits the bed and there is a very uncomforting crash. I rush over to make sure there's no damage. Everything looks in order. After some quick alterations it's strapped in place. Rob takes the truck back as everybody swarms over the boat like ants, tools and paintbrushes in hand. A loose tarpaulin is draped over the boat as it sits outside on the trailer.

22nd September 1997

A decision was made last night to rip out the forward hatch and turn it around. The reason behind this extraordinary act of vandalism is because with the way the seats are positioned the hatch won't open. Alan starts bolting the rudder pintles while I epoxy the support ply on the sides of the rudder to allow for the extra width. After that I start cutting out the ply around the hatch as there is no other way to get it out.

Wait, what about the insurance?

"Brett, I've not insured the bloody boat." I said which causes Brett to raise his eyes before responding with, "Better do it

then hadn't you?"
Before I blink I'm on the phone to Hayes Parsons (Marine) trying to convince him it's not too late to insure the boat on it's transfer to Tenerife. Wait, we need personal accident and holiday insurance too don't we? This is a nightmare - I really need to start making an itinerary.

Back under the tarpaulin I see Brett staring at the one solar panel we have to give us power during the race.

"You do know this has a crack in don't you?" he asks.

"Yeah, of course."

"Is it going to work?"

"I'm not too sure." I said trying to mask my doubts.

"We should probably try it."

Before we have chance to test the panel Keith appears with the seats, sliding rails and other items connected with the footplates. Whatever we do we need to hurry-up. The plan is to be out of the house by 5.00pm - we have a long evening of reflection over fine food and copious amounts of wine and I'm not even in my tux!

23rd September 1997
I rise with a thirst you would normally associate with a desert crossing. Dressing, I realise today's the day I need to take the boat to Southwold on the East Coast where I'll spend the night in my Aunt's cottage then drive to Felixstowe in the morning. It looked as if I might even get away before sunset but looking out the kitchen window towards the boat, which now stands the other side of the garden wall I have my doubts. Not only do I still have the task of sticking the company names of the sponsors all over the sides of the boat I still need to finish the

forward hatch. The phone rings.

"Graham, it's Keith, how are you doing mate, you alright?"

"Yeah, good thanks, how about you?"

"Listen – I've got some great news."

"What?"

"I've organised an unveiling of the boat today."

"What?" I say again, this time with more conviction.

"I'll be over in about an hour."

This is the final blow to a swollen head.

By the time 1.30pm comes we're ready for the Town Hall, although we've not had time to test the trailer. As we are leaving the street a car's headlights flash. Naturally I look over my shoulder and prepare for the worst, but everything seems to be fine. What can he possibly be trying to signal…oh… it's Tony, thank God for that, I was really starting to worry about the marine surveyors report.

Having unhitched the trailer at Town Hall Square in the centre of Leicester we climb aboard the boat for a brief photo session. I'm sure this one will look as awkward as the last. Maybe if I grab the oars... Oh no, is that Champagne? I'm still hung-over – oh, it's Fresnet-Juillet too, I can't pass on that. We do really need to get a move on though.

"I think the local paper want to interview us after this Graham." said Keith as he handed me a flute of Champagne. Although I'd love to spend all day pretending to be a celebrity time is doing it's usual thing – relentlessly marching on. It's 4.00pm and the boat isn't even loaded full of all of the things we need for the race…food, water…and we can't leave tomorrow. If there's a problem with the trailer we won't have time to sort it out. Also, what if Margaret doesn't get up in time? Cups full of cold water splashed about her face have resulted in ear blasting abuse in the past. We need to get a move on. The latest I can deliver the boat to Felixstowe dock is 2.00pm. Come on Keith - that's enough pleasantries for now.

Pulling up outside home we're met by a wall of items of every shape and size.

"Ok." said Brett. Timber, angle iron, bottles, tins, cartons of resin, paint, filler, turps, glue, plastic gloves, hand cleaner, sawdust...errr, rolls of wire, tubes of silicone, mastic, sikaflex, boxes of screws, bolts, nuts, nails, electrical items, two tool boxes full to the brim...errr, electric drills, angle grinder, saws. Am I missing anything?"

"Clothes, food?' I said.

"Both here somewhere."

"'Ok, shall we load up then?" I asked anxiously.

9.00pm sees me closing the main hatch. I then come to the tragic realisation, we don't have a spare wheel for the trailer. Great!

Before the clock strikes 11.00pm Margaret and I are off to Southwold. The A14 is very quiet this time of day, well, despite the rattling of the trailer. It's not too loud as long as I don't go any faster than 45mph but that's resulting in a long drawn out journey. Another worry is every time I look in my wing mirrors I can see the tyres bulging. I'm having to stop every 30 miles or so just to check them. It's become very obvious that they're greatly overloaded, and, not only are they bulging but by now they're red hot. I allow them to cool down and do the only thing I can, drive on with caution. The long day's beginning to take it's toll – better pull over for a coffee soon.

24th September 1997
What started out as a straightforward drive to the coast has turned into an endurance test. I've decided to keep to the A14 rather than take my usual route from Downham Market, as there's more garages open at this time of night. The trailer tyres have to be kept blown up.

Finally we come to the A12 and begin heading north - maybe we're going to make it after all, even if I am driving at twenty miles an hour. There are no garages open at this time and I'm scared if I go any faster than that the tyres will get too hot. Just a bit further now…the floodlit church of Blythburgh standing above the silted remains of the old Roman port that Edward the Confessor once held now comes into view. With only five miles to go a certain irony unfolds as my mind goes through the thoughts related to one of the main attractions of Blythburgh Church: the carved armrest. If I remember correctly it depicts the seven deadly sins; sloth, slander, avarice, hypocrisy, gluttony, pride and drunkenness, wait that's not right is it? Is drunkenness a sin?

BANG!

Suddenly the trailer slews all over the road. Fortunately a lay-by appears almost immediately, and managing to control the swinging trailer, I pull up in a cloud of burning rubber. With no spare tyre or the chance to get one at this hour I decide to disconnect the trailer and carry on to the cottage, that way I can drop Margaret off and come back. By the time I get back to the boat it's almost 5.00am. I sleep fitfully in the car for two hours after which I try to jack the axle of the burned out tyre. As it is almost touching the road it is not easy to get the scissor jack underneath it. On my first attempt the light steel jack handle bends in half. Unloading a large proportion of the contents makes things a little easier. 8.00am comes round just as I remove the last wheel nut, place everything in the boot and walk back to the telephone box I passed in the early hours.

I have to make a decision now between two branches of a large tyre company. One's in Halesworth, the other is in Saxmundham. Looking at the map I can either head six miles north and take the B road or nine miles south on the A road.

I take the latter and 25 minutes later, after an extensive search, a very helpful sales assistant informs me that he is unable to find a tyre suitable to fit the rim of the wheel. The only progress in this dilemma is through a telephone call between this depot and that of Halesworth, yes, they have a tyre to fit. Good one Graham! From now on I think I'm going to ignore my instinct. Collecting the new tyre I return to the scene of our unhappy situation to find the jack on it's side and pushed into the ground by the trailer axle. The only positive decision I made on leaving was to carry more jacks. The entire unhappy incident is put behind us as I remove both jacks, hook up the trailer and drive back to Southwold. Parking the boat in the car park of the village hall, I open the door of the cottage to be met by an extremely worried wife. Unable to sleep she had sat downstairs and waited for the delivery of the life raft and collision flares. A hot drink, 10 minutes of reflection and we are off.

Ian Chater - another contender in the Atlantic Rowing race lives on the way to Felixstowe, maybe we should sneak a peek at his progress. I'm not sure if the Challenge Business would like it but it might calm my nerves. I've heard through the grape vine he's in a similar position to us.

Looking around Ian's boat I try and mask my nerves - it's so stout! If this is the standard, we might have bitten off more than we can chew. It's perfect. I need to get out of here, let's go for lunch. Leaving Ian's we head for the nearest hostelry. Before long we're talking about Ian's boat in between large mouthfuls of homemade steak and kidney pie. Glancing at the directions for the docks I can see Steve Richardson has left nothing to chance. The accompanying instructions are so clear. All the essential information is highlighted in big capitals. 'PLEASE DO NOT LOSE THE STANDARD SHIPPING NOTES. REMEMBER TO KEEP YOUR FLARES AND ANY OTHER HAZARDOUS GOODS EASILY ACCESSIBLE.'

"Do you want to stay here Margaret whilst we go to the docks?" I say with caution, as I know I'm providing a very large window of opportunity for her to go shopping.

"Sure." she said with a large smile.

Stopping at dock gate two I am directed to Dooley Terminal. As I approached, the other rowing boats come into view. Two of the six are covered in white wrapping paper looking like giant parcels waiting for delivery. Speaking to the people milling around these secret objects I learn that one is the *Endeavour* and the other the *Spirit of Jersey*. Good names. Maybe we should have gone with something a bit more universal, still, I back the boat in alongside *Sam Deacon*, number twelve, and *Spirit of Spelthorne*, number ten. Climbing out of the car I meet Roger and Charles from the *Sam Deacon* and Matthew and Edward from the *Spirit of Spelthorne*. After a quiet chat, and a quick look at their boats I walk along to number 27 *Bitzer*. There I meet Russ and Andy. Quickly I move onto *The Cornish Challenger* and meet Michael and Louis. In these brief introductions I have been trying to cyphon as much information as humanly possible about seat positions and heights. I'm sure they won't mind if I take a few photographs will they? Saying goodbye to the few rowers I have met I drive into Felixstowe, park the car on the sea front and walk up the narrow winding road towards the town centre. It doesn't take me long to find Margaret window-shopping. As time has raced by again the afternoon is drawing to a close. I arrange to meet Margaret later and head for the second hand book shop to indulge in one of my favourite pastimes - collecting stories of voyages across the world's oceans along with any other maritime adventures. I buy a couple of books before realising I should be looking for paperbacks for the trip. My search is half-hearted and I come away with just a few books, none of which I really want to read. We discuss the few items I have bought over a cup of coffee at our rendezvous, including the quality tools for the boat from the pound shop. Salt water will only ruin them anyway. Looking out of the café window I notice that the shops are closing and I've not even bought anything to commemorate the day! Rushing out of the café and across the road I dart into one of the only shops that hasn't had time to put it's closed sign on the door. Right, my choice is pretty limited; at least it's not a clothes shop. Looking around, my eyes stop at an extraordinary flying machine bobbing up and down on a long spring. It seems out of place and probably would be better placed at a market stall. it's strange wooden wings are attached to paddle wheels. In it sits a little wooden chap with oversized goggles. Neatly fitted behind him are all necessary traveller's comforts; an old black cooking range that was common 50 years ago, not to mention the toilet which also has a 50 year history, being a high level cistern with hanging chain. What could be more ideal to commemorate the day? Feeling contented with my purchase I decide to treat Margaret to a nice meal. Without further ado we stop at a suitable looking establishment, order a bottle of red wine and two large bowls of Spaghetti Bolognese. A piece of garlic bread and two glasses of wine later the meal arrives.

25th September 1997
I rise early and walk to the beach. There, I enjoy a quick dip in the sea - nude, of course. There's not a single job to do on the boat. To be honest it feels rather strange. For the past few months I have been so anxious. Today will be spent recharging the batteries with some light reading and a few pints of beer.

26th September 1997
The day is spent trying to obtain small items for the crossing. I've no luck with sea soap or shampoo at Fox's Marina, Ipswich. Better look elsewhere. Maybe they have some in West Mercia. There, I can also check on my thirty-seven foot

sailing smack, *Albion*. I know it's still high and dry on the slip after seven years of re-building but it'd still be good to have a look at it. Arriving in West Mercia I take the opportunity to look in at Wyatt's Chandlers - soap and shampoo, no problem. Wait, there's some strong steel fittings for the rudder over there, I've been intending to change them.

27th September 1997
An early morning walk around Southwold harbour and a cup of coffee at the wooden teashop. As I stand drinking my coffee my eyes fix on another item for the crossing - a crab line. Now I'm not the best fisherman in the world but crab lines are pretty simple, you just tow them behind the boat.

Back on the road by midday means we get back home to Thurmaston at about 5.00pm. Great - pieces of timber, bricks (used for support), paint tins, mixing pots and tarpaulins, scattered about our front garden. Now the boats gone I can really see the mess. In the mad rush to get the boat on it's way everything else had been discarded.

"Don't worry, I'll sort this mess out in the morning." Is my candid response to the look of disappointment on Margaret's face.

29th September 1997
I tided away our mess yesterday. Bob arrives and we quickly start discussing some of the things I saw at Felixstowe to combat the oars which were too long to fit into the boat.

"So I'm thinking if we can make a 6"tube to fit into the forward cabin where the spare oars are going to be kept that'd be great." I say.

"What just to hold them?"

"Yeah."

As we now have no boat we must revert to the plans to acquire the angle of the cabin wall in preparation for making the gasket and end piece. You see - if I were more organised or innovative I would have done this weeks ago. Still, I check the shed for some tubing. I know there's some around here somewhere. Aha! It just needs a wash. What else did I want to do? That's right – raise the height of the seats, I don't think ours are high enough.

Early evening sees me trying to pack some clothes, although it is going to be hot I need to think about the two working weeks in Tenerife, a possible three months at sea and another couple of weeks in Barbados. Ok; Sunglasses, suntan lotion, passport, driving licence...books! The phone rings.

"Graham, it's Keith, look I've had a bit of a nightmare with these flights."

"Go on..."

"I don't think I'm going to be able to get one until the 7th of October."

Great. That means the two weeks prior to the race where we're supposed to be putting the finishing touches to the boat Keith will be absent. I need to sleep - being awake is just far too stressful at the moment.

30th September 1997

At last I am leaving to join the boat. I'm not worried about the physical aspect; fear's something I don't really have time for. It could crop up in situations along the way but I'll have to deal with it if and when it occurs. The financial side however, is a different matter. At first I had assumed that sponsorship would come to our rescue, by now I realise it's not going to happen. At least Rob's very kindly agreed to fill in for Keith in Tenerife. We shouldn't lose too much time that way. Where's Hugh? He said he was bringing me those books I need.

"Graham?" ' said a voice. I turn around.

"Thank God for that."

"Thank God for what?" asked Hugh.

"Oh, I'm just starting to panic a bit. Have you brought the books?"

"Of course." he said, handing me two volumes of 'The Sight Reduction Tables for Marine Navigation'. I was hoping to brush up on my astro-navigation already having packed my plastic sextant. Hugh had agreed to try and bring all the relative publications in his possession but unfortunately the two sight reduction books he's just handed me are for latitudes 30 to 45 degrees and 45 to 60 degrees. I need volume one, 0 to 15 degrees and volume two, 15 to 30 degrees. The other book Hugh has under his arm is 'Reed's Ocean Navigator', maybe that'll be more useful.

"Are these going to be alright?" he asks.

"I would think so and either way, Kim's agreed to send a copy of 'Nautical Almanacs Astro Navigation' to Keith."

"Who's Kim?" asks Hugh.

"An old sailing friend."

"You don't happen to have a book on star navigation do you?"

"No, sorry mate.'

Everything is packed by midday. Rob pulls up in his Range Rover. Joanne, Rob's daughter, is coming with us to the airport to bring the vehicle back. We still have to pick up the hand pump water-maker and solar vent from Sawley Marina near Nottingham though. Unfortunately, when we get there, we are greeted with the disappointing news that they've not arrived yet. Well I guess that makes two more items for Keith to bring. Empty handed we head for the airport. More bad news – the plane's delayed. Nothing ever seems to go as planned. Still I guess we have time for a quick beer. Four hours later it's time to board the plane. A quick thrusting noise of engines and we are above the clouds. Seat belt off and time to relax. It seems only seconds ago that I booked a similar flight with the intention of joining a charter crew of friends to sail around Tenerife, unfortunately I had to cancel at the last minute due to a typical confusion with dates. My two holidays, one sailing and one skiing in Italy were supposed to follow one another. It was only when I came to study the tickets I realised that I was due to fly to Italy on the Saturday but the return flight from the Canary Islands was not until the Sunday. Knowing my position on the boat could be easily filled I cancelled the sailing trip.

The skiing holiday would have taken it's normal route, skiing most of the pistes in what has become known as the Milky Way, were it not for the last day. After a long excursion to Claviere my friend John Smith and I were heading back to Sauze D'Oulx, our resort. We took the long drag lift up to Mount Fraiteve, which lies at 2,710 metres, and decided to ski down to the small drag lift and go back up under Mount Fraiteve. By the time we got there we found that the lift was closed. That meant we couldn't ski down the other side of the mountain following the pistes. The only way down is to Sansicairo. There, we'd have to take a taxi. John, my old business partner, was also an adventurous type of person so I knew at the time what his answer would be when I suggested trying to ski along the range of peaks keeping as high as possible. Guessing our approximate height was something like 2,400 metres as we knew Sauze D'Oulx stood at 1510 metres, gave us a 900 metre drop to allow us to ski all the way. Being reasonably prepared for the worst with rucksack containing wet gear and chocolate bars we set off slowly following the beginning of the black run 'Twenty One' through the high rock face we had seen on the way up. After that it was into the unknown. As it was only 5.00pm we had plenty of sunlight left. The first part of our journey was in good powdered snow high above the first tree line. We gradually descended into a wide gully thinly lined with just a smattering of trees. Skiing along the next rise again in powdery snow we could see the first wooded area. Turning and looking down beyond the trees we could see water cascading down between two large rock outcrops. Although our crossing was much higher we had to accept the fact that, at some stage, we were going to have to cross this gorge. Up to this point we had made very good time but now the trees were getting closer together. I remember coming to a standstill as the snow covered ground fell away and revealed a sharp rocky slope. The slope was about five metres long and disappeared into a fast moving stream opposite a high stonewall with snow-covered ledges. Looking up stream high above us was a much better crossing place but it would mean climbing through the trees. Looking down the mountain our options were no better. It was time to test our climbing skills and find out just how waterproof our ski boots were.

Looping a short rope around my skis and poles I slung them over my shoulder and started to climb. Grabbing hold of a tree to take a breath, I stood looking back at the gully. The climb had taken about fifteen minutes and a large proportion of my energy. We continued. Off we went through the snowy woods, which began to thin out the further we went, then at last we could see the open sky again. Keeping as high as possible we began to ski round some large outcrops to the left of us. The outline of the landscape became very confusing. What appeared to be a gradual slope turned out to be wind blown snow against a sheer stone face. Feeling a little agitated we slowed down. Then the horrible truth dawned on us. We had followed this snow plateau to the edge of a precipice.

'Bloody hell, another 30 minutes and the daylight would have started to fade - we would never have seen this' gasped John looking over the edge at a drop of probably sixty metres. 'Get back, get back!' I shouted which made John twist and fall backwards on his skis. Just at that moment the ski imprints left in the snow, at the very spot where we were standing, plummeted down the gorge leaving John hanging over the newly visible rock face. We had ignorantly stood in our skis, looking down, unaware that overhanging, compacted snow, was the only thing between us and the thrill of a free-fall without a parachute. Pulling John back to safety I realised we were only left with two options, up or down. If we went down we'd lose too much height and with that, the only chance of skiing back. It had to be more climbing.

The idea was that if we could get back onto the slope we'd be able to skirt around the rock outcrop, climbing up to where the snow formed a large slope. Staring across the gorge, light was beginning to fade. Dropping down in the snow and gasping for air I slowly began to get my breath back. I dug into my rucksack pulling out a couple of chocolate bars. John and I set off on what was now to become a real pleasure, slowly skiing around the vast gully with a crisp wind blowing on our faces after our arduous sticky climb. Trees then started appearing in small groups before ultimately surrounding us. As we begrudgingly lost height another gully came into view. It was much smaller than the last and still covered in snow. Although we could still hear the water trickling down we were unable to see it. It was obviously covered in ice, giving both of us an opportunity to ski down one side of the slope, along the bottom for a short while, then turn, climbing up the other side on an angle.

Having completed this energetic traverse we pressed on with difficulty due to the faint light, which had all but gone. This was brought home in dramatic fashion when, completely missing a small gully, my skis came to a stop as I reached the abrupt rise opposite, propelling me straight out of the ski bindings and reminding me of the human canon ball at the fairground. Luckily, a snow covered fir tree blocked my flight path. As the rustling snow finally stopped dropping from the branches onto my tree hugging posture, the only sound that could be heard was one of roaring laughter. It took some time to find my skis but when I did we were able to continue, thankful for a full moon. The lights of a small village then appeared as we came to the edge of a small wood. Guided by the lights, we found a small winding track skirting the village. Following this track took us roughly north. At last, the lights of Sauze D'Oulx became visible. Arriving at the base of the lift a large group of people gathered with torches. It had never occurred to us that anybody would know of our cross-country adventure. A friend had gone a separate way not wanting the long trek back from Claviere and we assumed he would think we were in a bar somewhere as when I'm with John; this is quite a common occurrence. In fact, what had happened was that he had gotten in touch with the Piste Guide when there was no sign of our return. The guide had in turn, contacted the lift operators and given them our descriptions. As the last drag lift was about to close we had asked if it was possible to get back to Sauze D'Oulx and the operator there had explained that we'd have to go down to Sansicario and take a taxi. With these few words the lift operator had made a mental note of our appearance and was able to explain our approximate position at that time. Not knowing whether we had gone to a bar in Sansicario or Sauze D'Oulx they had spent the last hour ringing most of the bars with details of our descriptions, without any luck, and now, unbeknown to us, were ready to start a full scale search.

By the time we had cleared the airport, bags in hand, it was 12.30am. We got in a taxi and headed for Los Gigantes. Arriving at the apartment we quickly checked in then set off for the main street. Hopefully there'll be a bar open.

1st October 1997

Better get in a final traditional English breakfast, probably won't have that luxury at sea. Looking out across the waters I begin to see more and more Atlantic rowing boats mooring up. Full stomached I walk along the front of the harbour. I'm eager to meet these intrepid rowers. I wondered what they'd be like. The first man I met was Daniel Byles, boat number 17, *Carpe Diem* - a fitting name for our imminent expedition. Next, I bump into two smiling and rather enthusiastic faces who are working on their boat, *Toc H Phoenix*. Passing them, and smiling back, three pontoons along I meet Richard and Isabel from *Stylus Mistral Endeavour*, number 31. Richard's father runs the type of business I've always dreamed of, Scuba diving and training. Not only that, it's merely yards away from the harbour in Los Gigantes. Walking on I realise I recognise the next boat, it's the *Hannah Snell*, number 7. I had seen it launched at the Bristol boat festival in 1996. As David and Nadia were very busy that day I didn't get a chance to introduce myself.

Time was getting on so we walked back to the quay side. There another boat came into view. Across it's side's written in big bold letters *Cellnet Atlantic Challenger.* I remember now, I missed an opportunity to see it last May when it was just 500 yards from my house having a paint job at a local heavy plant depot. It sat there waiting to be painted. Unfortunately at the time I wasn't aware of this until it was too late. Now was my chance to meet Simon and George - the men responsible for this beast. The morning was almost over spent meeting the other rowers.

I'm eager to see the space at the fishing port of Playa San Juan where the boats will sit whilst the competitors work on them. Rushing back to the apartment I go through my bags to find my driving licence and passport, this done, car hired, and off we go. The last rowing boat to meet our eyes as we approach the port gates is the aptly named *Mount Gay Rum Runner,* number eleven. After we park the car, Rob and I walk over and introduce ourselves to Jock and Duncan. Jock Wishart had sent me a letter back in February 1996 asking for a rowing partner. What impressed me most about his letter was his attached record of past adventures. America's Cup, European Dragon Boat Champion, power-boat record and an unsupported walk to the Magnetic North Pole. Unfortunately at the time I was in the process of organising my own challenge so I had to decline. My reply; *'I have no doubt that you will receive many offers from prospective partners in view of your past achievements, and I am confident that our paths will cross in the future.'* This last part of my letter now came true as we shook hands. Jock's partner was a 1994 Commonwealth

Games participant. I knew this from an article I had read in the Daily Telegraph describing his own challenge.

Steadily walking on after our quick chat Rob and I study the area put aside for storage. Ok, there's no power in here just a concrete floor to stand the boat on along with a slip-way. I guess it could be worse.

"It's not too bad." said Rob. "What now?"

"Well I called Alison this morning."

"Alison?"

"A lady from the Challenge Business."

"Ahhh."

'She told me that, because of the difficulties in port clearance at Santa Cruz and transportation to Playa San Juan, she's left the whole business in the very capable hands of Mr Fix it, Damien.

"Who's Damien?" asks Rob.

"That guy." I say whilst pointing towards Damien. Fortunately we've caught him leaving his shop. That means we now have a contact number. Damien assures us the boats are being transported as we speak; thus, it's time for a pre-boat inspection drink. For this necessity we didn't have to look very far. There, 20 yards away, that lovely word – 'BAR'. Hmmm, this might be a problem, what with it being so close to us. We still have quite a bit of work to do on the boat after all. Halfway through a cool bottle of local beer a large lorry pulls up in front of the port gates, unfortunately neither of these boats is mine. Unloading is well under way when a second lorry arrives, carrying a bright orange boat, *The George Geary*. Yes, it is here at last! As the boat and trailer are lowered down I notice that the jockey wheel is missing. I can't even complain as nobody will know anything about it.

The George Geary is finally backed into position, as two more boats arrive. The time is getting on. It's nearly 5.50pm, we better return to Los Gigantes. A quick swim in the pool followed by a trip to the Harbour Lights bar, which we've been told, was the meeting place for the majority of rowers.

2nd October 1997

Having now bought some food, it's Cornflakes, toast and coffee, which puts us in the right frame of mind. Maybe today we won't have such a hard time driving on the other side of the road. We're at the harbour by nine. There are now quite a few boats lined up against the wall, way more than there was yesterday.

"We better get cracking Rob." I say trying desperately to take my eyes off *The Mount Gay Rum Runner*. Until I saw it, I was certain I wasn't going to be intimidated but it was in such a better state than *The George*. Finally I manage to turn my head away and to my surprise Rob has already started unloading the boat. We're going to take the clothes, food and other mandatory supplies back to the apartment. When we return Rob begins fitting the switch and fuse box whilst I get to work on the floor. I can't help but feel sorry for the team on the right of us. *The Golden Fleece*, number 22, has suffered an unfortunate accident during transit and has a hole in the bow. Two unhappy figures, Daniel and Peter, inspect the damage.

3rd October 1997

Rising a little later than we should breakfast is a hurried affair. Just as I'm about to start the car engine we realise we've forgotten the bag of building materials. Rob turns and jogs off towards the front entrance.

"Hang on Rob, I'm coming with you." I say, "I've just thought of something else - the solar panels are jammed down the side of my other bag."

"You're unbelievable."

The morning starts seem to be getting later and later. It's 9.55am when we pull up at the dock. Rob gets out and opens the gates from inside. I drive in, park the car and begin to walk down the line of boats. By now there are many bodies fiddling with their boats. The boats I pass are finished and these guys are out earlier than us.

"What bloody time do you call this, your mate's been here for an hour?" said Pete from *Hospiscare*, number 21, our next door boat neighbour. When I get to *The George* I'm pleasantly surprised to see the deck cleared and tools out ready for action. Oh, and Phil's blown up the tyres on the bike I'd bought with me. Now I feel worse.

As Rob prepares to carry on with the electrics, Phil sorts out ply ready for my plan to reinforce the forward cabin. I decide on a burn-up around the harbour before starting the day's labour however, my cycling activity is cut short as the chain keeps coming off. Eventually this sees me crash land in a pile of cardboard boxes, much to the annoyance of two deck hands that are in the process of packing.

I begin measuring and marking lengths of ply from inside the forward cabin, passing them to Phil who immediately starts to saw away at them. Three bottles of ice cold beer and three packets of crisps later and the day comes to an end.

4th October 1997

Just as the breakfast dishes are put away there is a knock at the door. It's Phil and he's raring to go. We are at the dock gates at ten to nine. The coolness of this early hour gives me a chance to work in the fore-cabin while Rob starts to fit the brackets for the fire extinguisher and Eperb rescue beacon. As I've spent the last hour cocooned I decide to stretch my legs. Walking down the dock I meet, for the first time, Arvid Bentsen and Stein Hoff of *Star Atlantic*, number 13.

Having a lot in common with the two Norwegians we discuss boat building. They have some innovative ideas which I can tell are going to influence my plans for the fore-cabin. Maybe I should laminate the extra struts that strengthen the sides rather than use fixed ribs. Would that work? I'm sure Phil wouldn't mind re-cutting the ply.

1.00pm soon comes around. I don't think crisps will be enough today.

There was a nice looking café across the road. We cross and take our places under a large sunshade on the pavement where we're joined by Michael and Louis from *The Cornish Challenger*. Hmmm, it's not the most eclectic of menus. Burger and chips is the only real option, unless, of course, you fancy a burger on it's own. After our labours of the morning all of us are ravenous,

'Five beers and five burgers and chips please.' I say to the strange looking waiter trying desperately not to stare at what I'm sure is a fake leg.

Back in the fore-cabin fed and watered I mix the epoxy to stick the first ribs. I try to prop them in place after applying the epoxy. This stuff really hurts my eyes. Right, it's getting hot. Turning to put it down, drops of epoxy from the wedged-in ribs above me start to drop on my head and arms burning little rings of skin. Climbing out of my very own personal torture chamber I am met by a familiar face.

"Brett." I say. "You made it!"

After a quick catch up, and a look at the list we've made we head for a DIY store to get some of the things we need to finish the boat. Finding a suitable place on the way out of Playa San Juan we acquired most of the things we needed. But there are some items we can't find. Walking towards the counter we quickly discover the young lady there doesn't speak any English. Between us we don't know a word of Spanish. Trying to explain what a length of flat steel looks like ends with a frown. She must have misinterpreted our hand gestures. Shall we leave? Oh, she's smiling – maybe she doesn't think we're sex pests after all. We follow her through the shop and down some ladders. Before us is a mass of timber, metal and everything we could possibly need.

5th October 1997

I'm up before the sun. Walking onto the veranda I switch on the light and start to read yesterday's paper. Rob wakes at about 7.45am eight and walks across in his sleepy state to the kitchen. Our breakfast ritual is soon over. We clear the table and close the door behind us. Phil appears from around the corner and quickly starts asking me about today's project. On arrival at the boat Rob begins to make the battery straps using the steel we purchased the previous day. Phil fits the deck pump, cutting the plastic pipe to size.

1.00pm sees us back in the bar across the road, we ask the owner for the same meal as yesterday, only to be met with the reply 'the cook's on holiday.' I suppose even cooks need a holiday. Cold salad and sardines turns out to be quite a refreshing meal. While the crunching of celery and cabbage goes on I explain to Louis and Michael, who have again joined us, the startling fact that I have never sculled before. I try hard to reassure Louis of my experience with short wooden oars of which he appears doubtful. 'Don't worry, I'll take you out this afternoon seeing that our boat is in the water at the moment.' he said, still finding it hard to believe I've never rowed on the ocean before. A short while after returning to our labours Michael and Louis bring their boat along side the quay.

"Are you ready Graham?" asks Louis.

After boarding I'm soon taken out of the harbour. I've not had a go yet - I think Louis wants to wait until we are clear of all impending maritime disasters. On reaching clear water I could hardly contain myself from grabbing the oars.

"Right, I'll set the oars up for you, sit in the sliding seat behind me and strap your feet in." said Louis.

"Okay Louis."

"The main thing Graham, just follow my stroke."

Covering only a short distance, in which I clash blades with my earnest instructor many times, I find my persistence is rewarded as I slowly begin to row in unison with Louis, correcting the side-to-side motion every stroke. The more I become used to the lurching and pitching, the more I relax.

Thinking back to the last time that I had rowed in the open sea, the circumstances were completely different.

I had always harboured the idea of visiting the 1992 Sea Festival at Brest, the world's largest assembly of historical and traditional boats, in my own sailing smack 'Albion'. In the preceding month I had worked on her on and off whenever time allowed. Eventually, the realisation that she required a major re-build meant I had no alternative but to abandon the idea. Pondering over my disappointment a thought suddenly came into my head, why not take a part of the 'Albion' to the festival in the shape of her tender? When I say tender, do not picture a small lightweight craft of the inflatable or plastic type. This is a 14' clinker built rowing boat with traditional round seats in the stern, possibly as old as the 'Albion' herself, a mere 102 years old. I had inherited her when I purchased this consuming marine building project. I had already registered the 'Albion' together with a photograph for the festival therefore it was necessary to inform them of my change of plan. I assumed that they would notice the difference in length and width, 37' having shrunk to 14. Initially, on registration, I had received a parcel from the Mayor of Brest, which contained, to my surprise, a large piece of teakwood, 1' wide by 4' long. Enclosed was a request to carve or paint the name of the boat and port of registration including an additional note, which summed it all up. 'Your creation will symbolise the passion you have for your boat.' It stated. Before even considering the amount of repairing and painting that needed to be done to the 14' clinker, at present buried under a pile of scaffolding in the back garden at home, I began drawing a design for the wooden plaque. After this I took a brief look at Admiralty Chart 2675 showing me the entire English Channel. My original plan was for a short crossing from Rye to Bologne, slightly further than Dover to Calais but with far less shipping traffic. From then on down the

French coast, only rowing when the tide was in my favour. At that point I had planned to take five weeks holiday hoping that this would enable me to complete the trip one way. I was relying on my plumbing mate, Len, to drive car and trailer to pick me up. Route at that time sorted, I resumed work on the plaque, carving a picture of a man rowing on a similar boat with the words "Rye to Brest 500 miles."

Incidentally, the plaque survived the ensuing disaster and now hangs somewhere in the garage covered in dust and cobwebs.

Time now ran out on me as the festival approached, my five weeks sabbatical now became three. There was nothing else for it but to shorten the distance to Brest. With this in mind I changed the Channel crossing, Swanage to Cherbourg it had to be. Even then many doubts had already began to haunt me. I talked to my old friend Bob who had already started on his long voyage to Brest in his 30 feet motor sailor, 'Saffron'. He had painstakingly re-built her from a hull with just a few good planks, which he did over a period of six years at Syston boat yard on the River Soar just outside of Leicester. This was to be her maiden voyage, Syston to Brest. The boat was already at Boston in Lincolnshire having followed the inland waterways. After arriving on the French coast I would telephone Bob's wife Jenny and she would then contact Bob wherever he was to discuss a tow, providing he was behind me. With all the plans in abeyance we were now loading all the items necessary for the voyage of discovery into the clinker rowing boat that I had named 'Albion Two', after her new lease of life. This done I shook hands with Gaz who had one long drive home pulling the boat trailer. The time was 1.30am on the 29th June 1992. I rowed out to a vacant mooring with some trepidation, as it was now clear she sat very low in the water with just about six inches of freeboard in the centre. Although I had practised rowing the boat many times, it was always empty, as it was a last minute rush there was no time to test it fully loaded. I quickly put the oars together, dropped them in the crutch at the stern and into the mast. I threw the tarpaulin over the oars, tied it down, pulled out the folding board that was to be my bed, climbed into my sleeping bag and tried to go to sleep yet the rain was driving in the open end of my make shift tent and drenching the sleeping bag that was housing my feet. The rain eased off at about 4.30am, leaving me with wet feet and an uneasy feeling. I lit the single Calor stove, put the kettle on and had a cup of tea. Feeling more positive after my tea I packed the bedding away and fitted the 20 horse- power mariner engine to the transom and connected it to a five-gallon petrol tank. The last thing I wanted was a super tanker bearing down on me with a bow wave like a wall of water. This then was the plan. I would row to the shipping lane whereby I would start the engine and motor across the westbound and eastbound shipping lanes and, upon reaching the other side, stop the engine and start to row again. The sky began to turn a lighter grey as I began to row out of Swanage Bay, it was 5.10am. The wind - probably five miles per hour with only a light breeze from the north- west. I shipped the oars at 5.50am and turned on the radio - nothing. I fiddled and twisted the knobs, replaced the batteries in a last desperate attempt, but still nothing. The shipping forecast was at 5.55am, there is only one minute left to get the spare radio out of it's water tight container. But even that wasn't working! The one thing that was essential to me was the weather forecast. While I was mulling over what to do a fishing boat chugged by, grey smoke and water bellowed out of her exhaust. I remember shouting across and asking 'What's the weather doing today?' The reply I got was extremely vague.

"It won't come to a blow 'til later."

Before I could ask him what "'til later" meant the boat pulled out of earshot. I had to make a decision then. If I didn't go that day and waited for the next, the weather might get worse. Taking the gamble I started to row eventually clearing Anvil Point. Before setting off I had tested the electric pump and the automatic float lever. I charged the battery before leaving home, the inflatable dinghy was half pumped up underneath my seat, a new pack of flares lay in a watertight container together with a hand held VHF radio.

The portable hand pump, spare life jacket, harness, waterproofs, dry clothes, torch, spare stove, gas lamp, gas canister, charts, pilot books, almanac, Danforth anchor, chain, fifty metres of nylon rope, food, water, not to mention the medicine chest, containing a box of plasters, bottle of whisky, passport and cheque book. All of this was stashed under the front waterproof cover, which in turn was attached to my improvised mast. Twelve feet of hardwood handrail topped by my diamond shaped radar reflector above my all round white light. For night rowing I attached two bicycle front lamps with green and red paper stuck to the front positioned in boxes port and starboard. To add to this multitude of equipment I had also brought along another extra item just in case of engine failure in the shipping lane, my two horsepower Seagull outboard motor, usually attached to the inflatable tender. In hindsight I realise I was riding so low in the water because of all of that equipment. Two hours of non-stop rowing left me exhausted, the headland had almost disappeared in the overcast light. I pulled out my hand held compass and took three quick fixes, St Alban's Head, Anvil Point and Handfast Point. Drawing my chart out of it's waterproof holder I promptly worked a fix taking off six degrees for variation, SA = 290°, AP = 307° and HP = 328°. Having rowed south I calculated that the tide had taken me east approximately four miles as it flowed east and west. My plan was to ignore the tidal drift having worked out a rough ETA at

Cherbourg based on rowing approximately two miles per hour and motoring in the shipping lane at five miles per hour.

The final difference between the east and west tidal flow was approximately five miles, putting this against the fact that it was impossible to row an exact course. Sea conditions at that present time were not too bad considering that I was much more exposed after leaving the shelter of the headland. When it started to rain I quickly put on my wet gear and continued to row. Rain and wind were quickly becoming more of a problem, both having increased. Three hours passed since my fix and my discomfort grew with every creak of the oar. Windblown rain rushed down the outside of my waterproofs while sweat trickled down the inside. One factor in my favour was that the pump was working perfectly. Shipping traffic had increased in the area I was entering so I started the engine. Amazingly it started without too much trouble especially considering the amount of water that had covered the engine. The bow lifts slightly as I open the throttle. Thirty minutes went by in a flash as I concentrated on the first large freighter. I didn't know if there was time to pass her bow or if should I aim for her stern, which I assumed would be okay in normal circumstances. In that case it would reduce the time required for crossing the bow of the following tanker. Thud, a loud hissing noise followed by another thud. Steam poured out of the engine casing. I grabbed the pull cord in desperation but it was jammed solid. For some unknown reason it must have seized up, probably due to lack of water. Distracted because of the latest disaster I failed to notice a giant wall of steel passing not twenty yards away. All I could do is watch in horror and think of what might have been. The near miss shot me into action. I unscrewed and lifted off that inactive piece of machinery, laying it on one side of the boat.

I lifted the small two horsepower Seagull over the transom and locked it in place. I pulled on the knotted piece of rope like a man possessed, again and again until, at last, it fired. Up until this point I had failed to notice the floor of the boat, now awash with water. I see the ply flooring has loosened jamming the float lever and stopping the pump. It hadn't dawned on me exactly how much I was relying on the pump. Leaving the boat to steer herself I began working the handle of the manual pump, at the same time trying to re-fix the floor to allow the float operating room. At last it was free! The pump started to work immediately. A quick look around soon confirmed that the boat was not in danger of being run down. Confirmation of my position just inside the shipping lane had already been established by the amount of shipping steadily steaming behind each other.

My next calamity was now upon me as the wind started to rise. Although the Seagull engine was still running it's position was now to become a problem. A suitable recess had been cut out of the transom to house these unselfish pieces of machinery, a good idea for most unladen boats of this size, but, unfortunately for me being a very laden boat, sea water was slopping over this regrettable alteration at an alarming rate. Adding to this unhappy state of affairs, every now and again the swell, behaved in a somewhat erratic way. It was depositing large amounts of dark green water over the sides of my impending submersible. It was time to make another decision. Turning back would not necessarily mean an end to my rowing extravaganza, there was always tomorrow. Fortunately decision making for me has never been a fine art and within two minutes I was heading north. This change of course brought the wind and swell on to my port bow, the highest part of the boat, which immediately reduced the chance of getting swamped. My enthusiasm for rowing was now very deflated. Miraculously the weather, as if by some feeling of guilt towards my predicament, then began to clear up and the sun tore it's way through the clouds. As the boat made her way through the extremely choppy sea it was time to make up my mind where exactly I was going, the obvious choice was Swanage. Making a rough calculation, I figured tide had taken me east approximately seven or eight miles. The obvious destination is not always an acceptable one.

The vague outline of the Isle of Wight was visible. I planned to head for Christchurch Bay passing the Needles Fairway buoy, aware that the tide would be still running out of the Needles channel and then west. Once in shallow water I would drop the hook and I could eat. I passed that strange object known as The Wave Research Structure that stands about a mile off the beach and began to unravel the anchor warp, which had knotted.

The time was now 4.45pm and it seemed inconceivable that twelve hours had passed since I rowed out of Swanage Bay. In a desperate rush I pulled the dinghy from under the seat and pumped it up with the same agility as if the boat were sinking. Once loaded with my food box, paddles and life jacket, I unceremoniously chucked it over the side and duly followed. 30 minutes later I – a contented rowing apprentice - now lay on the beach.

Back on board, dinghy tucked under the seat, the hook came up without too much trouble and I continued my journey. The tide had started running through the North Channel so I decided to motor towards Lymington. When I came into sight of North Point the tide was almost at high water allowing me to motor straight to Lymington Yacht Haven.

Outside the dredged channel marking the entrance lies a very famous beacon known throughout the sailing fraternity as "Jack in the

Basket," it's easily spotted by it's barrel like top. "Jack in the Basket" was made by one of Lymington's historical iron smelting industries. It was beaten out with great hammers and worked by water wheels from the hammer ponds. "Jack in the Basket" was the departure point for the 'HMS Pandora' sailing out in 1790 to search the Pacific for the mutineers from the 'Bounty'. A small merchant vessel purchased by the Royal Navy. The 'Bounty' sank after hitting a reef whereby making a new meaning for the saying, Pandora's Box, as the box like cage kept on the deck to hold the mutineers, was opened as the ship sank.

Coming into sight of the few lesser-known but still interestingly named beacons, 'Tar Barrel', 'Seymour's Post', 'Enticott's Pile' and 'Bag of Halfpennies', I stop the engine and begin to row, thankful of the peace and quiet disturbed only by the occasional distant murmur of marine engines. I pulled harder on the oars as the tide turned against me. At last I tied up along side a visitors mooring buoy. After about an hour and a half of toil and sweat I was about to blow up the dinghy when the Harbour Master came by in a small dory collecting mooring fees.

"Stopping overnight Sir?" he asked.

To which I replied, "Yes, I think that's the plan."

"What's your length Sir?"

"A little over three metres."

"I'll charge you for three, seeing as you are probably the smallest boat mooring at the town quay this year."

10.00pm saw me showered and fed at the Ship Hotel. I left the decision as to whether I would make another attempt until the morning.

If I were to try again the twenty-horse power mariner engine and quite a few other things would have to be left behind. Around midnight it began to rain heavily and once more my feet were cold and wet. Not letting that put me off I dozed off until I was awakened by a loud sloshing noise underneath me. Wood had jammed the automatic float resulting in twelve inches of rainwater, at least, I thought most of it is rainwater.

Black turned to grey as dawn approached. The rain had finally stopped. I had already made up my mind by that time. The rowing was over for then. Not a disaster, more of a lesson that I am sure one day will be of service. There was still time to join Bob's record-breaking trip to Brest in his re-built motor sailor, 'Saffron'.

"Time to turn around and head back." Louis said. "You really don't say much when you're rowing." he added.

"Sorry Louis, I'm just trying to…concentrate. These oars are strange, they're like the ones used in the Cornish Gig Races."

I can only assume by the shape of the oars they intended to row with one oar each. I would have thought I'd feel more nervous. Obviously they've been practising.

Louis gave me a quick demonstration of turning fast into the wind, which had been behind us, back rowing with one and rowing forward with the other. If I thought rowing with the wind was hard, I was now in for a shock as we pulled against the wind. On the way out I had been watching Louis feather the oars. I had tried to copy him but after pulling with the blade horizontal in the water a few times by mistake, I gave up trying. This only confirmed the advantage of feathering as the wind almost brought the vertical blades to a standstill. After some strenuous effort I was glad to approach the harbour mouth and once inside the rowing became relaxed again.

Thanking Louis for his time and trouble I sneaked back to the boat, hoping nobody would notice my absence.

"Skiving again while we're sweating our balls off," Rob's jocular rebuke.

I see that Phil has crammed as much polystyrene into the two compartments so it is time to re-fit the cut-outs, drilling holes to accommodate the nozzle for blasting in the foam. Another long day draws to a close and time for a drink. Sitting across the road from the docks, swallowing ice cold quantities of amber coloured beer, I turn to Rob with a sudden thought. "After talking over exploits about the old clinker rowing boat with Louis today, I realise that I must replace the roof of the garden gazebo."

"You mean lift that ageing rowboat weighing a ton, turn it upside down and plonk it back onto the garden frame?"

"Got it in one Rob."

" I'd hoped that you'd consider letting me make it the centre of attraction on November the fifth, possibly a Viking funeral."

"How could you say such a thing after watching Keith and me row it up and down the River Soar?"

"Easy."

6th October 1997

At last, the position for the sliding rails has been decided. It's about time too; I think the lengthy discussions with our neighbours were starting to get tedious. Rob's planning to fit the solar panels today. Well, the one's that still work.

Thank God for Daniel and Peter from *The Golden Fleece*, they very kindly sold us two small panels at a very reasonable price.

By the end of the day we have the seats sliding on their would be position. All that remains, before they're fixed in place is; paint, silicone and a few screws and bolts. I'm sure I'm not speaking for myself when I say I'm determined to finish earlier than 7.00pm. I really want to go the Harbour Club. There's an event on.

7th October 1997

On our way to the port we stop to buy essential bits and pieces from our usual supplier. This morning's plan, Phil's going to fit U bolts for sea anchors. Rob is going to make the steel brackets to hold the VHF in place under the ceiling in the aft cabin, unfortunately I have to return to Los Gigantes. There's a meeting.

Arriving late I rush up the stairs and into the Centro Medico, now the Challenge Business office, there, I'm met by a crowd of enthusiastic rowers. Maybe I'm not the only one whose partner hasn't arrived in Tenerife yet. I'm not even sure why we're here, surely not just to announce the new title-holder.

As it begins to warm up it's becoming obvious that a lot of people aren't happy. The first boat that comes under criticism is *Wabun*. Her keel is deeper than the agreed size. Now this was one of the things I called Matthew Ratsey about for clarification, which resulted in clear diagrams and sizes faxed to me straight away. So I'm pretty interested to see what happens. Boris Renzelmann and Nikolai Wedemeyer's explanation is that it was simply a matter of interpretation.

The second boat to undergo serious criticism is the aptly named *Atlantic Challenge*. Pascal Blond and Joseph Le Guen have fitted fins to the lower aft section, which is definitely against the rules in my opinion. As for my boat, all this pales into insignificance, when considering my overall ambition is simply to be ready to start the race. With this in mind, I walk out of the meeting, jump in the car and race towards Playa San Juan. There, I find Rob still tinkering with the VHF while Phil screws on flat timber pieces around the hatch. Their job is to stop water running up to the hatches when opened. The afternoon was spent in another attempt to finish bracing the fore-cabin. To ease my discomfort Phil wafts air through the hatch to try and keep the temperature down. Packing away the tools and material only slightly earlier tonight keeps that guilty feeling at bay, for there is yet another function tonight. This is in the interest of competitive competition.

When we arrive at the Harbour Lights bar we discover that the arm wrestling contest was over, I'm pretty disappointed as this was the only competition I was prepared to enter. My days guzzling down large quantities of beer are over. Is that a yard of ale? Watching John from *Keilder Atlantic Warrior* tilt that elongated bulbous tube up in the air paints a grim picture in my memory of a Rugby tour on the Isle of Man.

I was already bloated by the consumption of enormous quantities of beer without trying to swallow that last pint that lay low in the bulb. I remember, I was so close - relief almost at hand. With the sinking of those last few dregs came an explosion, not seen since the breaching of the Mona Dam by one of the last bouncing bombs. Fortunately most of those encumbered were in no fit state to complain, apart from the Landlord. Snatching the yard of ale glass with one hand and fiercely pointing toward the door with the other, it dawned on me that I had probably peaked too early.

Not a good start to the Rugby tour, but in my condition, not the worst humiliation I was to endure over the next four days. Following the Publican's earnest wishes I found myself outside another fine establishment and regrettably my legs buckled underneath me. I can only commend my drinking companions, the ones still standing. They carried me the two streets home in a borrowed beach chair. The first night's sleep couldn't come too quickly, but unhappily I had missed the teams instruction – do not retire until 6.00am - apparently a regulation.

I contemplated the events of the night before over a sleepy breakfast, things looked brighter, that was, until lunchtime. Unluckily, due to my slow reflexes, I had been awarded more than my fair share of golf balls secretly dropped into my beer mug. The poor victim is forced to down it and the constant harassment results in a muddled brain. A tray-bashing contest is not the type of activity associated with a head like mine - being this particular shape it does not bode well for these endeavours. Four attempts at touching my ears, by bringing the tray down as hard as is humanly possible is all it takes. If this was not bad enough I was accused of bribery for buying one of the deputies a pint. On being informed of my punishment I was not at all happy.

I did not object to walking about in a comical hat but to have my head painted in the style of the Club's badge was not a pleasant thought. It had been a long day, trying to play rugby had not helped my condition. I decided to sneak off and bolt myself in. My two room companions would have to fend for themselves. Heavenly sleep. Crash! I am awakened with the top of the door crunching down on the side of my bed devoid of hinges or lock. I am unceremoniously dropped on the door and marched off, as if on a stretcher, to the edge of the banister. I was then unceremoniously tipped over the balcony, luckily just receiving a few bruises.

8th October 1997

Phil has decided to take a day off. I called for Keith and Jacqui, his fiancee, then picked Rob up and away we went. On reaching the port all the equipment brought yesterday is unloaded. Allowing Keith to drive to the airport to collect the oars leaves Rob and I to press on. Now that Keith has given me their exact length, I can fit the oar retainer - six-inches of plastic drainpipe, cleaned and ready for use. Cutting a hole in the fore-cabin I mix epoxy ready to stick the whole contraption together. It does not take long before smoking hot epoxy drops onto my hands and feet, fitting the hollow tube into the fore-cabin is far more difficult than anticipated. Arvid and Stein from *Star Atlantic* have helped me out on a number of occasions and today they are taking me out for a practice row. A last minute reprieve as Arvid shouts that they are ready to go out. It is not such a shock this time as I take to the oars, having had the practice with Louis and Michael. I ask Stein what he intends to wear on his hands and feet. In his opinion, if one's hands are used to working they should be okay without gloves. As for their feet, they'll leave them bare.

Over an hour later and after receiving some good rowing tuition, I am walking back to the boat, hopefully to see the oars. I'm not disappointed, there against the harbour wall are three pairs of oars standing upright, and Keith is already fitting the sleeves. After some discussion we agree not to epoxy them in place just yet. Next I begin to fix the bulls-eyes that will carry the grab lines down each side leaving three loops in each. Martin and Mark from *Salamanca* come to say goodbye as they are now ready to row to Los Gigantes. Both of them had previously offered their help but fortunately I had not had to take up their kind offer. Earlier I had watched Rob and Phil from *Kiwi Challenger* row out towards Los Gigantes setting a blistering pace. As the work progresses more help arrives in the form of David, a carpenter friend of mine whose contribution at the moment is transporting a regulator for the solar panels from England as the one we had brought with us is not really suitable. Good old Dave, he's considerately taken his annual holiday at this time, little does he know that in about five minutes he'll put to work drilling and fitting the rest of the bulls-eyes.

At the height of activity Brett arrives, camcorder in hand, filming begins followed by a generous offer to buy us all a beer, how could we upset him by refusing? By 7.00pm we all part company and head off on our separate ways.

Tonight's entertainment is a reception at the Royal Sun hosted by the Lions Club with the object of presenting the crews to the public, in doing so, raising as much money for charity as possible. Arriving late, as usual, I walk into the reception glancing at the lavishly decorated entrance hall and am informed immediately that I need to use the garden entrance. Strange, but we must all adhere to formalities at times. By the time I have climbed the steps the night's entertainment is in full swing. Is that James Brown? All these function bands seem to play the same songs; still, the setting is spectacular. There seems to be a lot of evening suits here, I hope nobody said anything about my t-shirt.

After a small search I find Keith and Jacqui sitting with the marines. After some light conversation a young bald waiter slips a small bowl of what I can only assume is caviar under my arm. Now I don't have the most seasoned palate, especially when it comes to delicacies, but that's good! Satisfying my appetite I excuse myself from the conversation and explore the higher levels of the venue only to find Louis and Michael seated with David and Nadia from the *Hannah Snell*. Engaging in conversation I'm sure they wished to avoid tonight, we discussed water-makers.

The evening is going very well as all the crew's signed tee shirts and menus were raffled to the public. Certain members of the crew are persuaded to reveal particular parts of their anatomy to raise more money for charity, something hard to refuse. A short and utterly chaotic five minutes on the dance floor is enough to finish me off as a day's work in the hot sun begins to take it's toll. Also, it's 1.30am.

Walking along the road that led to Los Gigantes I bump into Richard and Isabel from the *Stylus Mistral Endeavour.* We walk chatting for a short while before I forget my age. Just as we approach a steep, dusty incline, I'm challenged, probably as a joke to "Beat me down this drop!"

I set off at a reasonable pace, watching my steps as I zigzag down the side of the embankment. Looking around I can see Richard way up above me. He's not even racing me. I stop, now I realising there's no race. Not wanting to capitulate, I immediately think of another challenge. "I'll race down this way and you two go down the road." I say as I snake over the dusty ground. Dark is perhaps not the best of conditions for descending.

I'm told that approximately two thirds of the way down I slipped and fell. Apparently then I rolled over and over before my body coming to a sheer rock face, probably about fifteen feet high. Before anything could be done I was flying through the air, only for a few seconds as I hit something hard and my flight came to an abrupt end. I then began a vertical drop, bouncing off a few tree branches and landed in the street.

9th October 1997

Picking up Keith and Phil the next morning I looked up at the overhanging embankment with horror as the activities of the previous night come back to me. A cold sweat came over me when I considered the consequences of a broken arm or leg four days before the race. Well, work is the best therapy for aches.

10th October 1997

We arrive at the port at 9.00am, just in case our scrutineers arrive on time, although I am sceptical they will. Today Rob just needs to finish wiring the compass, Phil fitting the riggers and Keith the remaining rudder blocks and jammers. I need to finish fitting the footplates.

Two visitors turn up at the boat, Andrew Roberts and Matthew Ratsey, time for the inquisition. After checking the date on the life raft and water-maker they ask to see the flares. Unfortunately I can only show them the collision flares explaining that the others had been left in the apartment. Next to be inspected were the sea anchors and their relevant attachments to the boat, fore and aft.

"Can I see the fire extinguisher and deck pump?" said

Andrew. I point in their general direction. One thing I have not considered is a screw cover for the solar vent in case the boat capsizes. After the inspection there are still a few items that needed checking, this will have to wait until Saturday afternoon.

Rob has returned to Los Gigantes with Louis and Mike. There are two reasons for this. One, I have set aside this afternoon to finish the epoxy without Rob around as I think he's allergic to it. Last time he came into contact with it, his eyes looked bigger. The other reason is that there is a special race meeting at the hotel Los Gigantes at 4.00pm and it was impossible for Keith or I to go.

Taking the opportunity to relax over lunch at the restaurant and bar opposite the port it occurred to me that this was to be the last lunch. Thinking back over the past ten days I feel quite nostalgic. Apart from the first two days of crazy activity we had our lunch here every day, discussing the work on the boat with our crew, also Louis, Mike and any other crews that eat here. Still, mustn't think about that, I have too much to do this afternoon. One thing I definitely have to do is smooth all the bolts and rough edges in the aft cabin. A quick trip to the hardware shop solves this, pipe lagging is the answer. Dave has kindly agreed to do this for me. Keith fits the last bolt in the rudder while Phil and I mix epoxy and fit brackets to the bulkhead, now all the riggers are in place.

Tonight is the competitors leaving party and is being held at the Oasis Club. Brett is bringing his wife but Rob and Phil say they are going to the Harbour Lights. On the way to the Oasis, slightly late, I meet Ian and Nigel also on their way. They tell me that they rowed to the port today and that everything seems okay with their boat. Once inside, everybody looks as though they are having a good time dancing to the band. I join the queue for hot meat at the buffet. It has been a very long day and I pick up the plate. The waiter at the table asks me for a ticket and I tell him that I am a rower, expecting that will do the trick, but no, he still insists. It looks as if I will have to do a "runner," plate in hand, then another rower hands me a ticket. Keith comes up for a chat as I polish off most of the meat. Out of the corner of my eye I see Brett and Ann sitting watching the cabaret. Next it is Jock Wishart presenting every team with a bottle of Mount Gay Rum followed by a firework display.

11th October 1997

The last day before the race and Brett is waiting as we arrive at the port gates. The priority is to sort through all the material we have been using over the past ten days, picking out any items that we may need on the trip. A list is made, which seems endless. The sort starts with nuts and bolts and finishes with resin, hardener and paint. Next on the agenda - we need to organise what tools we're going to take aboard. All the water containers are unloaded, as yet, none of the compartments have been cleaned and there is still some painting to do.

We watch as *Star Atlantic* is launched, our turn next. As midday approaches we are ready. Clive turns up at approximately half past twelve and in no time at all the trailer is being backed down the slip with us sliding down beside it on top of a layer of green slimy seaweed. Everybody involved in the launching is aware that the trailer has to go fairly deep allowing the boat to float off. We're in! There is a small cheer from the watching crowd. I jump aboard, opening a bottle of beer. Keith aboard, the swell running into the harbour takes us back up the slip. We prod the boat back using the oars and the words "I name this boat The George Geary" are lost in the commotion. A whole bottle of beer is poured over the bow, well, almost a whole bottle. The swell now takes the boat up against the side of the slip and I look in numbed silence as the ensign and flag pole take the pressure. Fortunately it is well fixed and with a quick sweep of the oars we are away from the sides. Pulling out slightly into the harbour we decide to go back along-side one of the fishing boats using water containers as fenders, the plan works as we tie up briefly. I can't believe we've not sunk yet. Maybe we'll actually make it to Barbados! Jacqui climbs on board for the row to Los Gigantes and it occurs to us that we have not fixed the rudder, too late now.

For the last thirty minutes we have been watching the progress of Louise and Victoria from *American Pearl* who must have launched after us. They are steadily catching us up and may get there before us. Having rowed in a wide sweep angle we are now on the outside as they pull through on the inside. We just have enough time to cut in front of them which I must admit is not the sporting way. The loud cheering from all sides of the harbour took me by surprise as we rowed in. I know a few of the other crews thought that we would not make it, but this reception was very heart warming. We nose in amongst the impressive display of rowing boats, almost thirty, in a line. After tying up we are met by John and his wife, Ann, then Tony and his wife who bring along my spear gun - a last minute thought, and we all went for a quick drink together.

Final job, fix the rudder, which means turning the boat around. As soon as the boat's stern is next to the pontoon it does not take long to get the rudder in position. Dave carries on fitting the pipe lagging around the cabin and Phil tapes all the rough edges. I finish fitting the rudder by drilling and bolting on a rudder pintle upside. Next - the Argos Tracking Beacon. Phil bolts on the case. Outside the main hatch Keith refits the rudder controls. I must see David and Nadia Rice as, although I have fixed our compass in a place I assume to be the best position, I'm not sure. I think they'll be able to advise me.

Fishing kit! Something else I had overlooked. Running down the side of the harbour I was at Damon's Sports Shop in a minute, with hooks, swivel, lures, floats and lead weights in my possession I made my way out and came face to face with Steve from *Toc H Phoenix.* He had kindly offered to give us eight gas canisters suitable for our stove plus a few odds and sods and following him back to the boat I unloaded all his contributions. With so many things going on I had completely forgotten the final inspection, but I need not have worried, walking down the pontoon towards me were the scrutineers Andrew and Matthew. I hope everything is ok, there's still time to be disqualified. Everything seems in order apart from two items. One, which I did not agree with, I was told to remove the flexible covering on the scuppers which would let more water onto the rowing deck. I'm sure it won't, but I'd rather not argue about it. The other was the pump handle, which I had forgotten about. The two problems soon sorted, Matthew signs the Certificate.

Keith reminds me that the food is spread between my apartment and his. The car, where is it? The day has gone that quickly that I have not even considered it. I suppose that at the back of my mind I had assumed that Rob would bring it back when he leaves the port. Eventually Rob walks down the quay side and explains Arvid from *Star Atlantic* had asked him to bring their scooter back. He assumed Jacqui would drive back, not expecting her to come with us on the boat. Mary, always ready to help, said she will run Rob back to fetch the car, but unfortunately Rob has been celebrating our arrival and is not in a fit state. I'm not sure what to do at this point. Dave, who has just finished fitting the compass, has agreed to run Keith back to the port to fetch the car as he is staying on the other side of the island. At last we are getting somewhere. Wait, where's Keith? This is a disaster.

"Hello sir." said the voice of a small bearded man who I can only assume from the camera men following him is part of a television crew. "Can we film?" he asked.

"Errr, you see the problem is I can't find my partner."

"Ok, no problem we can come back at 8 tomorrow morning. Yes?"

I agree and just after they leave Keith turns up. It is now about 7.30pm, I looked everywhere for Dave but can't find him. I think he must have gone to his apartment. Summing up the situation with the hire car, which was now getting beyond a joke, I suggested to Keith that he stay here while I go and sort out the problem once and for all. With that I left, trying to get my mind round this latest setback. Phil had mentioned that as he was coming along the quay he had seen Mike from *The Cornish Challenger,* and his girlfriend, sitting outside the Harbour Lights. That is it! Mike still has his hire car, I'll ask him to drop me off. I rush down to the Harbour Lights, my luck is in, they are still there. Thirty minutes later I'm being dropped off at the harbour gates.

"Thanks Mike, I hope I didn't spoil your last night."

"Only too happy to help you out, Graham, will you be ready for the 10.00am start?"

"That remains to be seen." I say. Every time I look at my watch the time seems to be gaining on me.

Back at the apartment the endless job of transporting the bulk of our food to the car became a trial, as the distance from my apartment to the car must have been at least five hundred metres. At last it's loaded. Driving down to the harbour I notice that most of the activity around the rowing boats have ceased. We unload the car on the dockside while Keith goes to fetch the rest of the items bought from the Supermarket. Phil and I load the food under the floor in the aft cabin.

12th October 1997

It was 1.30am, all the final preparations have been made as I'm driving Keith and Jacqui back to their apartment.

"Last drink anybody?" I say, but there are no takers. Driving back to the Harbour Lights, the only bar still open, I park the car and walk over. There are still quite a few people left but no rowers. I order a drink, which is on the house, sign a few tee shirts, and have my photograph taken shaking hands with the landlord. I should book myself in for a mega breakfast at half past seven in the morning, it's free to the rowers. Right I better get to bed I thought finishing my last beer for some time.

What would it have been like to be a holidaymaker these past ten days? I must come back to find out in the not too distant future.

There was no time to look back over the past three months. They had passed so quickly. This seems to be the pattern of my entire life rushing from one thing to another. Now that I am fifty years of age it is getting faster. Is the Atlantic finally going to slow me down? No time for that I'd better sleep.

7.00am! Jumping out of bed I scurry around the room and grab everything I can find. Where's my passport...and my driving licence! I'm just going to have to press on without them. Dragging my bags out to the car the nerves suddenly begin to kick in. This is actually happening, are we going to die at sea? No time for that now, throwing my bags into the back of the car.

I pull up outside where Keith is staying and as I expected all is quiet. I ring the bell and Jacqui comes to the door. Although I have so many things I need to say, all I can remember to say is 'Tell Keith not to forget the film crew.' My mind is a mess. Running through the alleyways towards the seafront I have to stop as my flip flops keep coming off, putting them in my pocket I run on, maybe I'll be able to row barefoot after all. Looking at my watch it's 7.45am, which undoubtedly means I have no time for the big breakfast I was so looking forward to. I guess it's going to have to be Cornflakes.

Having made no passage plans for the ocean crossing I take out the charts for the first time and have a quick look just as the television crew arrives.

"No, don't stop." a small, rather strange looking man said.

"Excuse me?" I say.

"I want to film you looking at the charts.

"But..." Where's Keith? Oh thank God. I've never been happier to see him, hopefully now they'll just need a few shots of the boat, a brief and monosyllabic interview and they can leave.

I feel relieved to see them go as time is running out.

"Right, I'm thinking we place all of the less necessary items in the forward cabin, what do you think?"

"Sounds good to me...wait, what about toilet paper?"

"What about toilet paper?"

"Well that's a necessary item."

"Well where else is it going to go?"

"Good point..."

Our clothes, wet gear, books, camera etc are piled into two large waterproof bags. The theory behind the bags is that they will be placed either side of the aft cabin to prevent us from rolling about in the bad weather. Whether or not it'll work we've yet to find out.

As we are getting organised Teresa from the Atlantic Challenge company approaches us as she needs the customs forms, shipping forms, declarations etc. I was not aware that we had any, hold on, come to think of it Rob had given me a large envelope saying something about forms.

"'I'll have a look in the car." I say.

Walking to the car I begin to panic. But a couple of minutes later, I'm able to say, with honesty "Yes they're here. I've found them." Although when I pull them out of the envelope I am stunned into silence. There are probably about 14 or 16 forms wanting various information on the boat, us, passports that are yet to be filled out. Ok, that's a problem - I can't find my passport. Still, there's no time to think about it, I'm going to have to go without it. I'll just have to face the consequences when they occur. Writing down the first numbers that came into my head our party arrives. Keith and I manage to complete about half of the forms then in a last desperate effort I hand them to Dave to complete while we carry on preparing the boat. A final frantic effort to clear the decks now commences. We are oblivious of the activity around us as our fellow competitors begin to leave for the start line. I look at my watch - 9.50am!

Ten minutes before the start they are going to wave a flag with 'C' on it and fire a gun. Following that there's a five-minute warning, a flag with 'P' and a gun shot. Kissing his fiancee, Jacqui, Keith unties the mooring lines and pushes off. Sadly there's no time to shake hands or say goodbye to all the kind people who have helped me so much over the past three months. Let's hope they know how grateful I am. Paddling the boat past a few large cruisers moored nearby Keith begins to row out of the harbour as I prepare to follow suit.

"Keith, the foot plate's not even fitted." I say.

"I'll keep rowing while you fit it." Keith looks slightly concerned. I have envisaged this moment from the beginning, leaving the harbour to start the race. It was as I had expected – a mass of cheering people filling every available space on the harbour wall and quay side.

"Come on *The George Geary*, hurry up or you'll miss the start, come on *The Geary*."
The loud encouragement continues until we are, at last, among some of the other competitors. Finally, the footplate is secure, and I sit back looking and feeling totally relieved.

The first sight of what I assume to be start area is one of absolute chaos. Speed boats, sailing boats, passenger boats, all milling around. As for the rowing boats they are pointing in every direction with boats alongside talking and gesturing. Before we have even thought about looking for the official start line there is a crack of gunfire followed by cheering and shouting. "This must be it Keith, let's go."

Pulling on the oars we head out into the Atlantic. Our strategy for the first part of the race, I must admit, is rather vague. Discussing the start with some of our competitors it was clear that there's going to be two directions, north or south. The north sounded intriguing and seemed easier. The idea is to row along the west coast until you reach the lighthouse of Pint do Pargo, turn west and clear the Island of Gomera as fast as possible in a westerly direction thereby picking up the trade winds. Mulling over the options only an hour before the race we decided that we would go west clearing the north of Gomera and hopefully join in with a similar plan.

High towering cliffs are still our main view as we pull on the 12′ carbon fibre oars. We've decided to row as we had the day before, just concentrating on keeping a steady stroke. I occasionally look behind to see how Keith's stroke is following. I guess for us this is our training. We hardly had any time yesterday to practice our stroke during the short trip to Los Gigantes. What a way to start a race. We continue for some time before we're distracted by the spectator boat that passes us. We look up and there stands Rob and Dave waving.

Further along the deck is Jacqui waving to Keith, who's unable to wave back. Turning round to see how Keith was managing I catch a glimpse of another rowing boat, probably a quarter of a mile in front of us. It looks as if it's almost on the same course. Well, that's reassuring. At least one other boat has the same idea. The majority of the rowers had gone south followed by a flotilla of sightseeing crafts. A low thud of a distant diesel engine suddenly grew louder. Turning our heads a large sailing boat came alongside it was *3 Com* – no doubt our guardian in the weeks to come. Amidships sat the distinguished figure of Chay Blyth. As this famous boat of the BT Round The World Challenge slid slowly by, words I will no doubt remember for the rest of my life were heard over the short distance of water between us, "Only another 2,995 miles to go gentleman."

Three hours into the race sees a more relaxed rowing rhythm. Thirst has become more prevalent. We suck water mixed with glucose powder from a tube attached to our shoulders - a bizarre drinking method organised by Keith. I'm told it's called the Camelback Hydration System, a fitting name for such an awkward experience.

Occasionally small motorboats come alongside to shout encouragement or ask questions. Apart from them there's nothing to distract us from our own private worlds.

"What time do you think we ought to do a fix?" Keith asks. I look at my watch, 3.25pm. "Let's make it 3.30pm." I say before I immediately stop rowing and pull out my small bag from the aft cabin.

"That's it Keith, our first fix. I'm just going to record it in the ship's log.' Fix at 15.30pm 28° 16′ north 17° 02′ west. May as well get out a couple of chocolate bars whilst I'm putting the GPS back. There's no doubt about it, a chocolate bar tastes good when you haven't eaten for seven and a half hours. As we polished off our chocolate bars, the wind, which has been kindly absent until recently, starts to increase from the Northwest. Battling more and more against an increasing head wind we reluctantly made the decision to turn back and head Southeast. We both knew that we had to take this drastic setback in our stride, guessing, with good reason, to already be ten hours behind those who had gone north. I had estimated our position to be roughly four miles off Agulo on the island of Gomera.

The only chart we have is of the entire North Atlantic 4012. The island of Gomera is almost a pinprick on the chart. Wait, I have that tourist map showing Gomera.

"What the hell is that Graham?"

"It's a map."

"It's got cartoons on it!"

"Look, it gives us a good indication of what we are looking at."

Now that we have changed course the local current and wind are in our favour helping the boat to move in the right direction. The time is now about 7.30pm - a good time to start our evening meal. This thought brought an almost paralysing anxiety on. I've not lit the cooker. What if it doesn't work? Turning my head away from Keith in an attempt to hide the horror on my face I pull a small gas lighter from my bag. My hands are shaking. Please light…please. "Oh thank God." I say with a sigh of relief.

"What?" asks Keith.

"Nothing."

Out comes Keith's new saucepan with that weird clamp on lid, a quick dip in the sea, then on to the round grill. If I can just get the three revolving arms to lock the saucepan in place…there. So far this cooker's all of the things the advertiser said it was, perhaps it is "the ultimate sea cooker", apparently it's designed to work in the worst sea conditions. Right, let's get cooking. Tonight will be our first glimpse of what's to come. Neither me, nor Keith have tried a Wayfayrer boil in the bag meal before. Let's hope they're bearable. It's chicken casserole tonight. I remove the outer plastic bag and place the two pouches into the boiling water. Both of us sit staring at the boiling saucepan, one either side. Fatigue now holds conversation at bay. The calming sounds of the waves are the only sounds for miles.

Anybody now passing our boat would have seen two bodies facing each other, sitting, as if locked in place by rigor-mortis, holding spoons as if they were swords ready to begin a duel.

The pouches are taken out and ready to eat. As soon as the tops are torn off a delicious smell filters out. This is it…my first spoon-full actually comes as a surprise, this is really good food. By the time the kettle boils the light is fading which leaves us in an eerie shadow. After a small search to find the switch for the navigation light we discover that it's not working. I guess we can look in the morning.

"I'll start the first shift, probably for two hours, but we'll see how it goes, it's almost 9.00pm." Keith said before yawning and climbing through the hatch.

Great, the wind would pick up now. That's got to be 20 miles an hour. The swell's increased considerably too. It's not too worrying I'm used to five-foot waves, still, it's not the most pleasant experience for my first night alone. I begin to row a course of Southeast. Having got into a certain rhythm rowing with Keith I find that I must start learning all over again trying to correct myself every time I am thrown from side to side. The first hour drags on. My mind is slipping in and out of the memories of the last few days before our departure. Soon my body becomes acclimatised to the boats' movement. Looking at the sky I am slightly disappointed, I had imagined the first night's row to be under a star covered sky. The reality is much different. Low grey clouds cover most of the night's sky leaving just a few faint glimmers of light that burst through from time to time. The second hour passes faster. Time to shout to Keith, who wakes suddenly making strange noises. Pulling the oars through the rowlocks so that only the blades protrude I climb over to the hatch. Keith sits up half way out of his sleeping bag.

"Perhaps I shouldn't have woken you, it's just that we were going to decide on two hours or three." I say,

"Personally I don't think another hour's rowing would kill me, which would mean a change over at midnight and then I would come back on at 3.00am, how do you feel about that?"

"Sounds okay to me." Keith said.

"Sorry I had to wake you Keith, but at least it's now sorted."

Midnight came along much sooner than I had expected. "Time to get up Keith." I said. "The wind is still the same, our course much the same, south east, I can only guess that we are about three to four miles off the coast of Gomera. See if you can make better adjustments to the rudder, feeling the length of rope hanging out of the jammers I can only assume it's locked off dead centre."
Rubbing his eyes Keith climbs through the hatch. "Are we ever going to get used to this climbing in and out Graham?"

"I'll let you know in a month's time." I replied. Lying down under the sleeping bag I soon get used to the side-to-side motion and fall asleep.

13th October 1997

"Graham, Graham wake up!
My eyes open but my brain does not register wooden sides and face looking through the square aperture. Before long I realise where I am. Pulling on a sweatshirt I climb out. "How are we doing Keith?" I ask.

"We seem to be coming to a point on our port side where the coast drops away."

"Let's have a look at the tourist map."
Keith sighs and hands me the map.

"Hmmm, ahhh, I see, that must be the port of San Sebastian." I say pointing into the distance. "So as soon as we pass the point I'll change direction, north west." I say with a blind optimism. Although the wind won't be behind us we'll at least be sheltered by the land.

"Okay Graham, see you at 6.00am."
I watch Keith's awkward climb through the hatch as my stiff muscles are coached back to mobility. Constantly adjusting my position the sliding seat is squarely positioned under my backside and I begin to pick up a rowing rhythm. The long sliding seat movement is interrupted by alterations to the rudder and the occasional drink from the backpacks containing the water, which having been removed when we ate our evening meal, now lie to hand nearby. There is not much change in the night sky – overcast, a faint glow from behind the clouds. As my rowing labours continue my mind becomes obsessed with thoughts of the other boats. We lost sight of the last boat, ahead of us, about eight hours into the race. Who would have thought that could make me feel so lonely? Well before 6.00am, my head starts to droop, shaking myself I try to keep my eyes open. Maybe a dab of salt water on my face will do the trick. There we go. Relieved when the end of my watch arrives, Keith appears with a disgruntled look. Sleep comes quickly after my enthusiastic entrance to the aft cabin.

"Graham, tea up."
I wake to a picture of white and blue sky through the half-open rear hatch. I could murder a cup of rosy lea. The sun is still fairly low in the blue sky and dotted here and there are small puffs of white cloud. The wind has dropped considerably which allows a much smaller swell.

"What about a banana to go with our tea?" I say before climbing over the rowing seat and opening the forward hatch. The last item packed was the six man life raft after everything else had been thrown in. In hindsight that was a bad idea but it had all been so chaotic.

Pulling out the life raft I discover that the net bag containing our fruit has sustained some damage - three squashed bananas and a very oddly shaped orange. Another brew and two empty yellow skins later, Keith retires for a morning sleep and I'm back on the oars rowing Southwest. The island of Gomera is slowly getting smaller, although the high rocky interior is still clearly visible. I find it amazing that in 1492 Christopher Columbus left from this island to discover the New World.

At midday, it's time to think about food. After a brief discussion on the delights of various meals, beef stew and dumplings in gravy, is our choice. Organising the cooker pots and kettle was a very uplifting activity. It served as a time to relax and discuss our progress. Boiling bags of food are soon lifted out of the saucepan. Kettle on, sitting and eating our food in the sun seems to be a real luxury.

"How do you think we're doing Graham?" asked Keith. Now, I know we're not doing too well - we are still in sight of Gomera.

"I can't think we've done more than 25 miles since our last fix.' I say in an attempt to leave it to interpretation.

"Ok, we'll take another fix in a couple of hours." he said which clarifies he knows we're not doing too well either. As long as we take a fix roughly about the same time each day it should give us a good indication of speed.

"While you're rowing Keith, I'll read up on the Magellan 3000 GPS."

"You mean to say you want to stop using the backup?"

"Well it is a back up."

The more of the day we lose the more I start to worry if the race has been called off. The last time we saw a living soul was about eight hours after the race began. Still, there's no time for that now it's almost 6.00pm – time for a bite to eat, then bed.

Before 9.30pm arrives I am up, with dreadful stomach cramps. Luckily there's just enough time to climb out of the hatch and unceremoniously hang my backside over the edge of the boat.

"Don't worry Keith, I'm downwind."

"Oh, at least that then…that doesn't sound right Graham."

"I think I've got a serious case of the montys."

"See how it goes and if it gets any worse I'll open up the medicine case," is Keith's uninterested reply. Just as we are about to change over I have to rush to the side again.

"Right, I'll leave you to it." he said as he climbs into the aft cabin. The only good thing about this sickness is that it gives me a break from rowing every now and again.

Midnight can't come soon enough. I'm hoping that I can sleep for a couple of hours without disturbance from my stomach, no doubt some wishful thinking - we all dream.

14th October 1997

Time to crack open the medicine case. Now do I take two or three Imodium capsules? What a gracious start to the race this has been, still better start rowing, hopefully soon my misery will be over.

I'm starting to lose all perception of time. Having climbed out of the cabin I sit contentedly - a light breeze refreshes my sleepy head. The sky is relatively clear; the sun's bright glare warms the surrounding air. Keith has decided on half an orange for breakfast, this goes down nicely with a steaming cup of coffee. Adjusting the straps on the footplate I begin my three-hour row, secretly hoping that this is the beginning of my recovery.

The afternoon fix takes my mind off my bowels. 2.15pm: 27° 48′ north 17° 24′ west. The same situation occurs when it's time for the evening meal resulting in me hanging my backside over the edge of the boat. As Keith is normally in the aft cabin when this frenzied activity is taking place I make sure that I am wearing my harness. Dehydration is now becoming a problem and to combat this loss of bodily fluids I've doubled my water intake. Keith has also started me on a course of Dioralyte EFF tablets. I row on into the night knowing that I am becoming weaker.

15th October 1997
Gathering my clothes ready for the morning watch I make a definite decision not to eat any more food for at least two days in the hope of flushing this bug out of my system. Once on deck Keith informs me that there are lights ahead. It must be El Hierro, the most westerly island in the Canaries - that's some indication of our progress at least.

We were correct; the first sight to greet me in the morning as I scramble out through the hatch was indeed the Island of El Hierro. The lights that we had seen during the night belonged to the capital, Vulverde. Sitting down in the early morning sun, my day of abstinence begins by watching Keith drink a warm cup of coffee. This is the first time I have noticed the delicious aroma of freshly made coffee.

Midday comes without any joy, I'm merely relieved that I have finished my morning rowing shift. There's no food for me to look forward to today, my only distraction being the view of the rocky, bleak, windswept island. El Hierro's only claim to fame is that this was the last sight of land on Columbus's voyage of discovery, not unlike ourselves I should imagine. The Arab scientists in the early seventeenth century decided that all maps should begin or end at El Hierro and made it nought degrees longitude for the rest of the world. It took another two hundred years before the standard meridian was moved to Greenwich.

Progress is being made in the southwest direction as the last sights of civilisation slips past in the shape of Punta Restinga, the islands' main fishing port. My fix at 2.15pm confirms good progress, 27° 28' north 18° 01′ west. The swell is now quite steep, the wind must be gusting at thirty miles an hour. From time to time the tops of breaking waves are blown along in streaks of foam still northeasterly. Rowing with the swell, in a somewhat contented mood, my attention is suddenly diverted by a large yacht bearing down on us approximately two miles away on our port beam.

It must be *3 Com*, the 67′ steel sailing monster. This was one of the fourteen identical yachts to leave Southampton in a thirty thousand mile race around the world, crewed by people from all walks of life. Thinking back to the race, which was highly televised, I can see the crew celebrating on the beach at Rio de Janeiro after coming sixth in the first leg, a position that was to be their best. Seeing her sail towards us I am surprised at the amount of sail she displays in this wind strength, which I can only conclude is nothing compared to the Southern Ocean.

Sailing behind our stern and tacking round, one of the wet weather geared crew shouts to ask if we're okay. Responding with an affirmative gesture I suddenly realise that we're unsure if our VHF works. Shouting against the wind I ask if they could give us a radio check.

"Keith, switch the VHF on channel seventy-two…that's it."

"*The George Geary, The George Geary,* this is *3 Com,* this is *3 Com,* over."

Keith, asking for confirmation of our signal, gets the immediate response,

"*George Geary* coming through loud and clear, over."

After some update on the race and a few close circles, which results in loud metallic noises as boom and foresail swings over, they depart around 4.45pm.

Tonight's meal; water and Dioralyte EFF tablets but I'm comforted by our progress through this windswept sea. The wind's got to be about 25-30 miles an hour, surely. My short excursions to the side of the boat seem to have abated for now. All my hope is now pinned on a quick recovery over the next two days. Even drinking water has necessitated spells of sitting out over the edge. Mindful of the situation, should my body resist all of this stomach cleansing, an estimation of two days is all that I have before rendering me useless.

16th October 1997

Trips to the side of the boat are becoming less frequent in the early hours of my rowing stint. Sleeping more contentedly, with no stomach cramps, I rise at 8.30am. Looking through the hatch the sky is almost clear of cloud - a good omen. The wind is still northerly now probably only five to ten miles per hour. I shout to Keith, who is about to put the kettle on, "I fancy a coffee this morning."

"Are you sure Graham?"

It feels like my body is hydrating at last. Eagerly setting up the cooker after my stint I boil a meal for Keith and then prepare two steaming cups of minestrone soup for me. What a taste, it is incredible. Keith sleepily climbs out for his meal while I tell him the good news. Buoyed up by this positive attitude I decide to have a wash and a change of underpants, as hygiene has been forgotten over these last few days. After washing with sea soap - which I must admit, is somewhat disappointing due to it's lack of lather, I embark on a swim.

The sweat, toil and problems of the last few days drifts off in this water, which is much warmer than I anticipated. Climbing onto the boat is not as difficult as I had imagined with one foot on the safety lines, two hands on the bulwarks, a quick pull and, hey presto, I'm back on board again.

My hands seem to be coping with rowing pretty well, although I can't say the same for Keith's – they've blistered quite badly. By moving the foot straps I have managed to keep my feet blister free which I'm pretty proud of considering I'm still rowing barefoot.

With the meal over and everything tidied away Keith begins to row while I fiddle with the navigation lights, which have not worked since the first day. Last night a large cargo boat passed very close, and studying her navigation lights, we had assumed her to be on a possible collision course. Without our navigation lights we were left no option but to illuminate our boat with the searchlight, hence the urgency to get it working. A slight adjustment seems to have done the job.

There is just time to re-fix the outer casing before we lose the daylight. Our watch system appears to be working apart from the constant acrobatics required to climb in and out of the aft cabin. Four days of practice has produced a method fairly acceptable and reasonably quick. Having just completed another trial run I climb into the sleeping bag shared by the two of us. Not my choice, but as Keith acquired both sleeping bags, I go along with his theory that when this one gets wet we can use the dry one.

17th October 1997

With no bowel movements through the night I am starting to feel A1. Let's hope half an orange, a chocolate bar, and three cups of coffee will not change that.

I'm finally starting to relax, I wonder if that's partly due to the motion of the boat – we're almost still; the wind has mostly died away. That reminds me, suntan lotion…if the sky stays clear it's going to be a very hot day. The morning passes without any distractions and finishing my stint early I go for a swim to cool off. Stripping off my shorts, I'm pleased to see that the sweat rash around my groin and dangling bits has cleared up due to a thorough wash and plenty of cream the day before. I really did think that was going to be a problem. Following a refreshing swim, soap and a fresh pair of underpants I feel ten years younger.

Right, time for food. Preparing the cooker I can only just restrain myself from tearing open the food pouches and eating the contents cold. It does say it's already cooked...then again beef stew and dumplings probably taste better warm.

18th October 1997

Keith wakes me at 6.00am. I put on my sweatshirt and hat, quite looking forward to this watch. All indications are that it is going to be a good sunrise - my first on board. As the sun comes up it becomes trapped by long grey streaks of cloud. There, amongst the shattered clouds, a bright burning ball shooting shards of yellow light is just visible - time for a cup of tea. Half an orange and a chocolate bar make a splendid breakfast.

This morning I plan to start reading one of my paperbacks. With such a hurried departure I'm not sure how many I've brought without searching through everything. Guess I'll just have to go with the first I can find. 'Zeebrugge: A Hero's Story' by Stephen Homewood. I still remember seeing it on the news - at that time there was no indication of the scale of the tragedy. Fixated, I watched as the camera rotated around the fast channel ferry which lay on it's side.

Falling asleep, clutching the damp pages of my book, I'm eventually woken by shouting;

"What do you fancy for lunch today?"

"Chicken casserole, I reckon."

One of the things that struck me as strange, apart from the visit by *3 Com* and meeting the cargo boat, was the fact we had not seen another boat or ship. We've not even seen many birds or fish. If it is like this two hundred miles off shore what is it going to be like in the middle of the Atlantic? Changing places with Keith I take the daily fix at 3.15pm, 25° 43′ north 18° 14′ west, 31 miles since yesterday. That means we're still only averaging a mile and a half an hour…I can't imagine that's going to win us the race.

19th October 1997

Not long after midnight, the wind began blowing from the Southwest, we rowed against it all night. By 8.00am it's blowing force seven. We decide it's time to put out the sea anchor but unfortunately we only have 20 metres of rope and the same for a tripping line. As we are short of rope the large sea anchor and the small one are tied together then streamed out on the port bow. This allows the boat to lie at a small angle to the waves. Keith tries out the fishing kit while I read, having by now become accustomed to the erratic behaviour of the boat in this rough weather. Following a relaxed lunch Keith puts his head down for a couple of hours, leaving me to read on deck. Page 199, *'I believe the British seaman is second to none in the world and that when it comes to the crunch he will do his duty unto death, I went to enough funerals to know that proved true on the night of 6th March 1987.'* Searching through my bags I discover that my total book supply is much lower than I thought. Nine books, considering that I've already read one, I don't think they're going to last me for long.

I take the afternoon fix with an overwhelming sense of dread. 25° 42' north 18° 15′ west - it could be worse. We've at least moved a bit, even if it's only a mile. What else is there to do than start on the next book? *'The Ghost Road'* by Pat Barker.

The wind continues blowing in the same direction - against us. I earmark the page and put the book away. Keith has been back on the fishing line changing and trying all the lures.

"Any luck Keith?"

"Yes, then no."

"What do you mean 'yes then no'?"

"Well one escaped, a large one," he said before gesturing the size with his hands.

"Fishermen's tales are all the same" I answered with disbelief. "Right I'm going back to my reading for the last hour, after that I'll slap the dinner together unless of course you have something more appetising to eat by that time Keith."

"Graham, the worst thing about fishing is a disbeliever, anyway it's your turn next."

Returning to my seat just inside the aft cabin I pick up my book although the sound of Keith rummaging through the toolbox for pliers is rather distracting. This is followed by a further exploration under the cockpit seat where the boat repairing kit is stored.

"What have we got in the way of wire Graham?"

"I'm just thinking."

"I know, if you pull out the large white plastic container with the electrical spares in, underneath you'll find two rolled up jack stays, the original ones that I was going to put on the boat." I had had second thoughts on their strength and had changed them for the beefy ones we have now. Keith was soon lost in the joys of DIY fishing tackle leaving me to continue reading.

Dinnertime - 6.30 by my faithful watch, which heralds the start of a noisy search for plates, saucepan and the cooker.

"What do you think to meat balls in pasta sauce Keith?"

"We were given those large bags of pasta before we left too."

"Good idea, see if you can dig one of the bags out." I say whilst starting to boil seawater. "I think they're in the third compartment along, under the aft cabin floor Keith."

Another enjoyable meal and three cups of coffee later we sit discussing the next plan of action.

"I think we agree then that both of us sleep through the night and make a decision in the morning after studying the weather."

"Sounds alright to me Keith."

This was the first time that we have both tried to sleep in the aft cabin. The plan is to sleep down each side leaving all the bags stacked in the middle, and, as always, we'll leave the main hatch open. I can only hope we never have to lock ourselves in the aft cabin because of horrendous weather conditions.

20th October 1997

I am awake at 7.00am. I climb out with difficulty after re-arranging the bags. The sea conditions are pretty much the same, wind probably about force six, the sky getting lighter. Sitting on the leeward side, harness on, I start to wonder if Keith prefers the bucket. He assures me he'll remember which bucket is which, we only have two and one is used for washing. I decide to have a quick swim. With the sea conditions as they are and Keith still sleeping, I tie a line to my harness. Over I go – woah that's cold, before the seawater always felt quite warm. After a good dry down I feel refreshed and set about making the breakfast.

"Tea or coffee Keith?" I yell.

"Tea please."

Looking at the wind, it seems to have dropped slightly and backed to the south, which will give us a chance at rowing west. As Keith climbs out of the aft cabin he said "We can both row now that we've had a rest over the last day and a half."

"We should take a fix before we start rowing and after so that we know exactly what we've accomplished."

Keith smiles and begins to pull in the sea anchor. "Well?" he said. Unsure of what he's implying I wait for him to continue,

"Take the fix."

"Oh right."

10.45am, 25° 43′ north 18° 06′ west, quite surprising with the wind blowing from the southwest. The wind has pushed us back north only one mile and nine miles east.

"What do you reckon then Keith, due west?"

"There's only one thing Graham, it's your turn to row from the bow seat."

With the waves hitting us beam on, the rowing becomes really difficult. The way we've built the boat means Keith, as he's nearest to the aft cabin, can pull back on his stroke but only has a short range when striking the water whereas I have the opposite problem, I'm unable to pull back on his stroke. It means when we row together we're only capable of short strokes.

Knowing these difficulties we press on with a grim determination, but after only thirty minutes the pain in my hips is agonising. To counter this the angle iron had worn a deep groove in the side of my bare foot. There is nothing like taking one's mind off one pain by replacing it with another.

Suffering in this way we both continue deciding to give it all we've got until two o'clock in the afternoon. When it came I could hardly move. The pain in my hips is terrible and the sides of my feet are red raw.

2.00pm: Keith quickly puts out the sea anchor and I take the fix, 25° 43' north 18° 05' west. After three hours and fifteen minutes of torture we are one mile east. I guess now the only way to make us feel better is to have a good lunch, although I don't think that's going to be very easy.

After lunch Keith continues rowing. From now on we'll be rowing independently. Two hours of reading lifts my spirits and I begin to feel like my old self again, that was until I started to row…

21st October 1997

Although the rowing has been hard this morning I have been distracted. Three hours of rowing means I have a lot of time to think. Right from the very beginning of the challenge - the first day when I fetched the boat, my mind has been drifting off into the past. I turned 50, three days before construction began, is this what they call mid life crisis? Whether it is or not the seeds are planted. Why not use the trip as a vehicle to re-assess my past, good or bad? I mean, normally on a three hour rowing stint my mind races off in a million different directions. If I can cultivate my thinking patterns into just one situation from my past, the result could be recorded during my rest period. I have an A4 writing pad brought by Rob for notes on the construction, never used and thrown in my bag without a thought. I'm going to run out of reading material pretty soon.

By the time three o'clock in the afternoon comes everything's clear. I'm to begin my cognitive regurgitation on my next shift at 6.00pm. It's as if all the setbacks of the past few days have been forgotten with this new surge of positive energy. Ten minutes before my shift I was up.

"What's up with you - shit the bed?" asks Keith.

I smile and reply; "I can feel a new surge of adrenaline that's all. Have I missed much?"

"Not really – lights' of a ship in the distance. Oh, the wind's southwest again, I've been rowing west Graham and I think you should do the same."

Even though it's only been three hours since my last stint it takes me at least 30 minutes to get back into the gyrating movement. I've worked out now; to keep balanced it's necessary to throw your upper body forwards when the boat lifts sideways pulling back on the oars at the same time as the side goes down.

In these sea conditions 30 minutes seems quite an acceptable length of time to switch on the autopilot and let one's mind drift off in between short spells of rowing concentration. A dull grey morning slowly materialises. Trapping the handles of the oars in the foot straps with the body of the oar still locked in the rowlocks, a method we are using when changing watches, I jump over the side of a quick swim before preparing breakfast.

Eagerly climbing into the aft cabin I pull out the virgin writing pad, pen in hand.

1964: A cold bleak day with only a short distance to travel I was wedged between Vincent the labourer and Mr Lamb, my boss at the time. Soon after the pick-up truck was unloaded, lengths of planed timber, bricks, etc, I was dispatched. I climbed up scaffolding with the instructions to fit the barge boards and soffits - quite a confidence booster, as this was my first year as an apprentice carpenter. Industrious sounds of hammering and sawing filled the day. The mid-afternoon tea break had just finished with me about to ascend the ladder, when, to my amazement, Vincent, the labourer, began moving it to another position.

Left with no ladder, I could see my supervisor giving me a look from his position under the scaffold, his hands rolling a large piece of putty about to point the last window. Without a second glance I began to shin up the scaffold pole. On reaching the first cross section I gripped the cold metal tube with one hand and swung my feet onto the horizontal pole, mimicking those caged chimps you might see at the zoo. This procedure was carried out until I came to the last gable section of the scaffold, only pausing for a minute to get my breath. The scaffold had been erected in the standard method of the day, a row of long vertical poles approximately eight feet apart, fastened to them were horizontal poles the length of the construction. From these sprouted short poles with flat ends, usually banged into the wall joints when they were green. Planks would then be laid on top. Under normal circumstances the scaffold would run all around the house adding strength, but in this case big chunks had been removed, as some of it was needed on another job. A last leap, landing on the vertical pole there was an awful sound much like the screeching of a trains' brakes followed by one of the loudest crashing noises I have ever heard. My energetic monkey type swing had pulled all of the short poles out of the joints in the wall. The falling planks, bricks, blocks, sand and cement from the top started a domino effect. Fortunately my plight was not as bad as it might have been as I was left swinging from the end of the bent and twisted scaffold. Hanging onto the pole in stunned silence a lifetime passes before the noise and dust finally settled. Climbing down I was met at the bottom of what was left of the scaffold by Vincent, "Where's the gaffer, Graham?" he said.

"I don't know, he was there," pointing to what had now become a giant pile of bricks and planks. "Mr Lamb, Mr Lamb," I said in a trembling voice. Then, to my relief, I hear a muffled sound, then louder.

"When I get out of here I'm going to murder that fucking bastard."

"I think you ought to leave now and catch the bus."
This was Vincent's only suggestion.

Satisfied at my attempts to record the thoughts of my previous rowing stint I take a fix, 25° 28′ north 17° 59′ west. Fifteen miles south and seven miles east is hardly acceptable for twenty-two hours of rowing south. Our only excuse is the unhelpful wind, west to south west at something like twenty to twenty-five miles an hour. Climbing out to start the evening meal a group of dolphins swim towards us, leaping and diving around the boat. Three or four minutes later they are tired of the new object and they swim away. Suddenly, turning, they come back for a last turn around the boat and then go off again due west almost as if they are saying follow us, we know the way. Biting off a large piece of my dessert, a high-energy oat bar, I notice that the wind is slightly north of west, which gives us a chance of a decent row.

22nd October 1997

Great cumulous shower clouds sweep by. The rain curtains, just missing us, still contain some gusts of wind. I am always hoping for brilliant red and yellow sunrises. I should not complain though, this weather system does give us a decent wind to row with. I decide to take an early morning swim then on with the kettle. After three hot cups of coffee and a Peak bar I am eager to start scribbling. No sooner than I am ready to begin Keith has noticed this new pastime and shouts through the hatch, "What are you doing Graham, writing your memoirs?"

"No, this is just a bit of doodling to pass the time."

I'm reluctant to tell Keith about my idea, mainly because I do not want him reading over my amateurish accounts of my past.

1966: Pulling up outside a shop conversion in Syston, Leicestershire, a large kit bag strapped to the top of a dented petrol tank belonging to my old Triumph Thunderbird. That day I was to hang two doors - not too much of a task for an up and coming carpenter. The first door on, I inspected the second, and there, poking out through the door opening laid twelve inches of scaffolding pole. Looking through the shop, all that can be seen of this troublesome pole, is approximately four feet before it disappears under an array of building material that stretches all the way to the front window. I knew until I removed that object I would be unable to hang the door.

Naturally I thought why not save myself, at least an hour, by not moving the material on the top of the pole, but by striking the end and knocking it into the shop out of my way? Conveniently the labourer left some tools, including a large sledge- hammer. Without further ado I began to swing the hammer like a man possessed, moving inches at a time until suddenly there was a loud cracking sound. Stopping with shock, I stood motionless looking straight at the shop window, for there, in front of my very eyes, were two huge cracks in the plate glass window. Why did I not think, the scaffolding pole was longer than the length of the shop? Having money deducted from my meagre wages every week to pay for the damage is not what I call a happy ending to this short story, or for that matter was it a good start to my professional career in carpentry.

Putting my writing pad away it's time for dinner. Not long after our evening meal two dolphins visit us. Shouting "Keith" at the top of my voice has drastic consequences. He shoots bolt upright banging his head on the protected rim of the hatch. Although thinking about it, it's probably the first test on the protective pipe lagging taped over the protruding bolts – it failed. Conclusive proof of this is the sight of blood pouring down Keith's face.

"Graham come and have a look at this and tell me if you think it needs stitches."

Leaving the oars strapped up I climb into the aft cabin. Remembering the last time I attempted to stitch up my jeans I really hope Keith doesn't mind having a scar. By the time I'm close enough to see the extent of the cut, Keith has stopped the main flow of blood. The cut is only about one inch long and does not look as bad as I had feared. Three adhesive sutures and a squirt of antiseptic cream should hopefully do the trick…there.

"Don't worry Keith, I don't think it'll make any difference to your looks."

23rd October 1997
Rowing due west as the wind has veered to north, north, east, gusting up to 20 miles an hour. 3.00am takes forever to come around this morning. Looking up at a mass of stars the only constellation I remember is the Plough – it's top two stars pointing at the North Star. My early attempts at exploring the heavens have been few and far between and without a period of constant study the small amount of knowledge is forgotten. I promise myself that before this voyage is over a serious study of the night sky is essential. Sleep comes very easily as I change shifts with Keith. By the time 6.00am comes the wind has died down to approximately five miles an hour, which gives me an easier start to my watch. For some reason my mind races from past to present, work, weather, money. I decide to miss my writing today and will probably have a day on and a day off, this decision rests on my experience of the last few days by finding it difficult to maintain a constant pattern of concentration. Kettle on, I slice our last orange in half. Yesterday Keith had found several jars of Coffee Mate. Which at this precise moment is being mixed in coffee for me, and in tea for Keith. Before this exciting find we were using milk powder bought in the local supermarket in Los Gigantes. Not too bad as long as it was mixed thoroughly with cold water before administering it to the drinks.

The moment our breakfast is finished and our dishes are put away I eagerly climb into the aft cabin to continue reading. I am almost at the end of Pat Barker's *'The Ghost Road'* and the inevitable confrontation is about to take place, encompassing most of the principle characters.

"Graham how's the water situation?"

Pulling myself away I poke my head out, "We're using about a gallon a day each, more or less the same as when we started. I'll have a check on how the supply's going on my next shift."

"'Yeah, okay, it was just a thought."

Sitting back I pick up the book.

'He saw Kirk die, he saw Owen die, his body lifted off the ground by bullets, describing a slow arc in the air as it fell.' I read on drawn into this life and death drama. 35 minutes later the last two lines slip through my imagination, and closing the book I scan the chart in a forlorn effort to kick-start my enthusiasm for ocean voyaging.

I intend to calculate our progress using the data from these last 11 days. It's probably going to be pretty depressing though – I'll do it another day, maybe after some favourable winds.

"Keith, how do you fancy meat balls in pasta sauce?"

"Sounds fantastic." is Keith's enthusiastic reply. I think I would have found some difficulty to show my enthusiasm for a somewhat jaded feast considering the regularity attributed to these experimental meatballs.

Afternoons have now become something to look forward to, for me probably more than Keith. This is the time I plot on the chart our new position including the 24 hour run from the previous day. The information is then imparted to Keith, which usually begins a long debate on our subsequent actions. Up to this point there has not been a lot to celebrate, this afternoon's position is no great revelation, 24° 47' north 18° 47' west, 20 miles south, 37 miles west, but it is probably our best. Relaxing after a pleasant dinner of chicken casserole both Keith and I notice a large tanker passing approximately one mile off our port side. Giving it a casual glance we turn our attention back to after dinner coffee and a discussion on the merits of catching fish. That tanker must be on a completely different course.

"Keith, sorry to stop you in mid flow it looks like that tanker's going to cross our bows?"

"No, he' s turning more and heading straight for us!" exclaims Keith.

Transfixed by the sight of this huge tanker bearing down on us, her bow wave is getting smaller, "I think she's slowing down, I'll switch on the VHF and see what she wants."

"Good idea Graham, hurry though, before she decides to give us a nudge."

"Large red tanker on our port bow this is the rowing boat, *The George Geary*, come in please, over."

Silence.

"Large red tanker on our port bow this is the rowing boat *The George Geary*, come in please, over."

Ok this isn't good. Suddenly the silence is broken.

"What is your situation, we have come to assist your rescue, over?"

Our rescue? How... ?

"We are fine, there is no problem, over."

"We have come to your assistance, over."

"We repeat, we are not in need of your kind assistance, thank you for your kind attention, over."

"Please indicate that you understand our offer of

assistance, over."

"Keith, bloody well wave at them or we'll be here 'til midnight."

"If you do not need assistance we will resume our course, out."

"That seems to have done the trick Graham, he's backing up." said Keith.

"Keith, he's operating astern propulsion, remember we're at sea. When she came so close she was like a towering monster, strange that she must have been empty apart from sea water ballast."

"Bit like us then eh Graham? Let's hope that we're not carrying sea water ballast until we get to the other side.'

Tonight we have decided to change watch times again, starting with one hour from 7.00pm until 8, then Keith for two hours, change over for two hours until midnight; this will start the day with Keith instead of me.

24th October 1997

Waking at 8.30am, my nose immediately picks up an unusual smell. It smells like porridge. We don't have any on board. Poking my head out, all is revealed as Keith crunches up another oat bar and stirs it into a pan of boiling milk.

"'What made you think of such a traditional breakfast?" I ask.

"It was just as I reminisced about a good old English breakfast. Bacon, sausages, eggs, beans, mushrooms, black pudding, fried bread, all started off by a decent bowl of porridge."

"Yes, milk powder and oat bars, at least we have the first course."

Two minutes later a steaming plate of, what would pass as porridge in any eating establishment, was thrust into my hands.

"Delicious Keith, let's make it a regular thing."

"Okay, how about twice a week?"

"Done."

By the time I've taken my rowing position the wind has dropped to approximately force two and backed to southeast. Not a good start to my row.

Out comes pen and paper along with the log. Better take a fix first. Fix at 1.35pm, 24° 25′ north, 19° 19′ west, 22 miles south, 32 miles west, now we are talking. The miles have started to slip by. If we keep up this progress I am sure we will be in by Christmas, only 485 miles away from Santo Antio in the Cape Verde Isles. Having fixed our daily position on the chart, one look is enough to give anybody an idea of our progress.

March 1968: The first job of the day did not sound too bad. Deliver a sink unit, newly constructed in the workshop – I remember thinking things could be a lot worse. It was Tuesday, and I was working my notice, which the boss in all his wisdom deemed appropriate. The previous week I had returned to the office for my next assignment after completing the rebuilding of the bar and surroundings at the North Bridge Inn in my home town, Leicester. It had taken me two and a half months. During this time a lot had happened in my life.

I had left home to work and live in this establishment, working some nights for my keep. The Landlord and Landlady, Irene and Brian had accepted me into their family and I shared a room with their son Mark.

Their three daughters shared two rooms between them. The North Bridge was known to be quite a lively pub as indeed I had experienced two nights previous when a fight broke out between a few intoxicated locals. For a good view of the proceedings my position was perfect. Leaning back on the jukebox, which at the time was blasting out that classic Chris Farlowe song 'Out of Time'. I watched the men as they destroyed the furniture. A certain number of prostrate bodies began to fill the bar floor, but as I looked forward I noticed a large shape belonging to one of the few left standing. A smattering of blood from his nose rubbed down the side of his face - a perfect match to his bloodshot eyes.

Advancing on me now with a menacing look I could see his arm go back in what seemed like a slow motion retake and then catapult towards me. Side stepping this flying fist I watch as it smacks into the glass front of the old jukebox followed by a shattering of glass and a loud bang. The jukebox began to wind down, the slow speed singing getting slower and slower.

Realising where his fist had landed, my attacker immediately pulled it out and screamed. His hand was pouring with blood.

It didn't seem very long before an ambulance together with a police car were parked outside and the prostrate bodies were hauled and dumped on to what was left of the chairs. Was this to be the start of my new and colourful life? A local, fishing into the broken jukebox, and pulling out a blood stained piece of glass attached to which was a small piece of flesh and gristle.

Daytime hours also had their moments. The bar opened at 10.30am until 2.00pm and there was a constant stream of folks dropping in for a pint or two, shift workers, delivery men, quite a mixture. As you may well imagine, building a bar while people are drinking and enjoying themselves is far from easy. Eventually I would join their small groups, eating freshly made rolls and quaffing the odd pint of brown liquid. One of the most amazing things about this time was the way in which nobody seemed to mind or notice the absence of a bar, standing pulling pints from a wooden cage holding the pumps, the floor area under and around the bar a mass of scaffolding planks. Of course, there was a price to pay for this entertaining job of work.

Arriving back at the office on completion of this creative masterpiece the boss was waiting for me.

"Now me lad, the pub job wasn't too bad as far as the construction goes, but the fact that it took at least a month longer than it should have does seem to weigh heavily against you." he said. "For this reason, and my sanity, I am giving you a week's notice, but as your apprenticeship will be completed in four months I am going post date it." he added. "You can help in the joinery shop until next week, that's all I've got to say."

Walking out of the office I was a bit stunned to say the least and sneaking out of the joiners shop early I headed back to the North Bridge determined not to let this setback affect me in any way. After all, I had my whole life in front of me…time to get drunk.

Tuesday morning, I was on my way to deliver a specially made to measure sink unit. It took three of us to load the unit onto the back of the firm's old pick-up.

"Okay it's all yours." shouted the foreman, Geoff. As it felt so heavy there did not seem any point in tying it down. Six miles into the journey my route took me along London Road. Feeling at the

time a little under the weather, due partly to the previous late night. Living in a pub you feel obliged to join in any late night drinking sessions, making early starts increasingly difficult. To combat the boredom of driving I began to roll a cigarette, a habit I had started four years before. At that precise moment, to my horror, a car pulled straight out of a side street. Slamming on the brakes, which was all I could do, as my hands were at the top of the wheel - any erratic turns left or right were impossible. All outside noises were then drowned by the sound of exploding wood. Having stopped merely inches away from the offending vehicle, I climbed out of the cab with dread. There, before my eyes, was the biggest pile of broken and splintered wood I had ever seen. The emergency stop had sent the unfastened unit to the rear of the truck resulting in this abomination I now saw before me. Return and come clean was the only option. In retrospect it's no wonder he fired me.

25th October 1997

Not a good start to the day - wind westerly, force four. By the time my shift is over the wind has veered north and is now probably NNW. Feeling dog tired I climb into the aft cabin and fall asleep immediately only to be woken, in my muddled mind, what feels like five minutes later by the call of,

"Tea up. "It's light." said Keith.

I must face up to the dreadful realisation that my calculation is out by 2 hours and 55 minutes. Keith hands me a steaming mug of tea. Settling down to row has now become very unpleasant due to this rash all over my backside. Over the last few days I have taken to wearing cycling pants, and although the padding is not quite in the right place for sitting, they do soak up the sweat. Wear and tear on other parts of the body is, at the moment, not troubling me. Sunburn has not been a problem apart from the odd showing of white skin that occasionally appears when I change shorts or just wear underpants. One thing that does help my sore backside and cheers me up at the same time is my daily swim. Today has been no exception. After three hours rowing in this heat I'm covered in sweat. I cannot begin to describe the pleasure of diving into the blue sea and just floating beside the boat. Not only the enjoyment of the relaxing dip but also food to look forward to after it. One of our finds the previous day was a packet of cracker biscuits, half of which are going to be consumed today together with our slightly green supply of cheese and a mug of oxtail soup. To finish off the proceedings a pouch each of dumplings in butterscotch sauce swilled down with three mugs of coffee. Time to put thoughts to paper.

1965: Adventure seemed to be beckoning as me and three friends drove away from our makeshift campsite just outside Blackpool. A happy two days had passed. Football, funfair and a convivial atmosphere in some much maligned drinking establishments, me and my three participants in this two weeks expedition to the far corners of England's green and pleasant land. A liquid lunch in Chester, then on to Anglesey. Driving into the night we arrived in the early hours before cruising up the high hills above Holyhead. Leaving the single-track road we pressed on through coarse bracken to a rocky outcrop and a few hours sleep on the ground next to the car did not seem too bad. A Standard Eight is not the best car to try and sleep in. By 7.00pm we had pitched the tent and lit a fire.

Three glorious days of sunshine, swimming, fishing and an experimental sea journey using our ex-RAF flight-dinghy - it was time to move on.

Our eventual destination was to be Land's End, giving us approximately five days to visit as many interesting places as possible along the way.

There was a certain sadness at leaving our secret campsite. I say this because we had not seen a living soul the whole time we were there apart from when we took a trip into Holyhead for a few thirst-quenching pints. Four days later while reflecting on our journey, not without it's high dramas, a cameraman clicked away at our four adventurers posing under the sign of Land's End, sitting on the bonnet of a battered but not beaten overland express.

Perhaps this name, painted on the side, was a bit misleading, but it did show a good understanding of the word exaggeration. Our tent, camp beds and the dinghy were showing signs of heavy wear and tear probably due to the unstable fixing of the luggage rack. This resulted in much lost time picking all those items up from various places deposited along the road. Handing over a small amount of money together with our names and addresses for posting purposes we began the long journey home. Having started late, an amicable decision is reached to stop for the night at St Ives. Following a good sleep in the canvass beach huts on the sea front and an early fried breakfast we set off. 100 yards into our journey the problems began. The much misused Standard Eight now started complaining and would not climb out of this famous seaside town. The next hour and a half we spent unloading, walking to the top of the hill and depositing all the contents in a suitable pile. When the car was unloaded we began pushing it upwards, or should I say that my three trustee companions pushed it. Large clouds of grey smoke belched out of the exhaust accompanied by a continuous knocking noise drowning out the sound of the grunting and groaning. We arrived at the top in a thick cloud of oily exhaust fumes, not to mention the choking and coughing by the added manpower. Once reloaded, we were on our way. I remember thinking as the miles steadily passed by we were going to make it. This infectious unspoken feeling of optimism seemed to resonate in everyone. Yet regrettably it was to be short lived.

It must have been no more than 10 minutes before a long high incline came into view. I drove on with newfound encouragement and determination to make it to the top until, only a quarter of the way up we lost speed. Changing down, third gear, second gear, doubling the clutch, first gear. The car slowly crept on, grey smoke now obscuring the rear view. Optimistic shouts grew louder above the endless knocking noise, "She's gonna make it, she is going to make it."

Then the inevitable happened with just the last quarter left to the top. There was no time to dwell on our misfortune so we immediately began unpacking.

"'Right, let's push." I said reluctantly.

At the same time a large lorry passed us making that familiar crunching and revving noise associated with changing down through the gears. Stopping at the top of the hill the driver jumped down from his cab, "Do you lads want a tow to get your car started?"

It was time to face the truth and pulling on the hand brake I jogged up the hill towards him.

"To be honest the engine's knackered and we just don't know what to do, thanks for your kind offer though." I said.

The driver stood thinking for a moment.

"I tell you what, I'm on my way to Wolverhampton, I can tow you as far as Birmingham then all you'll have to do is get a tow to Leicester, how's that?"

I could not believe it; I was amazed by his generous offer. At that stage I'd not even considered a tow being so far from home.

"It sounds like a fantastic idea but won't it slow you down and cause you problems?"

"Not at all, I'll just carry on driving as normal."

"I won't notice any difference considering the weight of the lorry. I won't be able to see you in my mirrors so as long as you can control the car I can't see any problems." he said. With this I went back to my three companions. As we pushed the car the remaining distance the driver pulled out a large chain and attached it to the back of the lorry. 20 minutes was all it took to finish pushing, loading and attaching the chain to the front axle of the car. As we prepared to start our journey our towing saviour suggested that two of our number ride in the cab with him. At the time I could see no advantage but it would soon become obvious.

Although eager to set off I was somewhat perplexed by the shortness of the chain, a mere ten feet, as long as the car itself. As soon as we began our long haul home I knew this was going to be an ordeal I would remember forever. It's difficult to describe the beginning of this journey, staring through the windscreen at the back of this enormous lorry I had no indication of what was in front. Would we turn, go up, down, come to a stop? Two large indicators and two brake lights - one of which was not working, controlled my reactions. The only other guide was the constant squealing of the brakes. I will give you an indication of the conversation as we travelled through a small village. My co-driver was Len, a plumbing apprentice. Dave and Roy were comfortably situated in the front cab.

"His brake lights are on Graham."

"Okay, I can see, I am braking."

"Brakes squealing Graham."

"Yeah I know, I can hear them."

"Brake, brake, watch it, you're getting too close."

"Okay, my foot's almost to the floor."

"Look out, the bonnet's going under the back of the lorry!" *There was a final squeal of brakes as we came to a stop, the bonnet partially under the rear of the lorry.*

"Graham, I think the left wheel ran over the chain when it went slack."

"Are you sure?" I ask.

"Yes, I'm getting out to have a look."

"No, don't."

"Why?"

"You'll be left behind if the lorry suddenly moves, wind the window down and stick your head out…What can you see?"

"You're right, it's over the chain, pap your hooter at him."

"I can hardly hear it. He'll never be able to hear it's almost as knackered as the engine."

"Shout at him." I say in desperation.

"Too late, we're off, look out the front's lifting, turn the steering wheel we're going sideways now Graham!"

"I'm trying, I'm trying."

"We're going sideways."

"I know we're going sideways but nothing's happening."

"What's that black smoke?"

"What black smoke?"

"That black smoke! Graham he's going left, watch the chain it's moving across."

"It's alright I can see it."

"Careful, his brakes are squealing again, he's coming to a stop, brake, brake…"

"Stop panicking Len, I'm braking as hard as I can."

"You're too close Graham, there's masses of slack in that chain."

"Hang on Len, he's off, brace yourself."

Twang!

"My neck."

"Right, the next time we see that slack chain we're gonna have to slide down in our seats to brace our necks or we'll end up with that whiplash."

Sliding up and down in our seats became regular occurrences as we passed through numerous villages and towns. The main route back was vastly different in 1965 to what it is today. Straight new roads and bypasses have sorted that out. Our next problem was not long in coming. As the lorry made it's way down a long decline, keeping my brakes on the whole time produced a pungent burning smell.

"We're gonna wear out the brake shoes Len, can you smell the rubber?" I said as calmly as possible to try not to panic Len again.

"Of course I can."

As this nightmare progressed I became aware of the strain gradually taking it's toll as my head began to droop. Three hours had now passed since the start of this mobile endurance test.

"You're going to have to take over Len, I'm absolutely knackered."

"How are we going to do that, there's no way of communicating with 'Cannon Ball' our trucking superman?"

"We'll have to choose the best time, preferably a straight road with no junctions.' I said. This seemed to worry Len, however after a little bit of convincing he took out a map and began to work out where the best place to change over was.

"Ok ready? I'll stand up and climb onto the seat while you place your feet on the pedals, hotch over the gear lever and drop your backside into the driving seat. In the meantime I'll move over into the passenger seat, if you disagree say so now."

"Graham, I won't survive for three hours…"

The changeover did not go too badly and as soon as I got into the passenger seat I was asleep.

"Graham, Graham, wake up, we're pulling in."

"Len, before we go into the café, don't tell the driver all the horror stories ok? Just say it's difficult but that we're managing."

"Ok."

Sitting down to sausages and chips the difference between the two in the cab and the two of us on tow, regarding appearance and behaviour, was blindingly obvious. Two drawn and harrowed faces hunched over their food, in comparison our two cab dwellers were laughing and joking.

"What's up with you two miserable sods?"

"Here we go again Len." Two hours on, and two hours off, through the night. About 4.00am I was rudely awakened by a loud twanging noise.

"What? What?" I say quickly coming to my senses.

"The chain's snapped and the lorry's going off without it's shadow."

"Have you tried flashing the lights?"

"Of course I've tried flashing my lights."

"How about the horn?"

"Yes, Graham, I've tried that."

Luckily he realised we were missing and came back to collect us and finish our journey.

26th October 1997

Taking a good look around after climbing out of my comfortable sleeping arrangement, a white light appears on the horizon. At first I take it to be a star, but on closer scrutiny it's horizontal movement indicates it's probably a ship -

something to at least break the monotony. A cloudless sky is filled to the brim with stars and planets of all shapes and sizes.

Yet again I swear to delve into the bags and luggage that I have brought aboard in order to study the heavens using the Star Guide purposely packed and still unfound. A cool wind of probably force four from the northeast is steadily driving the boat along, encouraged by my enthusiastic rowing. Keeping a curious eye on my latest source of interest I see a second white light. A light on the horizon is beginning to gain more of my attention, which only confirms how sterile the mind can become when the body is engaged in some form of exertion.

27th October 1997

Nothing much to see tonight, the clouds obscure most of the sky. Even the moon rising into the heavens cannot be seen. Lunch has become the second-class meal of the day probably due to it's similarity to the previous days. The relaxing after drink of coffee and a bite of oat bar makes up for the lack of culinary excitement. Anticipation of our progress entices me into taking the fix half an hour early at 1.30pm, 22° 35′ north, 20° 51′ west, 41 miles south, 44 miles west.

I decide to leave the writing today and concentrate on the GPS. Having vaguely mastered the knack of inputting the waypoints my knowledge on the range of information available is practically nil. The first waypoint for us had to be the simplest after our departure. With this in mind we chose a fixed point sixty miles off the coast of Antao in the Cape Verde islands. I must say with all honesty that although we had chosen the waypoint, it came from a waypoint plan given to me by Mike from the *Cornish Challenger* in an act of true generosity. As I rushed to get the boat ready on time everything else had to go by the wayside including any thoughts on navigation. I realise that this plan can only be used as a guideline, knowing only too well that the forthcoming weather patterns will change and alter our route decisions. Therefore I considered asking Mike for his waypoint route in no way detrimental to the race. Since inputting our waypoint a large amount of information was available to us such as bearing to waypoint, distance, course over the ground, speed over the ground, course deviation, course to steer, course made good, velocity made good and cross track error.

60 minutes soon passed as I grappled with the task of assessing the Pan N Scan GPS functions. This gave me information relative to our position by placing the cursor over the waypoint as shown on the plotter screen as well as creating a waypoint viewing, a waypoint message and creating a 'Go To' from the Pan N Scan. This is getting awfully confusing.

28th October 1997

The weather has continued to keep us entertained blowing force six or seven from the northeast, not that we are complaining. Rowing in these sea conditions is extremely hard, countering the violent side to side motions always takes some getting used to when I begin my three hour stint.

1963: Early ideas of adventure came in many different forms. I say this because the start of this small experience was at the time an adventure itself. Swinging about, high up in a couple of birch trees, handsaw and axe tied to my waist, I was sawing and chopping. Whilst engaged in this entertaining work the owner of this particular country cottage was vigorously digging away at his vegetable patch, which was somewhat overgrown.

As I was about to tie the old hand saw back onto my belt I heard a shout along with a low rumbling noise followed by the sound of splashing water. Looking towards the direction where the sound came from I saw dust rising. Climbing down as fast as I could I raced over to the owner who thrust out his arm in the nature of a traffic policeman, fortunately, stopping me from going any further. Looking forward, the reason for his sudden shouts of surprise and the dust, now settling, were only too clear. A large hole had appeared, probably about five feet in diameter. The side of that gaping hole seemed to be very old clay bricks. Looking down to a depth of approximately twelve feet I could see murky brown water. Studying what was left of the covering it was easy to understand why it had finally given way. Timber bearers would have originally covered the hole but over the years it had rotted.

Above these old bearers sat large square shaped pieces of grey slate. What was left of the other two thirds of covering must have disappeared down into what I can only imagine to be an old well. After closer inspection, a lead pipe one and a half inches in diameter came into view, it was cut through approximately twelve inches from the top. Standing around chatting about this new discovery to the owner and the next-door neighbour, I spotted the boss's van pull up. Fading into the background I quickly made my way back to the trees. One thing that I have learned, standing around chatting when one is supposed to be working is not conducive to long term employment. It was the next day when I found out the conclusion of my boss's chat with the owner. An agreement had been reached whereby the boss could have anything out of the well and in return he would arrange to fill it in over a period of two months with all the rubbish left over from the jobs. This information was passed onto me together with my next assignment. The labourer, Vincent, was to drive me back to the cottage along with a motorised pump, paraffin lamp, scaffolding poles and clips and double extending ladders. Not forgetting two, gallon tins of creosote and a long brush. My first task was to help Vincent erect a tripod type scaffold over the well and hang the pump from it. I was instructed in the methods of switching it on and off and a gallon of petrol was left to keep the pump going throughout the day. In case I might feel idle the boss arranged with the next door neighbour for me to creosote the fence. I learned later over a cup of tea that the only reason I had been engaged to perform this seemingly easy task was because the creosote brought the boss out in a rash. Bolting the tripod together at the top, I tied the pump underneath.

"Vincent, I know I've not got much experience with wells but can you tell me what we're looking for?"

"25 to 30' down at the end of the lead pipe there should be a brass pump fixed in place with bearers. The boss said he's had one out of a well, similar to this one, before, the clue is that the lead pipe is still there so he's convinced that the pump is."

By mid-afternoon the water level was down to approximately 30'. Looking down in the dim light, I could just make out timber and slate wedged to the sides. When Vincent returned at about four-thirty he immediately set about lowering the extending ladders down into the well. When the first part had descended the next part of the extending ladder was fitted together and then tied so that they would not separate. As the ladder reached the debris Vincent told me to tie it off at the side of the scaffold.

"Right young-un, down you go." he said, smiling at me.

It had never occurred to me that I was to be the underground ferret.

"I thought you were going down?" I said, in the hope he might

change his mind. However all I got in return was the somewhat condescending reply; "What's the matter, you're not scared are you?"

To refuse would have only confirmed to Vincent and the boss what a sniffling little coward I was. Step by step I lowered myself down the ladder. Once inside, the noise from the pump was deafening. The overwhelming damp slimy smell was only dulled slightly by petrol fumes.

Once below the pump the air seemed fresher. Naturally, I assumed if I would be able to get to the bottom of the ladder, below the pump, the air would be fresher. Slowly descending I shouted to Vincent for a crowbar. It was not long before a steel crowbar was slowly lowered down on a piece of rope. Forcing the bar into the joints around the slate I was soon able to clear all of the debris and only left the bearer that was wedged.

As the water level had dropped another three feet I could see the lead pipe still descending down into the water. After climbing back up it took me a good five minutes to stop coughing.

"I think we're gonna have to switch off that pump the next time I go down."

"Okay, come on let's go home."

Back the next morning bright and early with some creosoting still to do. Vincent and the boss planned to return just before midday. I had broached the question of overalls to the boss dropping a hint that I smelt like a tin of creosote. His answer to this was that a tin of creosote smelt better than a sewer rat, intimating upon my impending trip to the bowels of the earth. Stopping for breakfast I decided to check the petrol in the pump, which at the present moment was swinging about way down in the well. Hauling it out I checked the water level.

As it was too dark to be seen from the top I lowered the paraffin lamp down on a long piece of string. To my horror, I found that the water level had gone down practically double the depth of the jammed bearer, the one I had previously stood the ladders on. As yet, not a sign of the mysterious brass well pump. I started the petrol pump and lowered it down even further. Fortunately, the out going pipe had quite a good length to it coupled with the fact that I had been given five or six lengths of plastic rain water pipe to take the pumped water away as far as the fields at the bottom of the garden. Arriving at about twelve thirty the boss and Vincent went to have a look down the well.

"Young-un, where's the lamp?"

"It's here."

"Hold on a minute, I'll bring it, I'm just cleaning the creosote off my hands."

"Bring the bloody thing here, we've not got time for your personal hygiene."

This time the lamp went out when it was lowered past a certain point. The same thing happened again.

"No bloody oxygen, I'll bet the damn pump's using what little there is."

"Vincent, get the torch out of the cab."

This time as the torch went down a pile of debris showed at about 70 to 75 feet.

"That must be it, I've never seen one so deep."

"Just shows you what the water table was like a hundred years ago."

"How about you Vincent?"

"No not me boss."

"Okay, let's get the big double extender off the back of the pickup and down the hole as quickly as possible."

The double extending ladders already down in the well were lowered even further, then, while Vincent and I held half of the next extender, the boss tied them together. This is repeated with the other half and lowered. Standing on the debris at the next level the ladder stuck out from the well by approximately four feet.

"Right, now take the crowbar and handsaw in case you need to cut the bearers."

Slightly apprehensive I question the situation.

"Did you say boss that there is no oxygen down there?"

"There'll be enough for you. Now get down there young-un before you wet your pants."

Halfway down the first ladder another thought crossed my mind. Now that the pump has stopped will the water rise before I can free the brass pump, if it is there?

"As far as we can see the water's well below the blockage, you've got plenty of time. Now get down there before I get Vincent to piss on you to cool you down."

Hand over hand down I went. Not that I considered that Vincent relieving himself over me any great threat, more, I had the distinct feeling that they were losing faith in my adventurous nature. Descending the ladder, which at this time was almost vertical against the side of the well, I could not help getting, not to mention the smell, a close view of the dank slimy brickwork. Looking up I was amazed at how small the well opening had become, but quite thankful of having the suspended torch. Reaching the bottom of the ladders at around 70' I began levering and breaking up the debris, which again had fallen from the well top. It did not take me long to confirm that the long awaited prize was here. I cleared the surrounding area around the lead pipe. The ancient pump appeared to be in excellent condition considering the length of time it had been here immersed in this murky water. I must have been down here no more than five minutes, but now I felt light headed and sick. I soon began the climb back up.

"How's it going down there?" A bellowing shout as I was about halfway up.

"I'm coming up for a breath of fresh air."

Arriving at the top I was grateful of the cool April breeze.

"You'll never make a miner, you've done nowt yet and look , you're covered in sweat."

"Why don't you go down then Vincent?"

"Hey, don't you get bloody cheeky with me you little snot gobbler. Right, here's the plan," the boss as business like as ever.

"Start down from the top and prize off all of the lead pipe brackets with the crowbar, looks like there's only four or five. When you reach the bottom saw through the timber bearers that hold the pump. In the meantime we'll tie the tow rope to the end of the lead pipe and flatten the lead around it making it impossible to come free, then, we can fit the old pulley under the scaffold and feed the rope through it."

I looked down to the hanging torch and could see that the water level had risen in the short time since Vincent had stopped the pump, although it had still not reached our prize. Down I went again, wrenching off the pipe brackets on my way, not a difficult task as the large copper nails came out of the brickwork joint very easily. Prizing the last bracket away had an instant effect on the redundant pipe dancing away from the wall, only to be brought to a standstill by Vincent and the boss hauling on the end of the rope now attached to the lead pipe. The urgency to free the prized object was now apparent as the water level was increasing quite rapidly. Sawing away at one of the two bearers went on for longer than I had planned notably because they were made of oak and also, of course, the fact that my saw had been used previously to cut off many branches in the surrounding trees and was now quite blunt.

"What are you doing down there?" The boss's booming voice.

"I've just got to cut through the last bearer. Are you sure the ladders are tied at the top because they're standing on the last bearer?"

"Pull the bloody thing off and you'll see it's tied up, get on with it."

I could sense from the agitated conversation that patience was not in large supply at the top. Bearing this in mind I began frantically sawing into this last bearer. Just as I pulled back on the saw my hand slipped off of the rung I was holding onto coinciding with a crack as the half sawn bearer gave way. It was holding my full weight and as I began to fall I made a desperate lunge for the nearest lifeline which at this moment held a torch. Stopping my fall I clung on with both hands above the torch hoping that the thick string would hold. It did not take long before I became aware that my feet were dangling in the water as it slowly penetrated my boots. The thought of losing the crowbar and saw, now in the water, seemed the least of my problems.

I could see that the pump, having been freed from it's bonds, had also dropped below the surface. I tried reaching out with one hand to grab hold of the nearest ladder rung, about fourth from the bottom but as the tips of my fingers were about to reach it the string gave way dropping me like bag of coal. My outstretched hand just managed to grab what turned out to be the bottom rung. The cold water hit me with quite a shock taking my breath away and stifling a shout. I hung on to the last rung of the ladder with freezing cold water up to my chin in total darkness apart from a small ring of daylight indicating up and down.

"What's happening down there?"

*"Pull the ladders up, pull the ladders up, no stop!"
Some sense was returning to my muddled mind. They would have to keep pulling up the ladders and untying them, not easy with my added weight. If they let go I would descend with these four lengths of heavy ladders trapping me and taking me to the black depths way under the water.*

Pulling myself up with both arms until about shoulder height I could let go with one hand and grab the rung above. This was the method I used until I was able to get a foothold on the bottom rung and climb up the vertical ladder. Some memories paint a picture that is stored in the galleries of the mind ready to be drawn out at any given time and gazed upon. On reaching the top of this dank, dark, hellhole and looking around at the tranquil picture of green fields, trees and gardens, was definitely one for the gallery. Vincent and the boss, staring at this soaking wet form shaking from top to bottom, I am sure, stirred their emotions.

*"Right young-un, pull the ladders up as fast as you can then on to the pump, you'll soon forget those soaking clothes."
Getting the pump out now that is was free was still not an easy matter. The 70' of 2" lead pipe combined with the weight of the pump was going to take some pulling. The boss's mind was already ahead as he backed the pickup down the drive and looped the rope attached to the lead pipe around the towing hook. Vincent and I were instructed to hold the scaffolding from falling over. The boss drove the pickup slowly along the drive and up came the elusive pump until the joint between rope and lead appeared before the pulley wheel.*

"Stop, stop, you're pulling over the scaffold."

*"Get out of the way, I'm not stopping until the pump comes to the top of the well."
That is how it was, scaffold and lead pipe being dragged along. I was*

THE TIMES TU

Chay Blyth, left, in one of the race boats with David Jackson, who enjoyed testing the prototype so much that he decided to participate

Blyth sets ocean challenge to rival Everest

BY EDWARD GORMAN

CHAY BLYTH, the first man to sail the "wrong way" around the world, yesterday announced plans for the longest and toughest rowing race in history.

The 2,900-mile Atlantic Rowing Challenge will pit two-man crews against the Atlantic, providing a test of willpower and stamina to rival conquering Everest. The race, to begin in September 1997, will start in the Canary Islands and finish in the West Indies.

Blyth has an incredible record of seagoing achievements. He himself has crossed the Atlantic by oar. In 1966 he and John Ridgway completed the trip from the United States to Ireland in 92 days in a 22ft open dory. Four years later Blyth completed the first solo non-stop circumnavigation against the prevailing winds and currents in the yacht *British Steel*.

Announcing the new event at St Katharine's Yacht Club in London yesterday, Blyth said the race would help to satisfy the increasing desire among ordinary people to embark on once-in-a-lifetime adventures. "There are lots who want a challenge," said Blyth, whose company is also the organiser of the BT Global Challenge, billed as the world's toughest yacht race.

"This will be the longest rowing race in the world and there will be plenty of adrenalin and plenty of challenge. From my experience with both the British Steel Challenge and the BT Global Challenge, it is clear that there is a big demand for unusual quests that people who take part in will remember for the rest of their lives."

The race is open to 30 two-person crews of any nationality, between the ages of 21 and 60. The £20,000 fee will cover the cost of the boat and a contribution towards a support vessel which will accompany the fleet across the Atlantic.

The boats, designed specially for the race, will be 23ft long and 6ft wide and weigh about 3,000lb when loaded. They will have a covered stern in which both rowers will be able to shelter, and stowage space for two months' supply of food and 80 gallons of water. Also, they will be self-righting in the event of capsize.

Competitors will be able to choose their oars and seats, but everything else will be standard. "We want the boats to be identical to ensure that the pair who win the race do so due to their rowing technique and courage, not because they have managed to raise suitable funds to build a state-of-the-art rowing boat," Blyth said.

The first confirmed entrants are David Jackson and Graham Burnett, both 25, from Tor Point, Cornwall. They have been conducting tests on the prototype boat for Blyth and enjoyed it so much that they decided to participate. Mr Burnett said he was impressed with the boat: "Instantly, when you get in a boat, you can tell if it's a bad one or a good one, and this was very, very good. We are very confident with it."

Was he looking forward to the race? "Two thousand nine hundred miles is going to be quite a slog in anything apart from a luxury liner," he said.

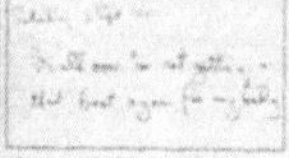

Blyth and Ridgway near the end of their voyage, which Blyth recorded in his diary

The newspaper article that started my adventure.

Chay Blyth launches the first Atlantic Rowing race in 1995.

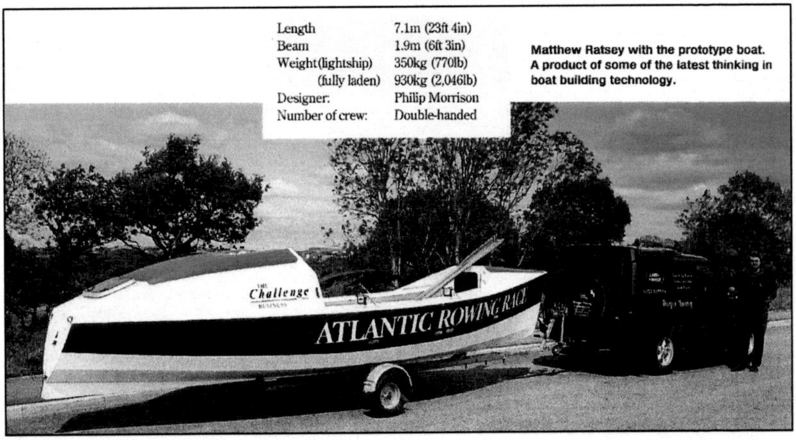
Length 7.1m (23ft 4in)
Beam 1.9m (6ft 3in)
Weight (lightship) 350kg (770lb)
(fully laden) 930kg (2,046lb)
Designer: Philip Morrison
Number of crew: Double-handed
Matthew Ratsey with the prototype boat. A product of some of the latest thinking in boat building technology.
ATLANTIC ROWING RACE

All the racing boats would have to be built to this specification.

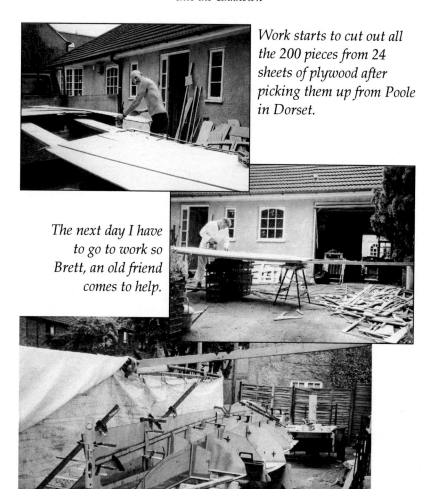

Work starts to cut out all the 200 pieces from 24 sheets of plywood after picking them up from Poole in Dorset.

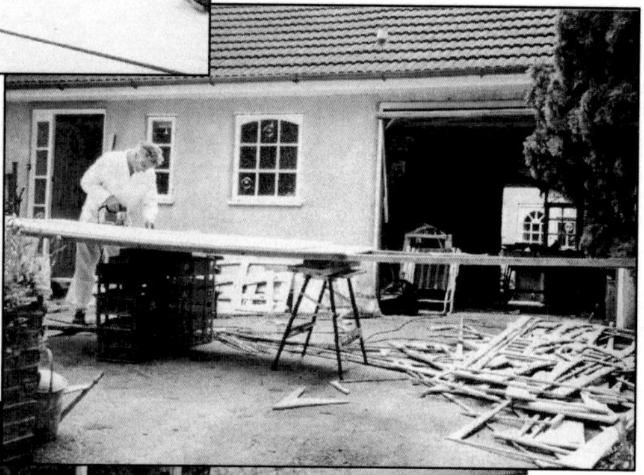

The next day I have to go to work so Brett, an old friend comes to help.

Things are starting to come together as the hull starts to take shape.

At last we can see progress

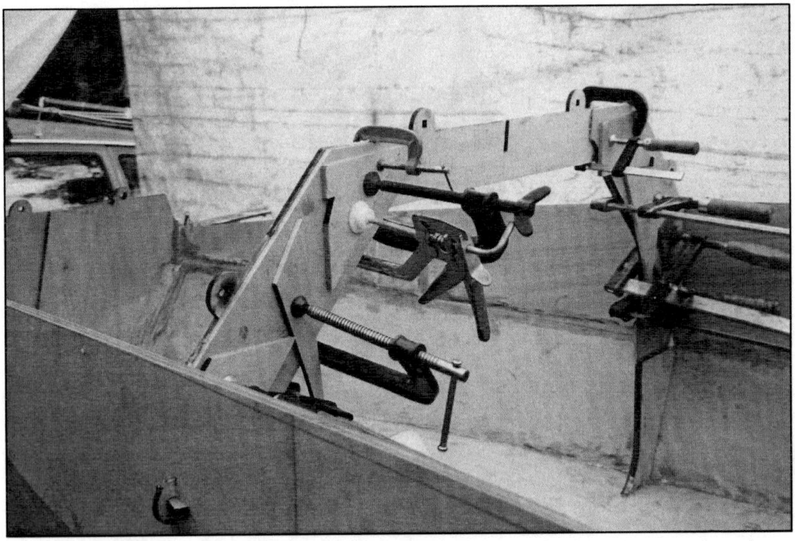

Now the boat is turned the right way up we can start to construct the cabin frames

The building tent for the boat in our front garden, something my wife and the postman were not happy about!

The basic boat is about finished.
It's time to cut off all the tenon joints holding it together.

Rob, another friend, welds a trailer together and borrows a lorry with lifting gear to get the boat onto the trailer.

We must not forget the rowing practice, using my old clinker dinghy after a few repairs.

And of course the gym!

Leaving the half finished boat at Felixstowe Docks ready for it's journey to Tenerife.

My friends and I organise a dress dinner before starting the row, toasting the journey ahead. This reminded me of Scott of the Antarctic's last dinner.

All the boats are offloaded at San Juan quayside, Tenerife where last minute adjustments were made to the boats before rowing to Los Gigantes for the start of the race.

Work continues on the boat.

Rob, another friend works on the rudder fastenings.

The boat takes to the water for the first time since being built. Just 20 hours before the start of the Atlantic Race!

Keith gingerly lowers the boat into the water with me on board so I could check for leaks

Next the naming of the boat. No champagne, just beer poured over the bow, I name this boat the 'George Geary' after my grandfather.

ATLANTIC ROWING RACE

The Longest Rowing Race Ever Staged

30 TEAMS AT THE START

With the start of the Atlantic Rowing Race looming just over the horizon, we are delighted to announce the final list of teams who will start the Race in October 1997.

Boat No	Boat Name	Team Names
4	*TBA*	Eamonn Kavanagh & Peter Kavanagh
5	*Endeavour*	Geoff Gavey & John Van Katwyck
6	*The Cornish Challenger*	Michael Elliott & Louis Hunkin
7	*Hannah Snell*	David Rice & Nadia Rice
8	*Cellnet Atlantic Challenger*	Simon Chalk & George Rock
9	*Toc H Phoenix*	Steve Isaacs & Mark Stubbs
10	*Spirit of Spelthorne*	Matthew Boreham & Edward Boreham
11	*Mount Gay Rum Runner*	Duncan Nicoll & Jock Wishart
12	*Sam Deacon*	Roger Gould & Charlie Street
13	*Star Atlantic*	Arvid Bensten & Stein Hoff
14	*Commodore Shipping*	Carl Clinton & John Searson
15	*Salamanca*	Martin Bellamy & Mark Mortimer
16	*Crackers*	Wayne Callaghan & Tim Welford
17	*Carpe Deum*	Daniel Byles & Jan Meek
18	*TBA*	Boris Renzelmann & Nikolai Wedemeyer
19	*American Pearl*	Louise Graff & Victoria Murden
20	*Kielder Atlantic Warrior*	Steven Lee & John Bryant
21	*Hospiscare*	Neil Hitt & Peter Hogden
22	*The Golden Fleece*	Daniel Innes & Robert Whitaker
23	*Key Challenger*	David Mossman & David Immleman
24	*Spirit of Jersey*	Ian Blandin & Robert Cassin
25	*TBA*	Rob Hamill & Phil Stubbs
26	*TBA*	Jean Marc & Marie Christine Meunier
27	Bitzer	Russell Reid & Andrew Watson
29	Atlantik Challenge	Pascal Blond & Joseph Le Guen
30	TBA	Keith Skidmore & Graham Walters
31	Stylus Misteral Endeavour	Richard Duckworth & Isabel Fraser
32	This Way Up	Ian Chater & Nigel Garbett
33	TBA	David Jackson & Jim Shekdar
34	TBA	Peter Haining, MBE & David Riches

A list of all the boats and their crews.

Spectators line the harbour wall in Los Gigantes ready for the start.

We cast off and row to the start line.

With a hurried start we pull away but within 20 minutes we are in last place. Considering we are the only team without a water maker and are carrying 100 gallons of drinking water, I suppose it was to be expected.

Two days into the race and we are still looking good.

My sailing smack 'Albion' looking in good condition but after I sailed her for a year she did not look so good.

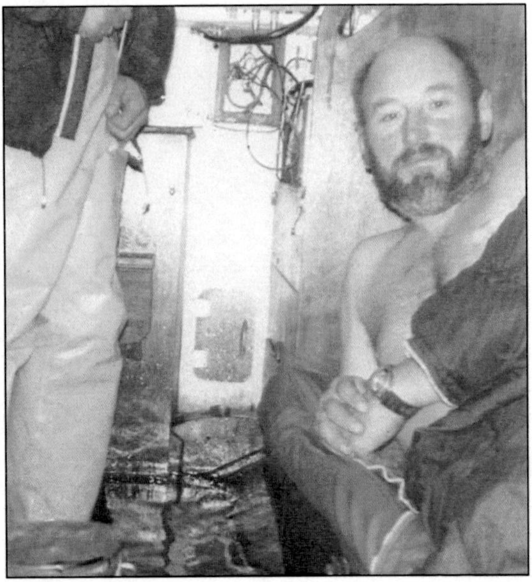

After a difficult voyage aboard the 'Albion' a drastic leak occurred and a crew member insisted that I unblock the pump, but I was happy relaxing with water up to my bunk

My first rowing experience after breaking the mast in heavy seas off Barra in the Outer Hebrides.

1934 at Lord's. England play Australia, King George V shaking hands with my grandfather George Geary. England won the match in three days with an innings and 38 runs to spare.

My grandfather George Geary on his way to immortality and an ashes record that I doubt will ever be beaten. In 1926 at Headingley George faced the strongest Australian attack in a ninth wicket stand of 108 with George Macauley to save the Ashes and square the series. In the final test George bowled Arthur Mailey a yorker splitting the wickets and the Ashes were won for the first time in 14 years. Two years later in Melbourne Australia, who should hit the winning run to retain the Ashes? Yes - it was George Geary.

Lunch break on SS Moldavia, 28 miles out in the English Channel.

Trying to catch the last lift skiing in a snow camouflage suit which I discovered was not such a good idea as people kept skiing into me!

My adapted clinker built rowing boat is ready for my attempt to row across the English Channel to Brest.

This photo was taken on a Rugby tour. In the opposing team was Keith who was to become my rowing partner. I am pictured in the centre on the back row.

The old Standard 8 taking a short cut to Anglesey before going to Land's End.

The Standard 8 being towed from Land's End to Birmingham. We can be seen reconnecting the broken towing chain. This was one the worst tows I'd ever undertaken.

Desert living can be a bit basic. I had hair when I was younger as you can see in this photo taken with my back to the camera.

The beginning of our trip overland to the Middle East. Unfortunately a lorry driver falls asleep and we disappear through a fence, roll down a small embankment and into the road below. We emerge from the wreck and feel lucky - no broken bones and covered in petrol as the impact burst the petrol tank, how lucky can we be?

My wife Margaret and me on our wedding day. She is still smiling considering I forgot to order the car from the church to the reception. I did not think about it until Margaret said, 'where is the car?' We are pictured in the back of a friend's Ford Cortina.

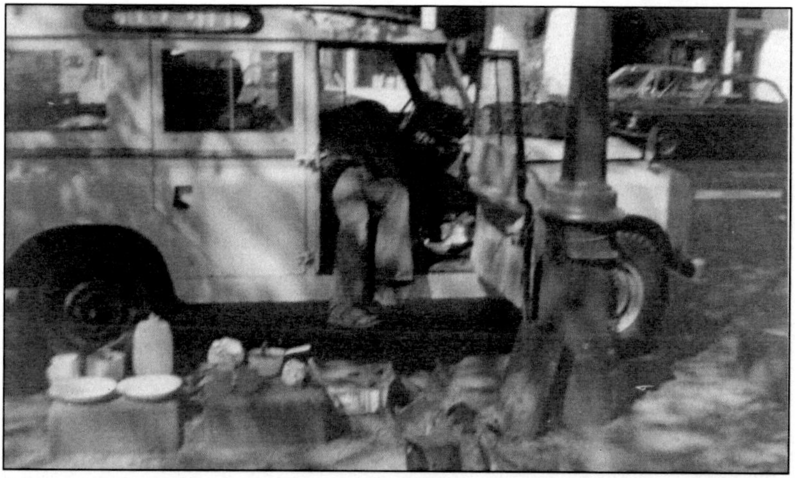

Margaret had a lot to put up with. Here we are living temporarily in a Land Rover in the centre of Amsterdam with a broken gearbox.

Margaret reluctantly volunteered to be towed back to England in the broken Land Rover.

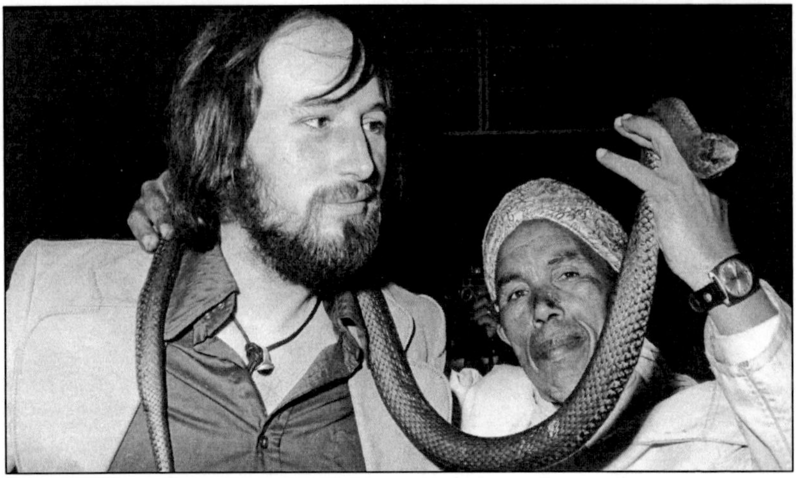

A friendly passer by introduced me to his mate as I drive to Algeria with a Belgian friend. I felt a little guilty as Margaret and I had only been married six months.

Contemplating the drive across Algeria to Mali, Central Africa

At Cropston Reservoir I'm not looking too confident in my wet suit. I am already freezing, so is my air supply.

Just getting the drinking competition underway in Arlon, Belgium.

The first time I've ever rowed a skip down the river for two miles. My four friends pose while I take the picture.

This picture taken just before my friend 'Little' Graham gets blown up welding the diesel tank. Fortunately he only suffered bruises, though they were all over his body.

Taking a sun sight with a sextant a few days after surviving a force 11 gale in mid Atlantic. I was assisting with a boat delivery from Antigua to Britain.

We explored the Zenobia ferry wreck in 1990 to search for the duty free store. The picture is taken just before she sunk in June 1980.

Before the ultimate cycle dive at Swithland Wood. In the picture I'm testing the drop before building the big ramp out over the water which would carry the lead weighted bicycle.

Kitted up and ready to go for a deep dive at Dorothea Quarry in Wales.

The raft race at Matlock. Just getting ready to board our raft 'police car' with our rubber truncheons and ready to dish out some good old British justice.

Preparing to dive on a D-Day shipwreck.

Diving the mystery wreck in Kalkara Creek, Malta. After a big search we came across it in low visibility still intact. From the engine room we brought up a full tool kit, finally identified as the wartime Italian MV Odile.

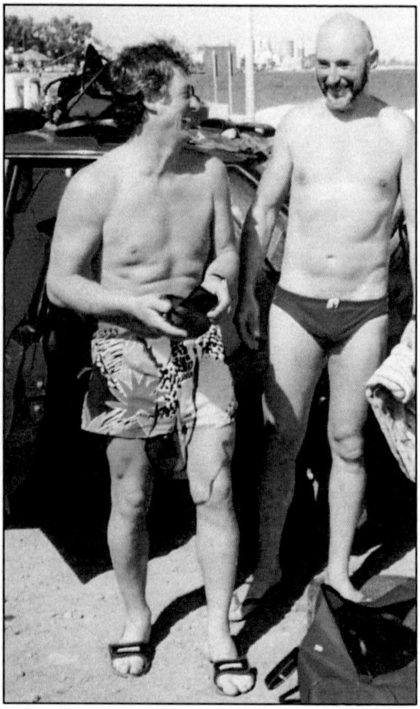

I'm pictured with John Smith before a dive into a lost cave not far from the Blue Grotto, Malta. This was to be a narrow escape as we both ran our of air with only minutes to live.

Good weather allows some much needed repairs about half way across the Atlantic.

Scraping the barnacles off the bottom of the boat.

A crafty cup of tea whilst Keith is still asleep.

15 minutes from the finish line at Port St. Charles, Barbados. We decide to stop and have a cup of tea.

The support boat '3 Com' came over to tell the sightseers to keep clear until we finish. This was only the second time we had seen the support boat on our voyage.

We've done it! Arriving at Port St. Charles, Barbados 60 days since we began this voyage of a lifetime.

As I stand up to get out my wobbly legs let me down and I end up in the water.

I didn't realise how thin I was, having lost three stone in weight.

The start of the race. (Picture from Rob's Hamill's book: The Naked Rower).

Peter Haining and David Richards try to get away from Olympic rowers Rob Hamill and Phil Stubbs (taken from Rob's book).

Rob Hamill and Phil Stubbs, the winners of the first Atlantic Rowing Race. (Picture from Rob's book: The Naked Rower).

The rest of the day I cruised about chatting to the rowers about their boats. The atmosphere was friendly, even buoyant, our competitors welcoming. There were loads of characters. Take, for example, Graham Walters, a carpenter from Leicester. Graham had collected his kitset only two months ago. Here he was complete with saw and hammer in hand still building his boat, *The George Gearry*. The first coat of paint was still tacky and while that was drying he was working out the best set-up for the rowing positions.

Graham had yet to fit any of the major items of equipment, including solar panels, compass and electrical system. I tried to offer whatever assistance I could. The enormity of the task facing this likeable man with the broad accent made me feel quite feeble and inadequate. However, I did manage to convince him that fitting a water desalinator would be a good idea. He was considering carrying all of his water across the Atlantic with him, the same way previous ocean rowing crossings had been achieved. This, I politely suggested, was not the way to provision with water this time. Though it was perilous to rely on this kind of equipment, one had to do so if you were going to have any chance of winning.

An article Rob Hamill wrote about me in his book along with a thinking pose of me. Article and picture also from Rob's book: The Naked Rower).

A chat about the race with race organiser Chay Blyth after the race.

Back to reality and back to work after the biggest challenge of my life.

hoping for some celebration to mark the occasion but this did not seem to the boss to be any cause for a display of extravagance. We hoisted lead and pump onto the pickup. Even a suggestion that I might finish early to change my ringing wet clothes was treated with contempt.

"Don't talk bloody stupid, you've got to get rid of the rubbish down the well. You'll have to catch the bus home, and don't say I never give you anything here's the fare."
He threw me a few coppers out of his pocket.

Getting involved in the past, I completely forgot the fix for today. Taking over from Keith I explained the missing fix. As the weather is still unchanged, force six gusting seven, we are still getting the odd wave breaking over the side giving us a small shower. The rowing deck clears very quickly of seawater so it is not necessarily a problem, apart from one small defect the deck-hatch covers all leak like sieves. I think of all the material we brought with us for emergencies. I know there are two coils of different sized O cord probably a very similar size to the O rings used on diving torches. Once the weather eases off I will try and fix them. Keith switches on the GPS and I log the position. It is a bit later than usual but in the
The wind still comes from the northeast - six to seven. Wait, the deck hatches! Opening the hatch I prepare for the worst. The water is two thirds of the way up covering the majority of the tinned food. How is it possible that they've rusted this quickly? I try to dry them without fetching off the labels.

The afternoon fix is not too bad but nowhere as good as yesterday's. Fix at 2.30pm 20° 58′ north, 22° 13′ west.

30th October 1997

"Graham, Graham!" exclaims Keith.

My eyes pop open.

"Your watch."

Most mornings it takes me a while to get my faculties together. After three minutes I'm ready to climb out and take over.

"Anything to see this morning Keith?"

"Unfortunately not Graham, but the Argos beacon has stopped flashing."

"That doesn't necessarily mean that it's not working though, maybe the power pack is running down."

Getting into position for my row I notice that the wind is dropping slightly. The Argos flashes once before I hand back over to Keith. Looking at my watch it is only 8.30am and the smell of boiling oat bars wafts through the open hatch. With my mind drifting from one thing to another I completely forget the time until a call for breakfast shoots me into action. Climbing forward with eager taste buds a steaming plate of porridge is handed to me. By the time I take over the oars the sun begins to rise in a cloudless sky, it'll be hot but at least rowing will be quite pleasant. The wind's probably no more than force two which means swell is vastly different to yesterday. The last 30 minutes of my shift is spent dreaming about a cool swim. Pasta and soup for lunch followed by the inevitable oat bar and three mugs of coffee.

"'Keith, I've just thought, the battery drill case is still in one of the deck compartments, I'll have a look for it when you start your row."

"I don't think it'll still be work."

"Always the pessimist Keith." I say with a sunburnt grin.

"No, just a realist."

As I located the right compartment one look was all it took to confirm Keith's prediction. The whole case was under water and already coated in rust. Opening the lid slightly at first to tip the water out, then wider, to discover, just as I imagined - rust everywhere. I pull the battery out and spray it frantically with WD40 hoping for a miracle.

Fresh water would be the answer, but as the water maker was still untested our drinking water was too precious a commodity to pour over a drill that may never work again. I dive into the aft cabin to get back to my book. The U Boat hunt during the last war and straight away the life insurance companies get in on the action. They estimate that the average life of a U Boat Sailor is 50 days. That reminds me, did I sign the race insurance papers? Looking over the page at my wrist I see that there's 20 minutes before change over. Time to do the fix at 2.40pm, 20° 39′ north, 23° 13′ west. After dinner the wind picks up again which I guess a good thing. The distances travelled rowing without any wind, compared to rowing in a force six are now quite obvious. Earlier I found a bottle of beer jammed in behind the side locker and decided that we would drink it in celebration when we reach halfway across. Who would have thought going two and a half weeks without a drink could be so hard.

31st October 1997

The early hours pass by without any distractions and soon I am settling down for my 6.00am sleep.

"Graham, Graham."

I open my eyes and it's daylight.

"Come and look." he said waving a fish in the hatchway.

I climb out wearily to inspect a rather slimy trophy. It's probably fourteen inches long with a bright yellow tail. The body is a mass of different shades of blue and a dorsal fin to match. A tasty Dorado if ever there was one.

"I reckon it's the lures." said Keith.

"What?"

"The lures. I've been using that pink squid one for about a week and nothing. As soon as I change to the blue..."

Over breakfast we discuss our ideas on the various ways to prepare and cook the fish.

"Let's fry it." I say, almost salivating at the thought of sprinkling some spice on the fresh fish.

"I think we should marinade it in tomato sauce."

Before I set myself up to row we decide that the preparation of our fish must come first. A plastic mat given to us as we left makes a perfect cutting board and we attach it to the bulwarks. An ideal spot - as soon as the butchery starts all waste goes straight over the side. Keith produces a recent purchase, a small sharp plastic handled knife in a scabbard. Testing the sharpness by removing the head he proceeds to bone and skin and finally cuts off the tail. Two large steaks remain. As this is our first taste of freshly caught fish we decide to eat one between us for lunch. Keith cuts one in half and places the two halves in the marinade. This is to be eaten with a small helping of pasta. For our evening meal the remaining steak cut in two and lightly fried. Soup is to be the entrée. I begin to row while Keith sets up two trailing lines using the lures, weights and floats from our collection of fishing tackle. Let's see if it really is the lure, or if it was just chance we caught the fish.

The morning row proceeds as the sun rises in another clear sky. Keith climbs into the aft cabin and sleeps until I call him at 12.30pm.

"Keith, time for your bon viveur talents, I'm going for a swim."

As I climb over the bulwarks Keith is juggling with pasta trapped between two plates and a saucepan of fish. As we only have one saucepan the pasta is cooked first in seawater then clasped between two plates to keep it warm. The saucepan then goes back on for the fish.

"Let's eat." Keith said as I finish drying myself.

The pasta is separated on to the two plates and the fish in sauce is spooned on to the top.

Over the last two nights and early mornings I have spent a considerable amount of time searching through my past and trying to write down as many of my early memories as possible. During the last two weeks I have found it difficult to get any kind of cohesion between the different encounters, but after consideration, have decided not to worry too much about continuity. As I put pen to paper Keith shouts through the hatch.

Turning around to look at the clock I realise that there is only enough time to fix our position before I begin my stint, 20° 13′ north and 23° 39′ west. There is something very familiar with these figures. I turn to the previous page. The position on the 30th October is 20° 39′ north and 23° 13′ west. The minutes of latitude and longitude have changed around. Some coincidences are incredible.

"You must have made a mistake Graham, I'll check it out.'"

Not long after I began rowing Keith comes back.

"Graham, do you know if we have a spare plug for the cigarette lighter socket?"

"Yes," I say, "if you open the tool locker and take out the two tool boxes you'll find a large white tub, take off the lid and inside, at the bottom, you'll see a new one still attached to the card."

As Keith pulls out the tool kit to find the plug it occurs to me that I failed to ask him what he wants it for. Saying something about batteries and charging I assume that it must be for a battery charger. Keith disappears again into the aft cabin, until reappearing, about 20 minutes later, to tell me that the GPS has gone down. Now I know that Rob wired the two cigarette lighter sockets on the same circuit. One has the GPS attached to it and the other was the one that Keith was going to use.

"Keith, what have you plugged into the other socket?"

"Oh it's my CD player. I've no batteries left and I thought I'd wire it to plug it into the cigarette lighter socket that's not being used."

With this latest piece of information it was not hard to understand why the GPS had ceased to work.

"Take the fuse out of the control panel switch with the word LOG Keith, and swap it with the one named NAV LIGHTS. I'll find the spare fuses later and I'd better give you some batteries so that you can test your CD player in case you've blown it up."

The daylight has soon slipped away again making the search for the fuses difficult. Keith agrees with me that we leave the search until tomorrow. Tonight we have decided to fit in three rowing periods to change the watch system again, giving me dawn and dusk.

1st November 1997

By the time I finish watch it's 3.00am and the wind has come back with a vengeance, it must be blowing force six or seven. I'm glad to climb into the aft cabin, yet it seems the very next thing I notice is that the cabin light is being switched on, a sign that it is time to change watches again. Pulling on a damp T-shirt, I force myself out. I hook my harness off from the cabin wall and climb on to the damp pitching and rolling seat. Forcing the oars back I begin rowing hard with the wind first one side and then the other. Straining hard on the left side I get hot shooting pains down my left side, damage I must have sustained on the earlier row. I try to trim the boat so that most of the pulling pressure is taken on my right side, not easy in these conditions. I'm relieved to see the grey dawn with the knowledge that it is only a short time before breakfast. Drinking coffee and biting into my oat bar, I relax, explaining to Keith in between bites about my pains. He suggests a course of painkillers. With breakfast over Keith sets his fishing line before starting to row while I try my hand selecting one of the last pink squid lures on the opposite side to Keith.

"That's not going to work you know." said Keith rather patronisingly.

"Why?"

"I was using it for days."

"Maybe the fish are aware of our intentions."

"What, after catching one."

"We need new tackle then, if you're so sure…how about those meatballs."

"Do fish eat meatballs?"

"I don't know. Do you?"

Picking up the discarded packet of meatballs in pasta sauce I force one onto the lure. Goaded into action by Keith's contemptuous stare I challenge him to a contest.

"The biggest catch wins." I said.

Getting carried away with enthusiasm I recklessly suggest that the loser buy the winner a pint. Keith in an act of over confidence insists on two as he carries on with his version of Polaris Two. I am surprised that he is not using the leftovers.

"Why don't you use those dumplings?" I asked, however I get not reply. Making his spinner out of a green plastic bag he's cut into pieces he carefully forms it into a torpedo shaped body and the silver remains from the food bag are cut up. Keith decides on three hooks together attached to the body of the new squid decoy. Hooks and spinner are all bound with wire strand, as we have no traces. By the time Keith has almost completed his work of art my home-made lure has already been in the water for about 30 minutes. I cannot help but taunt Keith.

"I suppose you know that the only fish to take an interest in such an unusual underwater object will need to have an IQ of one 150."

"Look Graham, you can take the piss but the proof of the pudding is in the eating."

Undeterred by my attempts to belittle his efforts, he ties on the lead weights.

"Wait Graham, what about floats?"

"I dunno, I only bought two and they're both gone, hang on."

Rummaging through the kit locker I find two small pieces of neoprene. 'Try one of these.' I said as I throw Keith the cloth.

"You know, when you put that lure over the side there'll be loud gulping noises coming out of the water all around the boat."

Keith turns around with a quizzical look on his face.

"Why is that Graham?"

"Because all the fish will be laughing their heads off."

Keith lowers his lure in and starts to let out the line. Before it has gone down three feet he has a bite. Hauling on the line a bit too enthusiastically, the fish flies aboard and starts leaping around the deck. Keith is ravelled up in fishing line so the bludgeoning is left to me.

"Looks like you owe me two pints Graham."

"Not likely it's only about eighteen inches long."

I begin the afternoon's rowing stint, and as the recent activities have taken some time, we decide on two hours each. After extracting his lure Keith continues to fish for a while but has trouble getting his spinner to spin.

"It is ill catching of fish when the hook is bare." I say.

"Honestly Graham, where do you keep getting this crap from?"

"It's a fishing proverb."

By the time 4.00pm comes and I climb off the rowing seat I find that I have lost interest in pulling and fiddling with my fishing line. As soon as I am in the aft cabin I take a fix off the

GPS, 19° 52′ north, 24° 15′ west, and then get back to the submarine story of Alastair Mars. It is amazing how quickly the time flies by when one is engrossed in someone else's adventure. I can feel the tension and sweat as German destroyers drop depth charges all around. The only reason I can think of for becoming so closely involved in all of these stories is the lack of outside interference normally associated with the telephone, people calling and the television.

Once on deck again I open the cooking and food locker, pulling out the stove, plates, pan etc. I am determined to try and duplicate one of the seafood chef, Rick Stein's recipes. The nearest I can get to Dorado is grilled tuna with soy sauce dressing. I know that we do not have any fresh herbs or vegetables but we do have brown sauce, Tabasco, black pepper and salt. Also we have no means of grilling. A minute dash of oil in the bottom of the pan with a splash of saltwater, a sprinkle of black pepper, a spoonful of brown sauce mixed with Tabasco on the side of the plate was as close as I could get it. It may sound pretty basic but it tasted delicious. To finish off we decided to have a pouch of dumplings in butterscotch sauce. During the afternoon I had checked under the floor of the aft cabin to see how many packets of this rich sweet were left. Counting them out I discovered that there were only enough for one a week. A treat, we decided, for Saturdays.

Rowing on into the dying light the wind began to increase. A pattern had emerged over the last few days, falling during the day the wind increased at night or early morning. Along with the increased wind the return of my pains attacking my left side completely. Keith fetched the medical box, and before he turns in, hands me two painkillers suggesting a top up in the morning. I swallow them reluctantly with a drop of water. I am not one for taking pills always hoping to rely on my body's natural immunity.

2nd November 1997

Rowing through my shift, midnight until three, I feel a strain in my left shoulder. I can only assume that I am subconsciously using more shoulder movements to compensate. Rising at 6.00am soon brought back the hot shooting pains down my side, and against my better judgement, I take more painkillers. I am that pleased to see nine o'clock that I make porridge using the method we've adopted - two oat bars and powdered milk. After breakfast I climb into the aft cabin while Keith sets up a fishing line with what he's now referring to as the 'super lure'. Only a few minutes into my slumber I'm woken by Keith shouting,

"I've caught another fish…a bigger one!"

It is lunchtime and I find that Keith has caught another fish, much the same in colour and shape as the previous catch, all, we assume, from the Dorado family. Keith prepares the first catch for lunch, and, while he is gutting, a few small worms are found prompting him to cut away more of the fish. There is, however, a fair amount left to make a decent meal. I devour a good helping of soup and fish and am ready to row. Keith offers me more of the painkillers but I decline as I feel able to cope with the strain to my shoulder and side, and the fact that the weather conditions have improved considerably with the wind dropping slowly since the early morning. The afternoon fix shows that we are moving more out into the Atlantic, 19° 33′ north, 24° 57′ west, with a westerly gain of forty-two miles compared to a southerly gain of 21 miles. Our plan to row west seems to be paying off. The pattern of life always appears to be the same, in my life anyway. What is given in the left hand is taken away in the right. At this precise moment I am referring to the wind, which is veering Northeast, but unfortunately dropping to force three or four. I do not need to offer odds on guessing what we are going to have for our evening meal tonight.

3rd November 1997

The wind picks up as I start the first watch of the day. No stars in the early hours, the sky is completely overcast. Two hours into my second watch and the wind has carried on veering. It is now east, southeast. Working on the assumption that the wind will take us north of west, we have decided to row southwest all day. I look to the right hand side of the aft cabin and see that the eastern skyline has started to change from black to grey. The time approaches for me to put on the kettle and I decide to have a quick swim first. Putting on my harness I clip the carabiners on to the hand lines allowing me almost free swimming range of the boat. I look in the direction of the wind and see a large wave approaching the side.

I leap over the bulwark and land right on top of the curling wave, which immediately drags me under the boat due to the pressure of the water rushing underneath.

Just as I pass the keel I am brought to a halt by the harness jerking tight below my armpits. I swim back under the boat and surface on the windward side pulling myself over the bulwark. I make a mental note that tomorrow I will try swimming on the leeward side - might be safer. After breakfast it is back to the Mediterranean in the submarine 'Unbroken'. Studying a photograph of her Captain, Alastair Mars, I am amazed at how young he looks, and, reading back, I discover that he is only twenty-six. A sudden lurch of the boat and I awake to find the book still in the exact same position and page held by both my hands. I think my body is trying to tell me something so I put the book down and lay back. I was fast asleep in seconds.

"Graham, Graham!"

Waking with a shudder my first thought was who the hell is calling me now. Of course it soon dawned on me that there was only one person it could be.

"What's up?"

"Can you get some grub out for dinner?"

"Okay, what do you fancy?"

"Beef stew, what about you?"

Lifting up the foam cushions I dived underneath with the square key to open the lockers. Even though we had re-packed all of the food pouches we were still unable to remember which locker we had put what in. After trying two on the left I shout to Keith.

"Which locker do you think it's in?"

"Second from the front, port side."

Marine expressions. Saying left or right may be okay on land but when you're afloat it just doesn't sound right. Apart from that it depends entirely which way you're facing. Trying the second without much luck I open the third and there it is. Taking out two pouches I re-fit the lid and lock the two small turn bolts. I check all of the others that I have opened, which takes time and effort re-locking the lids. My main reason for being so obsessive about re-locking is the thought that we may capsize. Obviously, if the tops to the lockers were left open and, God forbid, the boat did turn upside down, every item stored in them would be spread about the aft cabin. This in itself does not worry me. My main concern would be the watertight integrity of the boat, which revolves around the airtight compartments. All of these I know to be airtight having tested them for leaks when we individually filled each compartment with water.

I have always known myself, as well as reading about capsize drills, that the aft cabin must stay watertight if the boat is to right itself. Since the very first day we have kept the hatch held open. Even the stormy weather has not deterred us from leaving it open. The only problem is; should a rogue wave hit us, and we capsize, the hatch will be open. At this moment in time there have been no near misses from capsizing. I suppose if it came to a near thing, we would be forced to close it. I am forgetting, yes we had closed it simply to test the conditions inside. It was like sitting inside an oven combined with an overwhelming sense of claustrophobia. The small solar vent fitted in the roof hardly seems to make any difference.

"Graham, Sherlock Holmes of the food supply. Have you located the beef stew and dumplings?"

"Yep I've found them."

They taste fantastic. I'm convinced that the more you look forward to a particular meal the more you enjoy it. Over the meal we discuss the wind direction compared with our position, although I have not taken the fix. We both have a good idea of where we are, and come to a unanimous decision. Point the boat at Barbados and cross the ocean. Thinking over the trip in my head after just starting I had decided to split the crossing into three parts. The first, Tenerife to the Cape Verde Isles, the second, halfway across the Atlantic, and finally, the last part, the middle of the Atlantic to Barbados.

One third of the trip was completed. For me this was no celebration, more like another beginning. he ocean lay in front of us still to be crossed.

"Keith, what about a mid-Atlantic celebration? We know we have the bottle of rum that Jock's company gave to us, and the bottle of beer that I left by mistake. Let's drink the beer. We'll have to tow it behind the boat to try and cool it down."

"Okay, providing it doesn't drop off."

With that thought in mind I put away all the cooking apparatus and climbed onto the sliding seat. My rowing stint passes quickly. The 2½ hours pulling at the oars seemed quite refreshing. I can only assume that my rowing enthusiasm has been brought about by the start of the second stage of the trip, seeing us boldly setting out across the Atlantic. The first thing on my mind on entering the aft cabin is the fix, 19° 23′ north and 25° 59′ west. Incredible, 62 miles west, it must be the best days' run yet. Looking at the chart it is hard to believe. We have already travelled one third of the distance. We still have this vast ocean to cross. Only 130 miles separates us from the lighthouse on Antao in the Cape Verde Isles. Our present course is taking us parallel to the 4000 metres, contour line around the islands.

4th November 1997

The wind begins to die soon after I start my midnight stint, the swell's slowly going down. I keep telling myself how we can take advantage of the changing conditions, but the trouble is that I'm not very convincing. I'm much more composed now I'm not being thrown around, neither am I getting drenched by the odd breaking wave. The oars are harder to pull. More pressure on my arms and shoulders now the wind is not helping to push the boat along. The sky finally starting to clear, the clouds are dispersing which means I can see the stars.

My second stint starts with the moon just brightening the surface of the sea giving it a grey oily appearance. As the oars strike the water there is a strange splashing, gurgling, accompanied by a squeaking from the rowlocks. It's becoming rather annoying actually. Rummaging around in the kit locker I find the can of WD40. Normally the overriding noise belongs to the wind and sea. As for the squeaking sounds from rowlocks and seat these are taken care of by the liberal doses of saltwater administered by nature. For breakfast this morning, after a five minute dip, I settle for porridge. Something to look forward to as this is our biggest early morning meal just once a week. Usually breakfast consists of an oat bar for me, and a chocolate bar for Keith. Once breakfast was over I was keen to start doodling, the common expression now every time Keith sees me with pen in hand. I had sat rowing in the early hours chuckling to myself recollecting two comical situations that had happened to me many years ago. To be precise 1977.

I was working in Bath at this particular time finishing a loft conversion on my own. Most of the work was complete. My saw was left be accident under the eaves, a small space that was now more or less built around. In cases like these one must weigh up the pros and cons, which in this case was how much would a new saw cost against the effort to retrieve the old one? Unfortunately sentiment came into the argument, not always a good thing. It was, after all, one of the first saws I bought as an underpaid apprentice on a small wage. After this thought process the argument was over, I must get the saw at all costs. I had two options. Take off a ridiculous amount of roof tiles and cut through the felt and lath or try to reach the area by crawling behind the wall. The area in which I'd have to crawl through is tiny. I say through, but there was only one way out, the same as the way in. To be honest I had not really considered getting out.

Once my decision was made I crawled in using methods carried out by the Army, forearms and sides of feet. To make matters worse the whole area was covered in new fibreglass. I soon reached the end. There was my saw. I picked it up and started back using the same method but backwards with my feet going first. I think I must have managed about five feet before I came to a halt. The shuffling backwards action had caused the fibreglass insulation to push up and drag along with me, forcing it's way around my body turning into a compressed mass. As my arms were forced out in front of me I was totally helpless. The final realisation of my predicament took about five minutes. In this time I had tried to move one way then the other, stopped, rested and tried again. Fortunately I do not suffer with claustrophobia, the main thing on my mind was the embarrassment. I knew that at some time I would be found so there was no danger to my health. Deciding on a plan I began shouting, "Is anybody there?" about every minute. I knew that normally the lady of the house, Lesley, would be about and at some stage she would come up the stairs and ask me if I wanted a cup of tea. Eventually I heard somebody walking up the new stairs.

"Graham where are you?" she asked.

It took me a little time to explain from my position behind the wall, but at last, action. She phoned her husband Rob at work and asked him to drive home to help. Lesley informed me that he would be about an hour and asked what should she do in the meantime. I pleaded with her to go back to whatever she was doing. This was embarrassing enough already. That hour seemed to go on and on before eventually I heard Rob call; "Graham where are you?" Explaining my predicament I could do nothing else but wait to be rescued.

"Rob, if you can drop a slip knot onto the end of a length of rope over my feet and hitch back to where the roof opens out, you'll be able to sit with your feet against a ceiling joist and pull."

I remember how ridiculous I felt saying that but without hesitation Rob began making a knot in a piece of rope. The first pull felt like what I imagined a medieval rack used in a torture chamber would feel like.

"I think it's working Rob. Try again."

I finally popped through the compressed fibreglass, and when I emerged into the bedroom a very relieved Lesley was there to greet us.

The second incident did cause a certain young lady some embarrassment.

I was working on a loft conversion not far from Leicester with a friend of mine named Chris. We were at the early stages of the job putting in the floor joists when Chris called to me in a hushed voice "Curious." I scrambled over towards him, and by this time he was kneeling down looking at something on top of the ceiling. As I approached his leg slipped off the ceiling joist and went straight through the ceiling with a crack followed by a scream from below. I could now see the object of Chris's interest. There, below, sat a young lady in a bath half full of water trying to cover certain parts of her anatomy. We of course apologised and moved away from the spot allowing her to retrieve a bath towel. By the time we had re-fixed the ceiling and cleared away, the lady in question had dressed and brought us a cup of tea each. We all agreed not to mention the incident to her husband who might misinterpret the accident.

With the sea reasonably flat we decided to do all the maintenance work through the afternoon.

5th November 1997
My midnight stint becomes almost enjoyable, looking up at the stars I promise myself to look for the book of stars again. Breakfast over I eagerly pick up my book. Would I change places with one of the crew of the submarine 'Unbroken'? An hour later I decide to take a quick nap after finishing the last few lines.

Soup, the last but one, gets used for lunch. This I am glad about, not because it didn't taste good, far from it. By the time it was ready for human consumption it had a thick creamy consistency with a taste to match. A mug and a half each was all that a packet produced. It was fine over the first week when we had bread and the second, when we had cracker wheat and margarine, but on it's own it just doesn't satisfy my hunger. I guess I could dip an oat bar in it...or would that be weird?

18° 57′ north, 26° 59′ west. We have slowed a little since the day before and now the wind has decided to slow us down even more, backing to NNW. After breakfast, while I rowed, Keith was trying out more of the GPS functions, a most useful one being the Trip Odometer, re-set every hour to give us miles per hour. With a light wind blowing from a slight angle and a constant swell, our average speed appears to be about one and three-quarter miles per hour. Now the wind has backed and is slightly against us that has been reduced to one and a quarter miles per hour. Just before dinner our speed starts to go up, although the wind is more or less the same, it is now back to one and three-quarter miles per hour with the wind slightly against us. By the time I had the dinner prepared we were rowing at two knots. We discuss this whilst eating, Keith puts it down to a better rowing rate. The meal lasts about an hour but before we finish I check the Odometer reading.

"We're still doing one and a half knots even though nobody has been rowing and the wind slightly against us." I said.

"Then we must have picked up a new current."

"I'm not sure about your idea of an under water current Keith. Looking at the chart what you see is what you get. Half a knot rising possibly to one knot but no more. I'll row while you keep an eye on the GPS."

Over the next 2½ hours the speed has steadily increased, and after three hours, when I finish my watch, we are doing three knots according to the GPS. Usually at this particular change of watch, 9.30pm, the one coming off watch climbs into the sleeping bag, and as it is totally dark, switches the light on.

"Graham, I can't see a thing with that light on."

"Don't worry."

I hang my towel over the hatch.

"How's that?"

"Better… for now"

"Just give me a bit longer Keith, I'm going to take a fix and check our distance ran over every hour since the last one. I'll see if the speed tallies."

"What speed are we doing now?"

"Four and a half knots, I don't think even you could row that fast Keith and I can't honestly believe that we've found some strange ocean current."

I wait until 10.45pm at which time our speed, according to the Odometer, is 5½ knots. I change the GPS back to nav for a position, 18° 45′ north, 27° 18′ west, and add our last six hours, given to us by the Odometer in distance run approximately 22 miles, and re-calculate that the 4.45pm fix is bang on.

"Keith, the GPS fix must be wrong."

"Why?"

"It seems to be increasing our rowing speed every hour and then calculating our position from that. There is only one way to check for sure. I'll get out our GPS backup and see what position that said.' 18° 54′ north, 27° 06′ west, that's more like it. Did you touch something, were you going through the various functions?" I ask.

Keith looks at me with a uncomfortable stare.

6th November 1997

I start my second watch of the day with a lot more effort due to the wind's erratic behaviour. As the swell builds up so does my anxiety. The boat is starting to tilt at some alarming angles. The main hatch is always open. If the boat did capsize would it self-right after allowing gallons of water to enter the aft cabin? Thinking over these things leads me to decide on more ballast. After breakfast I will fill ten, six litre bottles with seawater. Up until now we have probably used about forty-three of them, our main ballast of thirty, six litre bottles still contain fresh water. During the nights, since setting out into the Atlantic, we collected quite a few flying fish landing on the deck, some of which we ate.

Over breakfast we discuss the problems with the GPS. Keith believes that it is now okay since he re-programmed it, but is still unaware of how it happened. I clear away the cooker eager to start my doodlings. As well as trying to pin down the year I had an idea to give my trips down memory lane a title. This one I decide to call 'The Burning'.

1967: At last, a nice cushy job in town - removing all the fixtures and fittings from The Pelican Hotel, a pub I had drank in many times in the past. It was situated in a central position on Granby Street very close to Leicester's clock tower. Two very substantially built bars were to be removed along with all of the shelves, mirrors and fitted seating. The end product was to be an empty shell ready to start it's new life as a shop. Firstly we removed the bars, I say we because for this endeavour Paul, a young scrawny apprentice had been assigned the job of helping. All of the sawn and tortured ornate timber was unceremoniously piled at the rear of the building awaiting it's final journey to the tip, care of the firm's lorry. Scrap and useful items were to be brought back into the shop. The copper scrap pile began to mount and a thought crossed my mind. Perhaps a little of the copper for myself could help out with my cash shortage. My instructions regarding where to start and stop ripping out the pipe work were, to say the least, a little ambiguous. I therefore settled for a more thorough job, which involved a speedy removal in the cellar. Certain copper pipes were targeted and two days of work left the ground floor clear. On the third day we began to remove the seats and bar on the first floor, a much more pleasant area to work. Opening the french doors onto the balcony to gaze at long forgotten architecture that filled the skyline in the heart of the city. Pigeons flew back and forth oblivious to the destruction we were to vent on yet another part of the city's history.

As the morning progressed with the removal of a very ornate mahogany panelled bar, we came across a chrome cylinder approximately two feet high. A small handle protruded at the top and our curiosity, at this stage, did not lie with the use or history of this object, but was directed mainly at the outer casing. Was it copper or were the innards made of brass? In no time at all the top was sawn off with a hacksaw. Two faces peered down at a multitude of brown sticky matter, the smell probably the discovering factor. Floor polish. A note of disinterest returned us to the removal of the fitted seating. Heeding the lunch time hour we sat by the open French doors eating our sandwiches to the hurly-burly sound of a city at work.

The last of our sandwiches and tea consumed we began the after meal ritual participated by at least fifty per cent of the population. For me it required a little preparation as I rolled my own, but for my helping apprentice this was not the case as he produced a packet containing several cigarettes. The next action is a little vague. When I describe the course of events, one of us, as I say I cannot remember which one, lit his cigarette with a match and nonchalantly flicked it across the floor. Before I mention it's landing place I must describe the condition of the room we were in. Having pulled out all of the seating areas, the floor was covered in packing material, broken timber and torn seat coverings. You have probably guessed by now where. It landed in the open top of the floor polish cylinder, and whoof, a flame shot as high as the ceiling. At that moment the situation was not necessarily dangerous, but my helping apprentice, startled by the sudden burst of flame, jumped up and kicked the cylinder over. I watched with horror as the burning cylinder rolled across the floor spewing out it's glowing contents and within a matter of seconds the discarded seating was ablaze. Looking at the open-ended water pipes curving away from the wall an idea came to me. I shouted to the apprentice to rush down to the cellar and turn on the water.

There was still a small passage across the floor that wasn't on fire and as we were near the open doors one had to negotiate a way through the burning room to the door. I waited on the balcony for the apprentice to begin a fire fighting action, not realising the amount of smoke that was pouring from the windows. With the bright glow behind me I turned around in amazement to see the centre of the city at a standstill. A large crowd had gathered blocking the traffic and somebody was shouting up to me. Over the roar of the blaze and the din of the crowd I managed to establish that the Fire Brigade has been sent for. No water had come out of the pipes so I assumed that Paul, the apprentice, was having difficulty in turning the stopcock. I decided to make my way to the cellar, there was still a path through the burning chairs. The biggest danger was the thick black smoke filling the space between the ceiling and three feet off of the floor. I tied a handkerchief across my mouth, and squatting low, made my way to the doorway and down the stairs, partially blocked by dismantled bars. On reaching the final cellar steps the first sounds were of running water. I opened the cellar door and was met by an incredible sight. Water was gushing from open-ended pipes, cut through and forgotten about in the previous rush for scrap. There in the middle of the cellar stood Paul, water now well past his knees and he was bending over with both arms in water up to his shoulders.

"What the hell's going on?" I shouted over the din of rushing water.

His explanation was that he had gone in search of buckets to fill, but by the time he had found one the water was already rising above the floor. He was now attempting to switch off the water.

"Leave it, just bring the buckets!"

As we got to the cellar door the familiar sound of fire engine bells were ringing outside and in a short space of time the fire was out. The stopcock in the street was switched off and a pump was running to empty the cellar.

After our account about the start of the fire the Fire Chief told us that we had been very lucky. The first floor was made of concrete with woodblock tiles, once the said tiles had burnt away along with the scattered broken seats and what was left of the bar, there was very little to fuel the flames. Also, the fact that the ceiling in the room where the fire had flared up was of very thick plaster, it held the fierce heat from breaking through to the next floor. If that had of happened, in his opinion, nothing would have stopped the fire gutting the whole property. The Fire Chief informed me that a full report would be forwarded to my employers, with this went my last hope of anonymity. I gave notice to quit by the end of the week, informing my trusty apprentice Paul of my decision. I went on to tell him that he should not be sorry at the thought of never working with me again, and, not wanting to sadden him any further, never mentioned the prospect of him having to face an inquiry alone. I suppose that deep down I knew that he would have to face a severe bollocking although his apprenticeship would save him from the sack.

The last of the pasta sauce had been planned for lunch together with the ubiquitous meatballs. I press on with the rowing soon after while Keith takes his afternoon siesta. A notable absence of seagulls and storm petrels since leaving the Cape Verde Isles has made me even more vigilant towards our feathered friends. So far three seagulls have had flying practice around the boat just before breakfast. More may have flown by, but my observations during the 11 hours I am on watch, has only brought about the three, yesterday and the day before were the same. Before I hand over to Keith along come our two storm petrels, dive bombing the boat at all angles. Sometimes flying straight at the boat and then veering off at the last moment. My first job, after climbing into the aft cabin, the fix, 18° 17′ north and 24° 00′ west. This looks the best run yet. I eagerly pick up the chart and begin to plot the position, yes, 71 miles. I shout to Keith to tell him the good news, although I know he has a reasonable idea after seeing him looking at the GPS. It comes as no surprise, his retort is slightly nonchalant.

"Yes I thought we must have made good progress."
Not letting his matter of fact answer deter my elation I write in the log 'Incredible run, 71 miles'.

Time for another book. A work of fiction I bought quite a few years before purely because of it's title, 'Albions Dream', the name of my east-coast sailing smack. The latter part being my dream to finally finish the re-build.

7th November 1997

My first stint over and my hips seem to be completely bruised. Sudden movements cause sharp hot pains down my side. It is not difficult to understand the reasons behind these pains. Over the last year my training sessions has consisted mainly of long and short periods on the rowing machine combined with much shorter activity on the bike and running machine intermingled with bouts of weight lifting. In all this exercise none of it put a strain on a side to side movement of the upper body. 50% of the time whilst rowing on the sea one's body is thrown from side to side in varying degrees. To compound this discomfort the soles of my feet have become very painful when wet and when I put pressure on them. Trying to keep them dry is almost impossible. At the end of each night's stint I dry my feet and put Ster-Zac powder on them. The trouble is we have only 30 grams, and with both of us having the same problem, it is not going to last long. As we change watch Keith gives me Brufen 400, my painkillers for my hips. Talking of ailments I might as well mention the other common condition, backsides, infected with what I can only describe as red bumps in a sort of rash and very painful. I usually begin my night's row by spreading Vaseline all over my backside normally leaving treatment until after my swim.

Breakfast comes and goes leaving me in a relaxing mood to read. As I get deep into the story based around an aged board game where characters in the game resemble real people, in the world of our main hero, Edward, life and death hang in the balance as Edward plays the game for good against evil. Reading through the book makes me wonder if I should have brought an odd game to play between us, although the only time we spend together is at meal times. As the constant day to day routine carries on with one rowing and one relaxing or sleeping, chess, I am sure, would have been the most entertaining game, pitting our wits against each other. Memories of nail biting fights to the finish until that final word the loser dreads 'Checkmate'. Perhaps it is better this way, as I haven't played a real game for twenty years. After lunch and more rowing I take down the fix hoping for another good run, 17° 32′ north and 28° 37′ west, only 55 miles since yesterday's fix and quite a difference from the day before of 71 miles. I don't know what I am complaining about, the last run is still five miles above our estimated 25 hour run. As the wind has decreased to force five over the last fourteen hours or so, it is understandable.

8th November 1997

Rain pours down, beginning after only an hour of rowing. As the sky had been cloudless all night there was nothing to indicate a downpour when I started my watch. When the outlines of black rain clouds appeared there was still a possibility they might miss us on their journey across the sky. Forever optimistic I have not bothered to put on my waterproof trousers. 99% of the time, we are bare legged, even when the deck is washed by largish waves. The seawater is always warm and does not necessarily bother us when we are wet up to the backside. The rain is a different matter altogether with the temperature being much colder one soon feels chilled. Relieved to finish my watch I hand over to Keith warning him to wear his salopettes. He said that he couldn't be bothered and shrugs his shoulders. I dry myself and climb into my sleeping bag. Waking me at 6.00pm I enquire how his watch has gone.

"No problems, not a drop of rain."

I could hardly believe it.

"You lucky bastard."

"I think it's cleared up."

'Okay, I'll take your word for it and leave my bottoms off.' It must have been no more than 30 minutes before another downpour drenches me again. The feeling of misery finally leaves me when the sky begins to brighten. By the time coffee is made my early morning dip had been accomplished along with dry underpants and T-shirt. After the drenching I feel a bit bleary eyed. A quick nap should see me right. Lying back against the sleeping bags, I am soon asleep. My next recollection is a raging sea. I'm thrown about like a rag doll. I hang on to a side rope, we seem to be in some kind of inflatable. I see a large wave approaching. Trying to shout out a warning seems impossible as if something is paralysing my mouth. I try again but it just comes out garbled. Before there is time to do anything else it hits, turning the inflatable upside down and throwing me into the water in the process. As I surface something ravels around my leg, the anchor rope. With the weight of the anchor I am slowly pulled under the surface struggling for my life. My eyes are open. Keith is looking at me with a smile on his face.

"I thought you'd got St Vitus's Dance, squirming and wriggling. Before that you were making a loud mumbling sound."

"Sorry Keith, I must have been having some kind of nightmare."

My short story of the past that I had been thinking of writing would have to wait. For some reason it seems to be tied in with my dream. I think that it's back to the book.

When lunchtime arrives, the dream is all but forgotten. I would describe our meal but I am sure you know the main ingredients, pasta will never be the same again. The first watch of the afternoon gets me back in my stride. When the time comes to change over my enthusiasm for a progress report has taken hold of me. I dive through the hatch and pull the GPS out of it's holder, 17° 07′ north, 29° 29′ west, sixty-two mile run, seven miles improvement on yesterday. With this encouraging progress report I decide to carry on writing.

1985 Lucky Escapes: A sunny April morning, a brisk chilly wind was blowing, not exactly strong but enough to make me regret that I had not put on my thicker jacket. Raising the big double extender at the rear of this reasonably large semi-detached house in Birstall, Leicestershire - the job, planting a new chimney pot and cementing it in place, what we call in the trade, flaunching. The wooden crawler ladder that I was now raising to the roof belonged to a friend as my metal one was on another job. Most crawlers have some sort of hook which fits over the roof ridge and holds it from sliding down the roof. This particular one that I had borrowed was home made, a common practice back then. When working on roofs made out of tiling lath, in place of a hook, a large wide piece of timber would be attached which simply dropped over the ridge. Having positioned the crawler on the roof I began to descend the ladder giving one last look as to how it was leaning against the gutter. By the time I reached the bottom a nagging doubt concerning tying the ladder disappeared along with the excuses, such as no strong tying points to be seen. Returning with the chimney pot my first trip to the top went to plan. Mixing enough mortar to fill at least two buckets in the barrow was soon accomplished. Filling one of the buckets approximately two thirds full I started to climb the ladder, trowel and pointer in my back pocket. The hardest part was probably climbing from the ladder on to the bottom of the crawler holding a heavy bucket of compo. Half way to the top of the roof an ominous creak distracted my attention. Momentarily stalled in no man's land on the roof, my ears now became attuned to a new sound as the creak grew into a groan. It increased in volume and I realised what was about to happen. I began to run up the crawler imitating Sebastian Coe still holding the bucket of compo as if by instinct. The race to the top of the roof coincided with the downward speed of the crawler. The horror of seeing the top of the crawler come away had been replaced by my sudden burst of activity. As the last rung slipped past me my balance was lost completely finally letting go of the bucket as I began to roll head over heels backwards down the roof slope. Preoccupied with my own destiny I failed to notice the sliding crawler knock the untied ladder away from the roof. As I became airborne I felt a fleeting sense of relief, probably due to the end of a short bruising roll down the roof. I say fleeting because the next thought was lost in violent shooting pains in both knees as they came into contact with the small lean-to roof. his affected my fall by propelling my body away from the back of the house, and with a final backward somersault I felt a severe stabbing pain across the front of my stomach. All of the wind in my lungs seemed to be forced out as if flattened by a heavy stone. A sudden sense of relief from this intense pain swept across me as the ultimate journey to earth came to an end and my fight for breath produced a haunting croaking sound.

Lying in that state with my eyes shut as the body, then with added vigour, started to commute messages of pain from all parts.

"Graham, speak to me, Graham, speak to me."

I open my eyes and looked into the imploring face of my client unable to say a word. My lungs were taking an awfully long time to fill up. Slowly the power of speech returned. The small gathering of worried faces insisted that I didn't try to move anything informing me that the ambulance was on its way. Looking around at my surroundings I see that I was lying on what was once the dividing fence between the two properties. Four or five fence posts snapped off level with the ground. Tulips that were flowering in a variety of colours lie squashed and broken. One half of the double extender ladder lay broken in two and the crawler was beyond repair. I asked if anybody had seen the unfortunate accident. The next door neighbour on the far side informed me that he had witnessed it. He had watched my backward summersault off the edge of the roof, and completion of this great feat by crashing my knees onto the lean-to bouncing off at an angle backwards and landing face down across the garden fence. The impact, when I landed on my stomach, tore down the fence and saved me, no doubt, from serious internal damage.

The pains were beginning to subside and I was convinced that there were no broken bones. The ambulance men arrived with a stretcher and before long they are going through the standard procedure.

"Does this hurt? Does that hurt?"

Bending my joints and sitting me up slowly they checked a few cuts and bruises. When they finally brought me to my feet it was a little painful at first but I soon began to feel better. Plasters were stuck and a trip to hospital was suggested for a thorough check up. Confident of no damage, and mindful of the jobs planned for that day I decline with the knowledge that I will have to sign a document taking responsibility. They then suggested that a visit to the casualty department at the hospital, reminding me that there could have been internal injuries to body or brain. After the ambulance left I hobbled back to the scene of the crime. That day I was lucky, a few inches to the left or right would undoubtedly have resulted in broken bones or worse. If I had landed a few feet away from where I did and had my neck landed on the fence I doubt that my head would still have been attached to my body.

"Graham…Graham" said Keith. 'I think it's time for a change of menu."

"What have you in mind, pasta sauce?"

"A packet of meatballs in pasta sauce."

"I may be a bit slow, but don't we already eat meatballs in pasta sauce?" I say.

"Yes, but only one packet, today we're going to have two packets."

"And that's a change of menu is it?" I ask.

Finishing my row I decide to carry on recording the lucky escapes I've had.

Ten months later I was working on a large house roof, there was no scaffold or ladders only a long drop onto a wooden spiked fence that encircled the garden. The ladders were on the opposite side. In the back of my mind were these pointed fence boards, but, as usual, time was short. Half way through the morning, to make matters worse, a mist appeared which left behind a slight frost on the surface of the slates. As I was bending my legs, both feet slipped backwards, throwing me flat onto the roof. This action sets off a slow slide that grew faster the nearer I got to the edge of the roof. Even trying to hug the roof with both arms outstretched would not slow me down. This feeling felt far too familiar, surely not again?Suddenly, bang, both toes of my boots forced themselves into the gutter and abruptly stopped my descent. It was far too slippery to climb so I shouted for help. No answer. Lodged in that position I heard a plastic popping sound. The horrible realisation sank in. Without doubt, that the plastic brackets had broken.

My body slid slowly further down the roof as the plastic gutter begins to bend. Shouting as loud as I dared I finally got a response, "Graham, what's up" said a voice.

"What do you mean what's up, can't you see? Get me a rope as

fast as you can, the guttering is giving way.
Another lifetime stretched ahead as I waited with my cheek to the roof. At last a coil of rope dropped around my prone shape. Pulling it tight gave the guttering all the excuses it needed as the remaining brackets gave way and I drop another twelve inches until the rope pulled tight again. Slowly pulling myself back up I could not help but think next time, I wouldn't be so lucky.

9th November 1997

Starting my shift at midnight the wind is still blowing a probable force six to seven. For some reason I am finding it more difficult to row even though I have altered the rudder more times that I care to mention. An hour of hard work goes by before I become acclimatised and begin to relax. Then like always, the tranquility of the ocean doesn't stick around for long and a larger than normal wave throws the stern of the boat up in the air. It could not have chosen a better time as I have just removed my feet from the straps to adjust them. I am hurled backwards in the air, landing on the bow seat. Lying there for a few minutes until most of the pain has gone I climb back to the rowing seat but discover that the pain in my lower back was not going to go away. The change of watch is appreciated even more than usual knowing that the constant movement related to my suffering back is about to cease. Getting up for my second watch means more pain as all of my muscles down the side of my back have gone stiff. Daylight brings some relief and, feeling the way I do, postponement of my daily swim is a must. Stripping off my shorts I decide on a quick wash. s I reach for the soap another wave leaps over the side knocking me over. When I regain my composure I discover that it had taken my shorts.

By the time we're sharing breakfast Keith has noticed my dejected look.

"What's the matter Graham, you look a bit pissed off?" Explaining my back pains and losing my shorts he prescribes more pills. I don't expect any sympathy for losing my shorts as he lost on the third day, but still, it's rather annoying. Sitting back against two rolled up sleeping bags inside the aft cabin is one of those moments of rare pleasure, the pains in my back seem to ease away. Time for some relaxing reading I think.

10th November 1997

1.00am takes an awfully long time to come. The first hour of my watch has dragged on more than usual. The sea is the same as it's been the last few days making rowing hard work. Rowing in the dark always creates more difficulties. I'm unable to anticipate the size and direction of the oncoming waves. There is no time to prepare a response with the oars. They are not necessarily high, but always with a breaking crest. This morning as the wind is northeast I am rowing north of west. This allows the waves a 45° angle with which to hit the starboard side of the boat in three general positions. The aft cabin produces a blast of seawater that usually hits one in the face having come over the top or propelled off the side.

When the express wave hits the centre it does one of two things, either shooting up over the bulwarks or rolling under the boat. As for the bow, generally it goes over the top of the fore-cabin, most definitely the least of all problem makers, as one does not get drenched. Not that one waits to be soaked, of course. As soon as it comes into view one bobs and weaves like some Prize Fighter.

The thought of climbing out onto the open deck to commence rowing does not seem quite as daunting as the midnight stint. This is probably due to psychological thoughts regarding the arrival of the dawn. After rowing for about an hour there is a shout from the rear cabin followed by some cursing. I have a reasonable idea what it is all about, and when the cabin light goes on my guess is confirmed. Keith is trying to mop up a layer of seawater lying over the blue waterproof covers with his towel. The cause of the deluge stems from the temptation to leave the rear hatch slightly open to cool the hot humid heat inside. The consequences usually end in being rudely awakened by a jet of seawater. Leaving the hatch open at the front does not seem to help the rear area of the cabin where our heads lie. We have already tried sleeping the other way round and it is possible to get cool air circulating around the area but, unfortunately, we have no cover for the foot well. This means that my head has to lie on one side of our bulging bags containing clothes, salopettes, sailing jackets, cameras and everything else we have brought that in no way represents a pillow. We do, of course, have the option of rearranging the bags. I suppose we have been spoilt so far as we were able to leave the top hatch open for three-quarters of the trip across to the Cape Verde Isles. I do not envy Keith trying to get back to sleep with the wet sleeping bags on top of the damp covers. Normally we would still have a dry sleeping bag but Keith came up with the idea of joining the bags together giving us twice the room. The advantages lie in the luxury of movement inside the bag. As they are designed to fit snugly around the body, the urge to change sleeping positions is due to the boat's erratic movement. The more the rower tries to gain speed by keeping the wind directly behind, the more chance there is that the waves or the wind will turn the stern this way and then that.

At last the day begins, always seemingly slow. A distant light appears on the horizon until bright rays burst through. A few low lying cumulous clouds, black and white, turn first grey, violet, then break into deep red and dark blue. The dawn makes me feel more alive, more in touch with the world. If I were a more pragmatic type of person I would have used these early sunrise images to predict the forthcoming weather usually associated with bright violets, reds and purples. Moist air, sometimes, may be an indication of bad weather. My attempts at reading the approaching weather took a backward step two days after leaving, suddenly realising that I had left the barometer behind. On appraisal of the situation, not being equipped with communication systems, unlike many of our competitors, a down to earth approach has been adopted. What comes along comes along. The seats, oars and deck buckets all have lanyards, a necessity in these conditions.

Over breakfast I suggest splitting the two sleeping bags so that if one gets drenched the other can be used. We both agree that this is the best solution, and with the sun shining the two bags are hung out to dry. For the first time on the trip I can write in complete privacy behind a screen of hanging sleeping equipment. Not that it makes any particular difference to my writing, but it certainly feels different to be separated from Keith.

1969: Me and two friends, Len and John arrived in Haifa, Israel after a journey by land and sea. It began with transport in Sweden when my car was squashed by a giant lorry near a town called Jonkoping.

The fast speed of the lorry when it hit us immediately forced us off the road straight down a small embankment. This was when the car began to turn over and over, I will always remember the dust it created. The car landed on its side then skidded 30 yards down the road before finally coming to a stop.

Opening the driver's door, which was now on top, I climbed out expecting two injured companions but they both managed to climb out on their own. Looking back at them, a look of horror came over us all, each one of us was completely covered in what looked like red body matter. Rubbing some off with my hand a slow relaxing look appeared on my face, to confirm my suspicions I tasted it - tinned tomatoes. There was a full box of them in the boot, the impact had exploded them, then with the fall spread them round the car. As we relaxed a strong smell was noticed, all three of us were thinking this time there was nothing comical - petrol! On impact I could not forget looking out as we skidded down the road and seeing sparks.

Acquiring our six months visas we travelled to Tel Aviv by bus to find the office of administration for work on a Kibbutz. We slept on the beach for a relaxing three days before travelling to our new place of employment, Kibbutz Carmea, which unfortunately for me was a predominately French speaking area. My schooling never included languages. With our somewhat lack of communication we were given compulsory language lessons once a week. The group of workers was quite cosmopolitan. We were taught odd words.

The day we arrived we were shown our quarters - a small bungalow on the outskirts. s we talked and discussed our new surroundings a message came telling us that our wake up call would be at 4.00am and we were to gather chickens for market. A message I'd not received before and suspect will never receive again. This was our first day's introduction to working on a farm.

The second Sunday of our stay we were a bit late in rising due to our first drinking binge the night before. We had saved our shop ticket allowance, 20 tickets per person per week to spend in the camp shop. As we had brought tea and coffee with us there was no alternative but to use our tickets to purchase much sought after beer. No alcohol was served with the evening meals so it was our first drink for two and a half weeks. I believe things have changed drastically in the Kibbutz since, these days being able to obtain virtually anything you want.

A little disappointed that we had missed the tractor that had taken us to the beach the first Sunday we decided to walk to the beach, guessing roughly the direction we set off. Tarmac road soon turned into rough track, cultivated fields filled the horizon as far as the eye could see, sugar beet, peanut bushes and vegetables. It took forty minutes of walking before signs of human endeavour finally gave way to arid dusty earth interspersed with sand dunes. Arriving at a barbed wire fence we roughly calculated that the sea could only be thirty minutes away. A track ran parallel with the fence. After following the track for a while it became apparent that we were following the coastline. The only logical route to the sea started with climbing the barbed fence. As I put my foot in a small hole in the wire ready to launch myself to the top of the fence one of the men I was staying with pointed to a sign attached to the fence. As we neared the sign we could see that it was covered in Hebrew writing, some big then small and in the right hand corner a drawing of a skull and cross-bones stood out. I remember so vividly at that point that what we were about to do was not a good idea. A part of me knew it meant danger but the less logical side of my brain thought maybe someone was trying to claim the land. When we got over the fence we headed for a rise in the land, sand dunes spread out right and left. Once at the top, there, before us and probably two or three miles away glistened the Mediterranean in bright sunlight. Lowering our sight a depressing scene came into view, a line of rusting, blackened and burned out tanks and lorries littered the ground. Walking towards them, more out of curiosity than anything else, we began poking at old shell cases and other bits and bobs. Impatient to get to the sea my companions set off. I was about to follow when, taking one last look, my eyes came to rest on the tail end of a mortar bomb. Quickly picking it up as a souvenir I ran to catch up with him.

We spent a pleasant two hours swimming and lazing on the beach before we decided to head back. Walking along the beach we at last came to the end of the fenced off area giving us a clear walk to the end of the road. That night at the dinner table I engaged one of the men I had been working with in the garage in conversation. Simon was one of the few who spoke fluent English and I asked him about the fenced off areas close to the sea. He eyed me with an interrogating look.

"What do you want to know for, don't tell me you've climbed over the fence?" he said with a look of utter disbelief. "Yes, why not, it's a good short cut to the sea?" I said.

"You are lucky to still be in one piece. The whole area is waiting to be cleared of mines and live ammunition by the Army engineers. You must know about the six day war?" he said.

I was not that ignorant of major upheavals in the last few years, but as for details, that was a different matter.

"Of course I remember but some of the stories are vague in my memory."

My working companion had shown me an insight to essential mechanical jobs required on the Kibbutz. These included fitting thick plating to the sides and underbelly of the tractors, a necessary protection against mines, an occupational hazard living so near to the Gaza Strip.

My mortar bomb souvenir still stands in our living room, it's journey back to England fraught with problems of my own making after some illicit dealing in cigarettes. I was left with some 2,000. Concluding our stay at the Kibbutz, a period of some six months, we decided to head for Elate with the intention of making money through hard labour. Certain things would have to be discarded before we began our journey south. All that I possessed was my old leather jacket, the mortar bomb tail, and, of course, the cigarettes. A large parcel was made containing these items and sent to England, six months would pass before I would discover that all of the cigarettes had been confiscated by the Customs. On arrival the parcel had shrunk considerably now containing only my souvenir and jacket.

The conversation between Simon and myself about the history of Israel is the only memory of discourse to an Israelite that has stood the test of time, some 29 years.

Pulling aside the hanging sleeping bags that, by now, are completely dry, the sight of a smiling face greets me with the usual banter.

"You must have got plenty of doodling in this morning. You've been silent for about three hours."

"No, it's not that Keith, I must have been nodding. I'll take these bags down before making the lunch."

"You know Graham, I think you'd make a great bon

viveur."

"I've never heard such colourful culinary expressions. Do you think I'd look good in one of those tall white hats? Anyway Keith it'd be no good to me, as they'd insist that I cut my fingernails, and trim my beard. I thought for a change today I'd keep the ingredients for lunch secret, just a small clue, three letters PMB."

Only an hour and a half into my afternoon row and there is another shout from the aft cabin. It is not necessary to see Keith at the hatchway wringing out his towel to know what has happened. By the time we change watches the bag is dry. The fix written down, 16° 21′ north, 31° 17′ west.

11th November 1997

It is still blowing like mad as I take over at midnight and the usual struggle begins. An early dip and porridge for breakfast. This once weekly treat certainly perks me up.

The wind still northeast, the sea state much the same with winds 28 to 32 knots, the fix, 16° 03′ north 32° 16′ west.

12th November 1997

Halfway through my second watch the wind begins to subside. This was what we had been hoping for. It enables us to have a short break, relax our aching muscles and allows us to open the rear hatch. Discussing yesterday's fix over breakfast we both come to the conclusion that we're losing too much of our westerly course. We are being driven south by the predominantly northeast winds, quite often backing north. We decide to row northwest, optimistic that the wind might change. Through the previous night's and early morning row my thoughts of the past seemed to be trapped in a time prison.

Not wanting to break the natural pattern of reminiscence I must write them as they occur.

1969: Following my stay at the Kibbutz Carmea, I joined a sightseeing group for three days while my two friends went to Eilat and found work. The Kibbutz had regular holidays staying at a youth hostel close to Eilat. This meant I could join my two friends in their labours during the evenings after a day of sightseeing. I visited the Pillars of Amran, named after the father of Moses. The gold coloured pillars rise above the hot sandy ravines of the Negev Desert. However it wasn't until the next day I was able to visit King Solomon's mines. Before me lay the ruins of a watchtower, serving as a lookout for guards supervising the workers. All around were large black mounds; the remains of the waste slag and parts of a wall intended to prevent the escape of Edomite prisoners who toiled as slaves in the mines. It seemed almost fitting that my night was spent unloading beer crates at a local distributor.

The last day of the short tour took us to Taba, four or five miles from Eilat, where I saw coral reefs from a glass bottomed boat. The first holiday in three months was over. My friends had secured a job on the local building site of a large hotel, five storey's high. Having worked in the building trade for the past five years I found it hard to accept the makeshift wooden scaffolding. It was little more than wooden timbers forced into the side of the building and braced with one angled timber. My first job of the day entailed the filling of buckets with sand and hauling them up to the fourth floor for the use of levelling a base to fit terrazzo floor tiles. Unnoticed by me, a few people had watched my arrival. On hearing it was my first day working in Eilat, coupled with the fact that I was not wearing a hat, exposed to the sun all day loading sand, they began to bet. What time would I retire or even collapse? All this was unknown to me until after the event.

6.00am was the starting time and only punctuated by a brief 15 minute break half way through the working day finished at 2.00pm. Looking back now I wish I'd remembered working in the fields on the Kibbutz. I was advised to drink plenty of water. It wasn't that the building site did not possess this priceless commodity, no, situated on the ground floor was tap for all to use. At 8.00am the water was still reasonably cool, however at 11.00am it was a different matter. I have never found hot water to be very palatable and declined to drink it. By midday my actions had slowed considerably but I pressed on undaunted. I failed to notice a gathering of workers on the scaffolding peering down at me from time to time. 1.00pm saw me more rubbery legged than Olive, Popeye's girlfriend. Struggling on for another 30 minutes of agony I collapsed at the side of the pile of sand. There I lay oblivious to the shouting and gesturing of the gambling workers.

Before long the foreman noticed that the floor layers were out of sand and came to find out the reason. The next memory I have is my head being yanked back by my hair and water was poured over my face. On regaining my senses I reached for the box like container filled of water. My saviour stood above me pointing to the water carrier indicating that I must buy one and I gather, with some difficulty from his broken English, that a cart comes every day with ice.

The once a day visit by the iceman was care of the construction company and the workers filled their water carriers with ice after breaking it up. Wobbling along the road towards the café with my two friends, the only sympathy conducive to my predicament was turned into ridicule.

"Only the first day and you've had it. How are you going to last another three months Graham?" I was asked by one of my companions.
Unable to find the energy for a witty reply I staggered on. No way would I be caught out again with dehydration and sunstroke.

Wait, that makes me think. When are we going to run out of water? We have 80 gallons of water. I'm drinking quite a lot, so is Keith. Maybe it's time to get acquainted with our water maker.

Reading the instructions for the first time, I drop the two open ended tubes into the sea, and place the small tube into an empty water bottle. I then begin a frustrating 10 to 15 minutes, as small quantities drip out every now and again. My doubts grow over the water intake, moving about as the boat moved through the water. My suspicions are confirmed after fitting a fishing weight to the end and getting a better flow but this only seems to work for a short time. There's only one solution, I need to fill a bucket of seawater and then try putting the intake in it. At last, a steady flow is secured. Counting the pumping strokes of the handle and making note of the time, I continue for a full 30 minutes. 980 strokes of the water maker produces one third of a litre. I probably sweated that out in purifying that. Well at least we now know the hard work involved in creating fresh water from salt water.

Putting the water maker away I suddenly realised that it was time for the fix. This was to be a special day. We had roughly estimated that half way was approximately 44° west, which we hoped to pass some time tonight. Having found a bottle of beer tucked away in one of the side pockets we agreed that this would be a good occasion to open it.

13th November 1997

My midnight shift gets off to a flying start as the wind picks up to force six to seven, approximately 25 to 30 per hour. White foam from breaking waves appears more frequently out of the black and surrounds the boat. It occasionally rides over the side to wet my backside, once again irritating my rash. I survive the first stint of the day without having to rub Vaseline all over my offending part.

I retire to the aft cabin feeling a lot better and looking forward to starting what I think may be the best of the books I've brought.' The Magic of the Swatchways' by Maurice Griffiths. I've read it before, but at a time when the pace of life didn't allowed me the necessary peace of mind to take it in properly. The situation now is perfect - thousands of miles away from any problems and without communication. I only have two books left after this. Maybe I should read every paragraph twice to stretch it out a bit. Or is that a bit mad?

15° 29′ north, 33° 55′ west, almost there, a run of 54 miles since yesterday, not too bad.

"Graham, time for food."
"What do you reckon Keith?"
"I fancy beef stew and dumplings."

While waiting for the food to boil I study the discarded outer packet, a thing I have never done before. Nutritional Information, Energy 503 kJ, 120 k cal, Protein 6.7 g, Carbohydrate 10.9 g, Fat 5.5 g. Well at least the nutritional value sounds good.

"You want to read the contents Graham, that'll give you an appetite."

"Diced beef and three herby dumplings with carrot, potatoes and peas in a rich onion gravy." I say, reading aloud.

"Get them out of the pan and let's eat before you put me off."

Today it's my turn to face the sea whilst we eat. Which inevitably means my food will soon be swimming in salt water.

Currently we have a southerly position, the wind is still predominately northeast. Rowing northwest should give us a better course but it will probably slow us down.

Reading notes on the predictability of tropical cyclones in Stanford's 'Pilot Chart for December', I have to feel sorry for any sailors who were in this area in 1887. Only seven tropical storms have been recorded in the North Atlantic during December over the last 100 years, three of those in 1887. Out of the seven, five reached hurricane strength. Knowing my luck I am prepared for anything. It was only when I began to clear away the stove that I remembered the celebration drink for being half way.

"Keith, we've forgotten the beer."

"We'll have it tomorrow Graham. I think it can wait considering we've not let a drop of alcohol past our lips for a month."

To be honest I wasn't bothered either and soon forgot about our drink of beer.

Not thirty minutes into my rowing stint before our old friends, the three seagulls came along. Flying around the boat, swooping and landing between the large waves. It never ceased to amaze me how these three gulls stayed together, calling on us twice a day, now something in the region of five hundred miles from any land. An hour later our second visitors turn up, also their second trip of the day. Two storm petrels darting about almost landing on the boat. These two groups of feathered friends have been our only visitors these past eight days.

14th November 1997

The new day starts badly for me. After only 10 minutes rowing my backside begins to feel raw. I slap on more Vaseline. I hope the tub will last. The wind is still approximately force six and not doing me any favours. It is driving seawater over the side exploding in small squirts coming up under the seat and washing off the Vaseline.

To distract me from the discomfort the sea kindly lays on other more painful experiences. One such event occurs five or six times every hour. The sea drives the boat onto it's side by forcing large waves against the starboard rear cabin lifting the pulling stroke of the blade clear. My left arm and shoulder are then freed from labour resulting in a violent twist of the body. My right arm straining to pull an oar that is now deep under the water as the wave now roars under the boat levelling the steep angle. Just before the stroke is completed, the waterless blade in my left hand is attacked by another wave crest coming from a slightly different angle hitting the exposed blade with a mighty force and jerking my left arm forwards twisting my upper body in the opposite direction. Three hours of this leaves me with pains down each side of my chest, upper arms and shoulders. What a relief lying back in my sleeping bag is after three hours of what seemed like endless torture. Feeling slightly recovered with the arrival of daybreak I decide on porridge this morning. Spooning the steaming, glutinous mass into my mouth compares with the most delicious fried breakfast I have ever had.

Picking up my pen after breakfast I find myself back in 1969.

I was picking oranges on the Kibbutz in a much more temperate climate. I can only thank my good fortune at this spell of convalescence. Having caught tonsillitis I was unable to eat. This had left me too weak to walk. My condition was then worrying two companions, who informed the hospital of my predicament. Suddenly from the quiet of a sunny morning came footsteps, slowly getting nearer and nearer. Lying on the earth in our small hut with my ear close to the ground every footstep sounded louder. Two shadowy figures crouched and entered the hut both dressed in white trousers and shirts. With a quick burst of no nonsense communication they laid out a stretcher, rolled me onto it, stuffed a blanket over my rigid body and hoisted the stretcher waist high. There began the long walk down the barren hillside towards the road. Stumbling and cursing as they went, I rocked about in the rather precarious canvas stretcher. Once in the ambulance it seemed like only seconds before I was lying on a hospital bed being prodded here and there. My efforts to indicate the problem concerning my throat did not receive much attention at first but once they had established that my condition was not drug related I was diagnosed very quickly. They stuck a largish syringe into my backside and pumped a large dose of penicillin into my bloodstream.

Three and a-half-hours later my two companions arrived to see how I was getting on and at this time I was feeling much better. It was then the doctor came in and explained that I would need a course of penicillin as well as probably three days stay in the hospital to alleviate my weak condition. Unfortunately all this would cost a considerable amount of money so considering the lack of finances the three of us agreed on an immediate plan of action. As soon as we were left alone we made our departure. An arm round both of their shoulders I hobbled out of the hospital and along the road to our favourite café to discuss the next plan. I would recover at the Kibbutz for a week by which time I should have finished taking the course of penicillin. Arriving back at the Kibbutz I explained my position and they were extremely helpful, and gave me a flat next door to a young girl from Belgium named Martine. Martine was tall rather slender girl. I still remember how her dark hair cascaded down her back. Many nights I sat trying to muster the courage to lead the conversation away from the meaningless exchanges of hellos and goodbyes.

After two days rest I began working in the orange grove picking oranges. Three days later I was given a day off and decided to spend it in the town of Gaza. Finally I had something to talk about. I discussing the trip with Martine, who showed a fair amount of interest so I offered to take her along. We set off early catching a lift on one of the Kibbutz tractors, which dropped us at the bus stop on the main road. The waiting passengers, two Arabs and three soldiers, gave us strange looks but never actually said anything. When the bus arrived it was about half full of men and women, some holding onto young children. Sitting down on torn plastic seats, the ageing bus lumbered on in a cloud of dust and black diesel smoke. The next stop was a frontier post and an armed soldier boarded the bus to look through identity cards. Outside groups of soldiers manned two fixed machine guns behind walls of sandbags each side of the road. Walking up to us we handed the soldier our passports. Holding both in one hand he looked up and said, "Why do you want to visit Gaza?"That question took us by surprise. After a long awkward silence I replied. "We want to see the town and maybe discover some it it's past history."

"This is no seaside holiday town. We cannot be responsible for your safety, this part of Gaza is still closed. Occupied territory. Understand?"

I tried to sound calm. "All these good people look happy enough to be returning to their homes. I am sure we will be accepted for what we are, just a couple of travellers."
And with that he handed back our passports. I remember then Martine's concern. She asked me if we were in danger and I remember so clearly saying, "If you really want to go back Martine we will, but you must understand that the Army is paranoid about anything unusual. They can't understand why we would want to come to Gaza."

We weren't looking out of the window at the arid landscape for long when the brakes squealed and the bus came to a halt on the badly pitted tarmac road. We were somewhere on the outskirts of Gaza.

Before we had gone no more than 50 yards we were surrounded by children who very quickly began pulling at our clothes, shouting and laughing. Fortunately, when we came to the end of the street, we came across the first Israeli checkpoint. Two soldiers immediately began shouting at the children and they ran off in all directions. Feeling much relieved we walked on. The centre could not have been much further away as soldiers, armed to the teeth, armoured cars, even tanks, occupied every street corner. The houses looked much the same as each other, grey, dusty, sand faced walls with boarded up windows that looked as if they had not seen the light of day for sometime. The shops that were open were little more than large openings at the front of the buildings, their cavernous entrances stretched back into a shadowy half-light. Inside odd tin cans sat on the half-empty shelves and dry looking vegetables were scattered about the bench type tables.

Walking in a westerly direction hoping to see what was left of the old port we came by the market. Some of the stalls were occupied, small joints of meat and small dried fish were covered in dust and flies. At first we did not notice a group of teenagers gathering outside until their chatter alerted us. At that moment they began pointing in our direction and shouting in Arabic. It was only then that I realised that there were no soldiers anywhere to be seen. Turning to Martine I suggested that we walk back the same way that we had come and she was only too eager to agree. As we crossed the road, whack, something hit me in the back, turning and looking down I saw that it was an old chewed bone. That first throw seemed to encourage the youths and soon tin cans and rotting vegetables flew our way. Unsure of what else to do we both broke into a jog. Half way along the next street stones and broken bricks started flying by. It was then I decided to stop and face our tormentors. To this day I'm not sure why I stopped. Part of me thinks it was just to impress Martine. Needless to say, I wasn't able to scare off the horde. Stones carried on flying in our direction and before long I heard Martine hysterically shouting "Run!"

As we disappeared round a corner I could hear the loud shouting behind when suddenly, from the side of the street, a voice called, "Over here." Looking left, there stood a man holding open the front door to his house. Neither of us needed any persuading as we ran inside. Gesturing for us to follow as he made his way to the back of the house, "Sit down here and rest."

Gazing around we found ourselves surrounded by a few small tables, his back garden was a small café. We could here him shouting from his front door at a large crowd that had now gathered outside and the arguing went on for some time. Whether he threatened to fetch the army or the Arab police I do not know, but the noise gradually subsided. I could not help but think this was a terrible first date. Perhaps it would have been best if we had never gotten past the meaningless conversations we shared from time to time.

15th November 1997

The wind seems to be dropping slightly. I must remind Keith to swap watches. We need a change. I will miss the sunrise and sunset but it will be nice to wake up to breakfast.

"Coffee up Keith, rise and shine."

"You say that to me every morning Graham, how about something different?"

I think it's time for a change of watch. I thought about tonight after dinner. What if we do three watches again starting at 7.30pm, one and a half hours a piece, you can kick off the day starting at midnight?"

"Sounds good to me Graham."

"Right, I'm going for a swim." I say before plunging into the deep ocean.

With Keith rowing and the wind blowing about 25 miles per hour it becomes more of a drag through the water than a swim. I must find my diving mask tomorrow. Back on board I pump out the water once again which half fills the deck compartments. The two plywood hatches in the centre holding our drinking water, with their makeshift wooden turn screws, appear to be keeping out the seawater. I eagerly go back to reading about Maurice Griffith's next boat, 'Wild Lone', a five ton sloop, before I realise that it is time for the fix, 14° 54′ north and 35° 30′ west. I put away the stove and prepared for my first watch, although I do have two to do before midnight they are only one a half hours each.

16th November 1997

"Breakfast up." Keith calls as I open my eyes to daylight. Coffee is over quickly and it takes me quite a while to become accustomed to morning rowing as the sun is still fairly low in the sky. I fiddle about trying to find my sunglasses without disturbing Keith. At midday I find myself covered in sweat and cannot remember it being so hot the last time I rowed in the morning. I guess I could try rowing naked. I'm sure Keith won't mind. Before long my backside feels uncomfortable and I have no choice to put on some underpants. Finishing off the morning row with a swim feels fantastic and towelling off, I apply some medication to my poor backside. Purely by chance I have brought a jar of Sudocrem, which does seem to alleviate the problem. A rapid brushing of the teeth, and out with the sea-cook to prepare lunch.

"What do you think about emptying the fore cabin after lunch Keith? We need toilet rolls and I want to find my diving mask. Anything you can think of?"

"No, not a the moment."

The operation of emptying the front is not an easy task considering the weight of our six-man life raft – in retrospect we probably shouldn't have left it so late to hire one. Fifteen minutes of cursing our possible lifesaver sees the life raft unceremoniously dumped onto the rowing deck.

"Hope we never have to launch this in anger Keith."
I find my mask straight away so it is just a matter of pulling out a pack of toilet rolls. These were one of the items that we had intended to wrap in waterproof bags, but like many of other things, they were bought and thrown into the fore cabin as they were.

"We're going to have to dry these out." I say as I hold up a white mush that barely resembles a toilet roll.

While Keith rows I plan to tackle the growth on the bottom of the boat. This time I am prepared, mask, fins, diving knife. I spend approximately an hour pulling myself around the bottom of the boat by means of a rope tied to the bow, all the time scraping away at the barnacles that I had noticed at least two weeks previous, close to the waterline. I was amazed at their growth as the steady stream of potential marine food flowed towards the rear of the boat. Two small pilot fish waited, both highly coloured and about twelve inches long. When we left Tenerife I had no idea that these creatures called Cirrupedia, or hairy legs, would become so attached. Finding a suitable place, the barnacle walks on it's antennae testing the surface, and satisfying itself, flips onto it's back and cements itself into position. After my energetic cleaning spree I take our fix, 14° 37′ north and 36° 17′ west, a run of 52 miles, which, to my mind, is a good average.

17th November 1997

The wind is still blowing 25 to 30mph but has veered to the east slightly. Nothing has been seen, as usual. I begin to think that we must be completely alone out here. The tranquility of the ocean surely clears your mind however I think without the task of journeying back through my memory I might go mad. 6.00am comes and I'm in the same wet condition. I'm grateful to climb into the aft cabin and dry myself and begin jotting down the thoughts I had during my row under the grey sky.

1969: Following my return from Israel I was invited by Martine on many separate occasions to visit her in Belgium. My trip firstly took me to Arlon, a town on the edge of Belgium very close to Luxembourg, later to Bruxelles, Liege and the surrounding countryside, for a period that spanned nearly 10 years. Subconsciously, I think now, it was because I found it challenging.

Something that has not changed to this day is my habit of driving the oldest and most run-down vehicles imaginable. Well past their 'use by' date, the consequences, only too obvious. Some abandoned in Luxembourg, some in Belgium, mostly at scrap yards, but one, a red, one ton post office van, on the side of the main road to Luxembourg and surviving for two years in that position. A few, brought back on tow by the good service of the Four Star AA. My habit, not restricted to the Continent only, caused some 30 vehicles to meet their demise during this 10 year period.

Dripping sweat puts an end to my writing, smudging the ink. Opening the aft hatch for a few seconds at a time is fraught with fear of chances of allowing bursts of seawater to enter, but then the relief is incredible. I take the fix before my afternoon row, 14° 34′ north and 37° 18′ west. Escaping from the oppressive heat of the aft cabin gives the rowing stint a slight pleasure, feeling the strong wind on the side of my face as I pull on the rubber handled oars. Keith looks over the

navigation, "Graham, you're three miles out here."
"So what?"
I know that my relaxed attitude to accuracy annoys Keith, but we all have to put up with each other's idiosyncrasies.

18th November 1997
Keith informs me that there are a few rain clouds about, 4.00am, an hour after starting, down comes the rain just as the wind increases. Pulling and tugging at my soaking sweatshirt, rowing becomes more and more difficult as the wind veers round to the northwest, which is directly ahead. So much for Keith's forecast. The rain clouds disappear and the wind backs to the east again allowing me to make some progress, handing over to Keith at 6.00am. He calls me at 9. I gingerly poke my head out of the hatch and what a desolate sight it is. Grey skies to the horizon that are only broken by the dark green sea. I try to suppress a smile as Keith, holding a steaming mug, is hit by the top of a wave as it separates, leaving most of it's body to roll under the boat.

"I don't know what you're smiling about this is your tea."

During the morning I try to gauge the height of the biggest waves, normally no more than three or four in a row and probably six or ten feet higher than the rest at about 30′. Fortunately the faces of these monsters were not steep sided, allowing our small boat to ride up them and down the other side. The greatest danger from these giants of the sea comes from the ones that break at the top. I'm trying to concentrate on their size and not let the boat broach to prevent it from capsizing. Time for the fix, 14° 22′ north and 28° 14′ west.

19th November 1997

Another stormy night, this time I decide to wear Salopettes. They're uncomfortable and noisy whilst rowing, but at least they keep me dry. Well, drier. Keith informs me over breakfast that he's managed to keep dry all night without his wet gear. Thankfully the weather cleared up for my morning row. By lunchtime, the sea had calmed a little. I think we'll both attempt to eat outside again today.

"Boat!" Keith shouts whilst we are drinking our coffee. I look over to where he is pointing and catch sight of a mast as it sinks below the swell. Watching it slowly grow we come to the conclusion that it must be *3 Com*, the race safety boat. As it nears I switch on the VHF. '*3 Com, 3 Com*, this is *The George Geary*, over."

Suddenly, through the crackling interference we make out a female voice, "*The George Geary* this is *3 Com*, how are you, is there a problem with your boat, over?"

"No, negative, we are both okay and so is the boat, over."

"We've had a signal from your Argos indicating a problem, over." she said.

"Not as far as we know. I mean, quite a few days ago the flashing light stopped working. I assume it's malfunctioning, over."

"No, as far as we're concerned it's giving out correct positions, over."

"Oh sorry about that... now you're here is it possible to give us any information on the race, over?"

"We're glad to hear that you're okay. The race news, well, your position at the moment is fourth. The leaders are *Kiwi Challenge* with Rob and Phil, second place *Atlantic Challenge*,

Pascal and Joseph Le Guen, third place *Christina* with Eamonn and Peter, over."

What? How is that possible? I can't believe we've caught up.

"How far are the leaders ahead of us? Over."

"Approximately 900 miles, second, about 500 and the third 100. We will give you some information on the others. The French husband and wife team on *La Baleine*, Jean Marc and Marie Christine Meunier were rolled over three times in big seas breaking the rowlocks and damaging the bulwarks. They have retired from the race and, unfortunately, we were compelled to fire the boat. The German team on *Wabun*, set off their emergency distress beacon and were picked up by the Spanish rescue authorities also suffering from exhaustion, but their boat was towed to El Hierro. The team of Ian Charter and Nigel Garbett on their boat, *This Way Up*, resigned from the race when their GPS began to malfunction. Peter Haining and David Riches on *Walter Scott & Partners* had to abandon ship when David went down with a case of food poisoning and seasickness. They got caught on the rocky shore of Gomera and were airlifted off. John Searson of *Commodore Shipping* is carrying on alone after Carl Clinton was evacuated by a safety vessel suffering a suspected slipped disc, over."

3 Com continued sailing around us in large circles.

"Keith, are you getting all of this?" I say.

"Most of it."

"Okay I'm writing down some of the details. 3 Com is that all of the boats that have pulled out, over?"

"No, we will give you a quick run down on the others. Matthew and Edward Boreham on *Spirit of Spelthorne* activated their Epirb beacon after losing power for their water maker.

They were picked up after a two-day search suffering from dehydration and exhaustion and their boat burned. The female team on *American Pearl,* Victoria Murden and Louise Graff retired after 24 hours because of violent seasickness and food poisoning. They were towed back and after a rest, re-started but because of continuing sickness were forced to retire for the second and final time. David Mossman has been evacuated from *Key Challenger* with sickness leaving David Immelman to continue single-handed. Another team, Daniel Innes and Peter Lowe, on *The Golden Fleece,* are out of the race after having power problems which left them without water, reluctantly asking us for water. That's about it, over."

"Before you go just fill us in on the situation regarding the burning of the boats, over." I say.

"With the sea conditions as they are and so far from land any towing is impossible. In accordance with Maritime Law the boat must be destroyed and the only guaranteed way of sinking is by setting fire to it, over."

With that we bid farewell to *3 Com* and I poke my head out of the hatch and watch it weaving and bobbing on their erratic course.

"What about that then Keith, fourth place, it's unbelievable especially after our disastrous start. Altering course after the wind changed we must have been almost last."

With the new information we now realise that the starting 30 boats have been reduced to just 24.

Keith finishes his third row while I sit studying the chart, thinking about all the other boats that are still in the race. We changed positions in silence, each one lost in our own thoughts after this mass of information. In all the excitement I had forgotten the fix and quickly jotted it down, 14° 22′ north and 3° 09′ west. Half way through my afternoon stint I can see rain clouds gathering in the distance and the last hour rowing was interrupted by small showers steadily growing worse.

Twenty minutes before dinner it grows blacker and blacker. The cumulus nimbus type clouds grow in size and their upper tops spread in all directions. As the sky fills with these menacing grey shapes I begin putting on my wet gear. Just in time. The sound of thunder is a brief warning before a huge downpour lashes our boat. The great rolling swell beats us into submission. The visibility is now reduced to a few yards. There appears to be no end in sight, just a slight reduction in the torrential rain, which gives me a chance to climb into the aft cabin and take off my wet gear.

20th November 1997

My stint is started under a grey carpet of shapeless clouds. The wind is still blowing approximately force six and is backing east leaving me the decision of rowing a course of west, north west or east, south east. It is impossible to keep the boat travelling on the same course as the wind and swell turns the stern one way and then the other. This allows the wind to push the aft cabin round so far. I've noticed how the sky's grey appearance often influences our moods, although this morning I feel pretty buoyant. I would imagine partly due to the recent news and the fact that we're set to reach our halfway position across the Atlantic some time tonight - that also means we get to open the bottle of rum donated by Barbados's Mount Gay distilleries.

Over lunch we talk about our fellow competitors. Are the leaders above us or below us? What kind of weather patterns are they experiencing? The truth of the matter is that we would not know any answers until the race is over. Retiring to the aft cabin I sit for a while deep in thought before retrieving my pen and scrapbook.

1976 The Beginning or the End of Normal Existence: This was to be the year that changes many peoples' lives and, no doubt, mine. I married a woman who had, I am quite sure, no idea that I would turn into some kind of reckless freak. I am positive that the first doubts crept into her head only hours into the wedding ceremony, which was to all intents and purposes the typical Roman Catholic affair. We had split the responsibility for preparing the food; I would prepare the savoury side, Margaret the sweet - a somewhat symbolic gesture to our future. A friend in the catering business had supplied me with large quantities of tinned meats, salmon, cheese and paté. Other donations came our way through a friend working at a bakery, sliced bread and rolls, vol-au-vents and sausage rolls.

Normally the food would be professionally arranged but as I'm always keen to learn something new I decided I would prepare the food. Taking Friday off from work I began the day by drinking a toast to my forthcoming marriage at my local, The North Bridge Inn, my home for a short while. By 12.30pm I had been joined by many of my friends and acquaintances who had supportively taken the afternoon off.

Closing time at 2.30pm, a plan began to emerge. Buying two crates of beer I gathered the enthusiastic group and explained to them that time was running out for the making of the sandwiches and rolls. In a flash we were triumphantly marching towards my flat. A table was set up and the industrious sandwich making commenced.

Saturday morning began, as most bridegrooms will experience, with pills and black coffee. Instructions were thrown in all directions. My task that morning was to go to the village hall and organise the arrangements for the wedding reception, unfortunately this involved more drinking. If it was not for Len, my best man, I'm not sure I would have arrived at the Church in time. The ceremony over, bagpipes fired up, we funnelled out of the Church and had our photographs taken. After photographs people started to make their way to the reception. Margaret asked me then about our transport arrangements - something I had completely forgotten about! Quickly looking around I saw one of my friends leaving in his old Ford Cortina and managed to attract his attention. Rushing over I explained our predicament, Derrick was only too happy to oblige, however the photographs of leaving the Church never made the mantelpiece.

Arriving at the hall we were surprised at the to-ing and fro-ing of people who had volunteered to make trifles, cakes and many other fine things. My friends had done a marvellous job of arranging the make shift bar. Earlier in the week, the landlord at the North Bridge had allowed me to use his card for the wholesalers. I spent £250, kindly given by Margaret's parents plus a further £250 from my own pocket. £500 enabled me to buy an enormous amount of alcohol, it was 1976!

All went well as the evening progressed and we had planned to leave at a reasonable time and go straight on our honeymoon. This was to be three days at a chalet belonging to my Aunt Barbara at Cromer in Norfolk. Dropping Margaret off to collect her things, I headed back to my flat for my suitcase. Passing the North Bridge on my way to pick up Margaret I could see the lights blazing above the half stained glass windows and I knew that a large number of friends from the wedding reception would have called at the pub to carry on with the festivities. I decided to join them for a last drink. Parking my old black Morris 1000 outside the front door, I entered the premises and was enticed to stay longer than I should. Realising that Margaret would wonder what on earth had happened to me, I rushed outside to begin my new married life only to find my car had gone, along with my suitcase and belongings. I rang Margaret to explain the situation, which did not look good.

My flat was full of friends from Bath who had travelled up to Leicester for the wedding and Margaret's parents house was full of relatives. So, for starters, there was nowhere to sleep. Fortunately for me Margaret had been preoccupied with problems of her own. Elizabeth, her cousin, had returned from the police station with the news that a very dear friend had taken up residence there for the night after becoming involved in a fracas with the manager of a local night-club. Elizabeth together with a large group of friends had apparently followed her and her captors to the station to state their case. Sobriety would have made for a better argument. After more discussion with the police over the theft of my car we decide to find a place to sleep, and at 5.00am we are standing at the reception of the Holiday Inn. Justice and my travelling arrangements were not to be the last before the honeymoon was over.

Travelling back, a detour had to be made to attend the Court of Justice in a small village 50 miles away from Leicester, a small matter concerning my now defunct J4 Post Office Van. It had refused to go up one of the many hills, due to a slight case of overloading, on the way to Bath. A possible quick turn, halfway up, resulted in the partial destruction of two cars, luckily nobody was hurt. Entering the court with the idea of a small fine led to my driving licence being impounded, and, to Margaret's surprise, she found herself the only eligible person to drive home from our honeymoon. At that time she was not aware that she would be called upon to drive a Bedford Van loaded with building materials each morning before she went to work and upon leaving at night. Such are the demands of married life.

Time for the fix before my rowing stint, 14° 08′ north and 40° 02′ west. Dinner comes and goes leaving us time for the halfway celebration, "What do you think Keith, drink the whole bottle now or savour it for a bit longer?" I ask.

"I think we should keep it for a weekly treat. It might last until the end of the race if we just take a nip."

21st November 1997

Climbing out at 3.00am I discover, to my joy, that the stars are once again shining down from the heavens. Annoyed at my ignorance of this heavenly picture, yet again, I promise to try to find the astronomy book. The clear sky unfortunately indicates a drop in the wind. A hot day is about to begin. A break halfway through the morning's row to pull out two, six litre water containers, and replace them, gives me a chance to cool down. 30 minutes into the second half of the stint I start sweat. Thank God for this hat. Thanks Arvid and Stein of *Star Atlantic* your gift is stopping the sweat from running into my eyes. Finally midday arrives and two minutes is all it takes to fit my fins and mask. No graceful entry for me, just a roll from whatever position I was in. Lunch over with and I'm sitting comfortably in the aft cabin - back to my book.

22nd November 1997
As soon as I poke my head out of the aft cabin I can tell that the wind has increased. I prepare myself for an oncoming tussle with nature. At least the constant spray and odd splash should keep me cool.

Back in the aft cabin I take out my pad.

1977 A Pattern Emerges: The first trip abroad after our marriage took Margaret and I to Belgium to visit the places and friends I regularly see each year. After 10 days with my friends we decided to take a casual trip back to the coast through Holland, arriving for a sightseeing trip in Amsterdam. We drove to the centre, then along the central canal past the massive Roman Catholic Church of St Nicholas. Looking at the canalised river of Amstel, dammed against the sea in 1275, needs little imagination to figure out where the name came from. We were hardly there when the forthcoming drama began to unfold as a strange crunching noise could be heard from the gearbox of the old long wheel base Land Rover I was driving at the time.

Almost immediately we were down to one gear, then nothing. Tackling a gearbox at the side of the road in central Amsterdam was, I now realise, a foolhardy mistake. Two nights sleeping at the side of the road was more than enough for Margaret. The outcome of my investigation revealed worn gears and broken teeth, which needed replacing. Enquiring at a Land Rover garage in Amsterdam did not help as I was informed that the only option was a replacement gearbox at a cost of £350. If I could take the gearbox back to England it was still under guarantee. Departing on the train and carrying as much luggage as possible we left the unfortunate vehicle at a local garage. My idea was to return with another Land Rover and tow it back. After making enquiries at a number of hire companies it became obvious that none of them had insurance to cover foreign travel so in desperation I bought another very old Land Rover for the sole purpose of towing. Now, normally when there is a chance of a bit of excitement I can rely on somebody to help, but after phoning round it became clear that this was not going to be the case. Pushing my luck to the limit I telephoned Margaret at her office and asked if she could take a couple of days off to help me tow the vehicle home. Stating my case, she was my only answer.

After a ferry trip of 10 hours we were back at the Hook of Holland followed by a relaxing drive from the outskirts of Rotterdam to the bypass of Den Haag. On to Amsterdam and by the time our convoy was on the road daylight had abandoned us. Parking in a lay by we slept in the back of one of the Land Rovers and decided that an early start would be an advantage, hopefully avoiding congested roads. I was to drive the towing vehicle knowing the route slightly better than Margaret did. A stout towrope, which I expected to have a life span of many years, was knotted in three places where it had snapped, somewhat slowing down our convoy. Turning left to leave the motorway a loud bang, followed by my head being jerked backwards, was the beginning of more delays. The brakes had failed on the Land Rover on tow. Laying underneath with a small spanner I could hear Margaret swearing to herself, completely putting my off my shouts of, "Press the brake pedal once more please." This was not to be the only tin of brake fluid we needed before we finally arrived back in Leicester.

Putting away my writing pad I begin my daily task of picking up the chart board and the ship's log in readiness to write down the next fix, 13° 38′ north and 41° 39′ west.

23rd November 1997

"Wakey wakey Graham!" shouts Keith.
3.00am still feels like an odd time to rise. Pulling on my wet gear I climb out onto the right side of the foot-plate while Keith climbs onto the left. A ridiculous performance we carry out day in, day out. With regard to the coffee arrangements I plan to be organised this morning. The cabin light stays on for approximately five minutes while the person in the aft cabin dries himself and arranges the sleeping bag before switching out the light. The light allows me to quickly fit the cooker, jam the kettle on, to avoid the seawater extinguishing the stove, get out the coffee and milk powder, not forgetting the Peak bar, which I place just inside the cabin hatch to keep it dry.

Taking my seat I am hit by the first wave as the crest breaks against the aft cabin and blasts water straight into my face. As I grapple with the oars water slowly trickles down from around my head on its journey to my backside where it lays trapped in my waterproof trousers. An hour of this constant struggle against the elements leaves my backside feeling raw… again. I must attempt to alleviate this discomfort.

To get to my backside I must first remove my wet jacket by pulling it over my head. This achieved it is time for the bottoms, and as they are Salopette type wet trousers, bib and brace, first the shoulder straps and then I have to pull the waist down around my knees together with my underpants. This effectively traps my legs together, which makes balancing on a rolling boat hard. At this moment I hear that familiar sound – express waves. I stand in dread of being drenched in this state of undress. It hits and goes under, lifting the boat and throwing me backwards. Coming to rest on the seat rails with my bare backside is absolute agony. Suddenly there is another clatter. The oar handles slip out of the toe straps and begin flailing about like Samurai Warriors. They are still locked in their crutches and I make a grab for them, catching the right. The left one clobbers me on the elbow and a shooting pain electrifies my arm. A one handed grappling contest now takes place as I try to strap the right oar into the foot-plate, my left arm hanging down without any feeling. Making a grab for the remaining wild oar I miss and it comes up under my chin, and wallop. At last I capture this wild stick. Blood dried and Vaseline found, I begin to pull up my Salopettes which means I fail to notice the next express wave approaching. Bang, in no time at all I am soaked to the skin, still holding onto what has now become, a small reservoir of seawater. I can't wait for this to end.

Waking for breakfast, the sight of daylight always makes the sea-state look better than the night before. I guess it's because I'm unable to see the surrounding sea so I paint the worst picture imaginable. After I've eaten I'm back in the aft cabin and settling down to read. The fix, 13° 50′ north and 42° 37′ west - another good day's run.

24th November 1997

Preparing for a similar row as the day before I climb into my wet gear, which has now dried sufficiently. The only enjoyable part of this first stint is the hot mug of coffee halfway through the watch.

"Graham, coffee?"

That familiar question instigates a bout of yawning, which

nearly ends with permanent damage to my jaw. Sitting in the aft cabin after lunch my attempts at writing are prevented as I fall into a restless sleep. Awaking with an overwhelming sense of dread, I happily realise I've only been asleep for 15 minutes. Time to get out the pad.

1977 A Desert Trip, Part One: Things don't always go to plan, an old cliché but this was definitely the case on my organised trip across the Sahara. I had managed to secure an agreement with Margaret, considering that the absence of her husband during the first year of marriage, for three months, is something that not many newlywed wives would put up with.

Lucien, a Belgian friend, and myself had planned to start in June. Lucien being a teacher was able to accompany me then, it was the beginning of the school holidays. Three months holiday for me was quite normal as I could close the Loft Conversion business and hopefully start it again on my return, a risk I was prepared to take. Unfortunately the gearbox on my Safari Land Rover was again defunct. The old Land Rover that I had towed the much troubled vehicle with was still parked outside my house waiting to be sold. I had a difficult decision to make. Should I take the old one instead? The main setback was in connection with the four-wheel drive, having had problems with the drive shaft to the front axle. Time really settled the issue, there just wasn't any left.

Setting out with the old Land Rover I stopped off in London at a firm who specialised in Land Rover expedition equipment and bought two jerry-can racks to carry three cans each together with a pair of sand ladders and head and rear lamp cages. Throwing them in the back I headed off towards Dover, an overnight sleep on the ferry refreshed me for the drive to Arlon.

It was late afternoon when I arrived outside Lucien's house. A brief trip to a local bar and we were underway. A little intoxicated we both fit the expedition items and loaded the Land Rover. Tools, food, beer, tent, stove, clothes, and presents for the Algerian family we were to be staying with. A hard evenings work saw us on the road by midnight, our destinations Metz, Nancy, Dijon, Lyon, in that order, the first night sleeping just outside Orange, 50 miles from the Mediterranean. Driving on in the early light of morning until late in the night, we arrived at Valencia. Taking turns in driving had still worn us out, sleep had become a problem. An early morning swim soon had us refreshed and we pressed on to Malaga, catching a ferry the next day to Melilla. An overnight stop outside Oujda in Morocco on a makeshift campsite gives us the chance to talk to fellow travellers going both ways. All travelling west said the same, be prepared for a long wait at the border crossing. Arriving at the frontier quite early did not help. Many vehicles had been waiting all night. We parked and waited, checking that all our documents were in order.

Eventually free of the paperwork we drove on through the Algerian countryside. It was quite a journey before we reached the smaller town of Ain-Temouchent. I remember so vividly the clusters of Arab and old French colonial houses. We parked outside a weathered French house and were met by Lucien's friends and their families. After a few glasses of mint tea everyone helped to unload the Land Rover - which we were informed must be housed in a garage during the night to ensure the safety of it's contents. Sadly, Lucien's friends did not possess any space so our host directed us to a night storage garage. Driving up we found a few spaces amongst the French and German cars. We parked in what must have been a large workshop - another leftover from French colonial times. The workshop was decorated with old French signs hanging down from the walls.

Unused petrol pumps, their contents now only rust were scattered around. It was quite a sight. The overnight charge? Something equivalent to 25p.

When we returned we were shown to a large round table, standing very low to the ground laid out in the courtyard. A huge round tray was brought out on which lay pieces of chicken intermingled with colourful rice and small chopped vegetables. Uncomfortably sitting cross-legged and looking very awkward I watched our hosts and it came to my attention that there were no women or children at the table, a custom that I was to get used to over my stay. Right handed they began to roll small rice balls and place them delicately in their mouths. My attempts to roll these balls were hopeless and I finally resorted to scooping up small portions with my fingers. The chicken pieces were much easier to manage. When we were finished the tray was taken to the kitchen where more rice was added before it was placed on the kitchen floor for the women and children to have their fill.

Our host, Amed insisted on sharing his bedroom with us while his wife slept with the children as is the custom, the best he could offer for our comfort, his duty would not allow any other. The next seven days were spent travelling around with trips to Oran, Mascara, and one place I'd always wanted to visit, having seen many French Foreign Legion films and read a good few books, Sidi-Bez-Abbes. It wasn't until a few days into our stay Lucien explained the situation regarding Montezuma's revenge. Not to put too fine a point on it, diarrhoea and vomiting, due mainly to unhygienic methods of storing meat and poultry combined with the standard of personal hygiene. Lucien succumbed to the sickness despite boasting of his 'bullet-proof digestive system' the night before we left. For three days he drank nothing but boiled water and took many visits to the toilet.

The desert trip went ahead but not without it's problems, and few fond memories of the oasis that are scattered amongst thousands of miles of diarrhoea.

25th November 1997

As soon as I am out of the aft cabin at 3.00am I remember to set up the cooker, fill the kettle and get the coffee ready for my mid row break before Keith switches off the light. The wind is still blowing force six and only 20 minutes have elapsed before I'm forced to find the tube of Vaseline for my suffering backside. Back on the rowing seat I try to take my mind off of the discomfort by watching the phosphorescence being flicked off of the oars, swirling by the boat and disappearing.

Breakfast is the call as I lumber towards the open hatch.

"When's porridge again?" I ask Keith.

"Not for at least another couple of days. Here, get your Peak bar, that'll fill you up."

Starting my rowing stint I am pleased to see the sun, now free from the low-lying cloud as it begins to rise. At 12.30pm I can hardly wait to get into the water. Fins and mask on I swim around in the large swell for a few minutes before scraping off barnacles with the old sweet tin. My labours soon produce a cloud of small shell like creatures, which are drawn to the rear of the boat as it moves through the water. Waiting patiently are two small black and white horizontally striped fish, approximately eight inches long, who immediately begin to dart about when the floating meal arrives. Every day for the past ten days I have noticed these two fish in the same position. After yesterday's swim I began to think about where I had seen photographs of these small fish. Suddenly it comes to me, a book I was reading on sharks. Pilot-fish, named after being observed positioned in front of sharks and mantas, presumably taking advantage of pressure waves formed as the hosts move their large masses through the water. These underwater waves provide a free ride, conserving their energy, and I presume they have chosen *The George Geary* for the same reason. They also conserve more energy by not having to seek and kill for their meals using their host as a free meal dispenser. Scurrying around for scraps of meat as great chunks of flesh are torn from the shark's prey. With *The George Geary* their regular meal comes at approximately 12.30pm on the daily hull scraping. We also have two more passengers, having hitched a ride before the arrival of the Pilot-fish, two Remoras, one each side of the keel. I have never seen them swim free of the hull. They are always in the same position, stuck on with their suction pads. Although their meals come by nibbling on crustaceans attached to the hull of the boat, they have been known to drop off when the sharks attack the prey and join in the meal, eating food scraps discarded by their hosts. Lunch over, I decide to do a few small repairs to the side of the boat, nothing drastic, only wear and tear due mainly to the wild movements of the oars when they escape my grasp. Work over, back to my writings.

1977 A Desert Trip, Part Two: We spent many cool nights under star-studded skies in Laghouat and Ghardaia before ending our trip to the Sahara in Algiers. I had been to some very interesting capitals, but never one like this. Such a mass of teeming people, every shop was crowded, every café was packed tight; the overworked waiters darted about like gazelles. Exhausted from the speed of the capital, I took a trip to the beach. Back in England I had swam many times in seas like these so I dived in. Swimming through the breakers, once outside, I swam in luxury. When I decided to return to the beach, after endeavouring to swim through the surf, suction pulled me back. I tried and tried again to get back to the beach but before long I felt completely exhausted. I swam back outside the swell and relaxed by floating on my back in order to get my breath back. Deciding I would make one more determined effort, and if it fails start shouting and waving my arms, I lined myself up and began my most vigorous front crawl. As I neared the beach a breaking wave forced me under, coughing and choking with seawater as I surface I was caught in the back suction. I turned upright and forced myself under the surface. When my head was approximately three feet below I felt the shingle under my feet and dug them in forcing my body to lock at a 45° angle. It felt like my lungs were bursting.

I hung on grimly as the suction pulled at my body and the backward pressure began to abate. Finally my head was out of the water gasping for breath, yet there was hardly time for a second breath as the next wave approached.

At last I was free. Staggering out of the shallow water I collapsed on the beach. Breathing in great gulps of air like an overpowered vacuum cleaner a man ran by and dived in through the swell, swimming strongly out to the calmer sea. At first I was concerned, but watching him swim out I assumed he was familiar with the area and a very strong swimmer.

Arriving back at Ain-Temouchent we bought a large chicken to celebrate our return to our hosts. We tried not to be put off by the sights we saw at the butcher's shop, dust and flies covered most of the products on display. Having both gone through the acclimatisation process, with regard to our stomachs, we should have been more concerned about our lack of toilet paper. Our supply had run out and I, in my forgetfulness, had overlooked the fact toilet paper was almost impossible to obtain here. Magazines and old newspapers were the only solution. The sanitary situation had been brought home to me when I visited one of the only public toilets I had managed to find. In Algeria, the bus station had it's own personal arrangements consisting of a small tin of water placed by the toilet. This was possibly changed once a day, not a lot to wash your left hand in.

During the course of the meal we were delighted to hear that we had been invited to attend a ritual ceremony, only performed about four times a year. Lucien had witnessed one before but would not tell me anything about it stating that I had to watch and gain my own conclusions from it. Slightly intrigued we walked to the outskirts of town arriving at a small square filled with local people obviously waiting for the entertainment to begin. Eventually a group of people emerged dressed in bright garb of wide pantaloons and a sash tied above their waistcoats. Some of the performers carried long curved swords some skin drums and copper cymbals. A rhythmic sound filled the air galvanising the sword carriers into action. They began a strange war like dance swinging their swords round and round, barely missing their companions. This activity went on into the night. The light from bulbs, hanging from odd wires, gave the dancers a strange appearance. Whirling shadows followed them everywhere. Finally, growing faster and faster until, without notice, the music abruptly stopped and so did the dancers. Walking up to us, first one and then another, they placed their swords before us, egged on by all of the onlookers. We were invited to test the sharpness of the blades by cutting pieces of paper, and feeling conspicuous, as we were the only Europeans, tried to act out the testing ritual doing what we assumed was expected of us.

Once the blade testing was over, a loud drumbeat burst out, catching everybody by surprise. The leader of the sword carriers strode to the middle of the gathering holding the point of his sword against his stomach. Then, suddenly, commenced hitting the handle with a pair of copper castanets. From our position the sword definitely appeared to be entering his body. I can only assume that the experienced swordsman knows where to enter the body without piercing any vital organs. When it was decided that the sword had gone in far enough, after consultation with his fellow companions, he began a slow dance leaving the sword sticking out of his stomach unsupported. The slow gyrating movement of his dance caused the sword to move up and down. Once over, the sword was slowly removed and a small amount of blood wiped from it. The performance was then repeated by all of his followers.

26th November 1997

Putting on my waterproofs I consider another three hours rowing. I really don't want to go out on deck. It takes a few more minutes pulling myself together, rationalising that there is no basis for my fears before I'm seated and pulling on the oars. It's not that bad I guess, I don't know why I was scared. Only another 15 minutes and it will be time for a refreshing mug of coffee. I'll just keep telling myself that. Suddenly, out of the corner of my eye, I catch the glimpse of a light. Wait, are there two? I twist round on the rowing seat to get a better view. Bang, off comes one of the wheels out of the track. That means another tedious job, untying the lanyard attached to the seat, sliding it right off, then fitting it back. The wheels, back into place five to ten minutes later, all is sorted.

Just as I put the torch away, whoosh, a wave hits the boat lifting it high on one side and sending me flying. I wonder if Keith has it this bad? It can't be just my bad luck. Luckily my knees prevented my whole body going over as the boat rolls back and forth. Thank God I'm wearing my harness. I try to steady myself by pulling on the harness lanyard, yet without warning I am on my backside again in the well of the boat. My harness is not attached to the holding straps. Time for some coffee. A cloudless sky soon warms me as I begin to row in a sea that looks a lot less wild than the night before. More hull scraping keeps my new fishy friends happy before lunch.

1979 The Black Hole: A trip to St Lucia in the Caribbean was to be the start of an all consuming interest involving my disappearance on every bank holiday for many years to follow, not to mention at least four weeks in each year. On that hot picturesque Caribbean Island I was to be introduced to Scuba Diving.

It wasn't until the following year that I was able to experience my newly found hobby again. After being told by a close friend I joined the local diving club. On this particular occasion I was at our diving location early partly due to the parking arrangements. Only the first six cars were allowed through the gate. Unfortunate people arriving a little late needed to either persuade those taking their cars to carry a little extra kit or carry it. When I pulled up in my battered old Land Rover there were only five cars waiting outside the gates, I was just in time. Soon after, a stream of disappointed divers drove up and began piling their kit into my Land Rover, not that I would charge for this small service, a small gesture in the pub afterwards might not go amiss. Six vehicles slowly made their way through Swithland Wood in Leicestershire, landing outside the wood gate that was always kept locked to stop anybody accidentally falling into the water. It was a clear morning with a little ground frost scattered about. A slight cold breeze made me momentarily shudder before we frantically unloaded the gear. My old friend Pete Tyson was the Diving Marshall.

"Graham, are you going down the black hole?" he said jokingly.

"Yes, must get some deep practice in before the summer." I replied.

"Okay, you go down with Paul and I'll tell him the bad news." He turned and walked towards Paul, a big grin on his face. Oblivious to all of the surrounding activity I busily worked away at arranging my kit having decided to take my two, seventy-two cubic pound cylinders, which at that moment I was trying to fit together.

"Paul and Graham, second pair down." Pete shouted.
Paul walked over with the usual smile on his face.

"It's you and me then Walters? Hope none of your kit fails today?"

"What do you reckon on stops Paul?" I asked.

"Let's say that we get to the centre at 46 or 47 metres, we'll calculate for 48 metres. How does 16 minutes bottom time grab you?"

"Sounds okay. What stops do we need to do Paul?"
I was unable to look at my decompression card as I had lost it some weeks previous on a dive.

"Five at ten and ten at five. Easy to remember. Probably only need to do three minutes at 10 metres if we come up at the usual rate."
Now that the technical side was sorted out all that remained was a small amount of grunting and groaning as I tried desperately to fit into my wet suit. More of the same was to follow when we entered the icy waters. A last cup of coffee and on with the two cumbersome cylinders.

Walking down to the water's edge two pairs of divers were entering the water whilst four more excited individuals were attaching their final bits of kit in preparation for a dive to 20 metres. For us it was to be a much deeper dive of approximately 47 metres in the part of the quarry nicknamed the 'black hole'. The reason being that the width at the bottom is probably no more than 10 metres restricting the light, which normally at best is only down to 20 metres. The first pair to go down into the black hole were just surfacing.

"Kev, what's it like down there?" I asked

"The usual, black and cold." he replied, shivering and shuddering.

"Last check then Graham. ABLJ cylinder filled, air on, full cylinder, compass, torch, knife, depth gauge." said Paul.

As I entered the freezing cold water, shaking and pulling faces, John picked up more dangling demand valves.

"Watch it Graham, it's icing up a bit."

"Will do John, shan't take a breath 'til I'm under the water."

Wishing now that I had taken the valve and cylinder into the warm house the night before, too late now, time to go.

"See you at five metres Paul." I said before I submerged.

I remember shivering even more as cold water slowly trickled down my back. Snorkelling over to the shot line I pulled the vent on my ABLJ, breathed in and slowly descended to five metres. The visibility at this depth wasn't too bad, slightly discoloured, range about five metres. In no time Paul arrived opposite me, smiling with the usual 'I'm okay' hand signal.

This particular dive we had planned to use a buddy line, a line, approximately two metres long, attached from person to person by the wrists. It is normally used at the discretion of the divers, having experienced losing our partners in the murky depths the last time we were here. As soon as we had slipped the buddy line around our wrists, switched on the torches, and gave the okay signal, we began to descend down the shot line. Darker and darker, and at 30 metres, only the torch light was illuminating the eerie darkness. Swinging my torch beam from the rock face to my wrist revealed the depth to be 35 metres. Carrying on down I noticed a small bubbling sound, which suddenly grew louder. Realising what was occurring, as compressed air began to be forced into my mouth, and at a very high rate, the divers nightmare was now mine. Freeze up. Slowing my descent meant that Paul now carried on below me. Stopping at 40 metres, and hanging on the line, my left hand stretched down bringing Paul to an abrupt stop. At that precise moment in time I felt helpless, one hand stretched below me, the other above me. If only I had compensated for my buoyancy by blowing air into my adjustable buoyancy life jacket. If I let go of the line it would result in me plummeting to the bottom. Free flowing air blasted into my mouth. The experience can only be compared to having a full bottle of fizzy lemonade tipped down your throat.

The drama continued in the dark as my torch now hung useless on its lanyard after dropping from my hand. Paul came up from below to find out what was the problem and he wasn't long in accessing the situation offering me his demand valve straight from his mouth. I knew three good breaths are about all I should take, even in these circumstances, before pushing one's buddy's hand back to enable him to take his turn. I knew something was wrong when I took the first breath. The desire to take deep breaths was overwhelming. Unfortunately, I could only manage shallow gulps, leaving me still gasping by the second breath. I pushed Paul's hand back and pointed with my thumb to the surface indicating that I was heading for the sunlight. I opened the valve to my ABLJ bottle, which instantly lifted me from the perilous predicament, but forgot to slip off the buddy line, dragging Paul unceremoniously upwards. He managed to slip it off his own wrist. Moments after the lift I felt my lungs expanding, blow out, blow out, I said to myself. The darkness grew lighter immediately giving me a sense of relief. There was no doubt that I would make the surface in very short time, but how much damage to my body would be any ones guess.

The only thing I failed to understand, in these fleeting moments of time was my expanding body despite me blowing out as hard as I could. Apparently, so they told me, when I hit the surface it was quite spectacular, flying out of the water and falling back in. My only memories of the event were of incredible pain and feeble attempts to ask to be taken out of here. Why was I worried, as divers had already jumped into the water, sussing out the situation on seeing the vast quantities of bubbles burst upon the surface? I was speedily towed to the side where many helping hands dragged me up the bank on my stomach. As they did, the biggest belch of my life started and went on for what seemed like an eternity. Instantly the pain began to subside and the benefits of speech returned. Decision time. The car nearest to the road was prepared to leave for the hospital or the decompression chamber at Stoney Cove. As I was now able to speak normally I entered into the debate explaining all the circumstances. Paul, my only witness, was hanging on the line affecting a ten-minute decompression stop. Stand by divers had instructed him to do so by means of hand signals and written notes stating that I was okay. The ongoing discussion centred around my condition as I had reached the surface. My pains had disappeared and I could finally speak normally again. The result was a vastly inflated stomach due to the amount of air that had been forced into it. The action of keeping the free flowing demand valve in my mouth had restricted my breathing underwater.

Part of me thought my stomach could not affect the muscular movement of the diaphragm inside my rib cage. There was also a distinct lack of blood and mucus associated with a burst lung. I couldn't have suffered internal damage. With all my heavy kit pulled off I began to feel like my old self, the main concern now was decompression sickness, commonly known as 'the bends.'

A short deep dive usually produces symptoms in the first few minutes, whereas a long dive produces decompression sickness hours after. As a car is always on hand to ferry unlucky participants to hospital it is suggested that I go for a check up, but while I appreciated the concern, a couple of pints in a quiet pub was my idea of convalescence.

Putting away the pen and writing pad I glance at the GPS, 13° 48′ north and 45° 17′ west, a 53 mile run. Still not too bad considering that the wind has dropped slightly. Climbing out to relieve Keith, I remember that today is a 'water-replenishing day'. In accordance with our rationing plan, we use two litres per day each plus a six-litre container purely for cooking, which normally lasts for about a week. Tonight's meal is an old favourite - chicken casserole.

27th November 1997

As soon as I began my watch at 3.00am, I could make out a small light as I scanned the horizon. I found no difficulty in keeping an eye on this ever-increasing light, after a good 10 minutes of observation the one light became two and they started to grow in size. Another five minutes go by before one of the two lights appeared lower than the other one. It is the one nearest the stern of our boat that is definitely lower, which makes it obvious that the ship is about to cross our stern some distance away. Roughly 10 minutes is all it takes before a red light appeared next to the two white lights. As these grew in size and smaller deck lights come into view it was time to switch on the navigation light just in case this lighted monster got too close. To my amazement, after flicking the switch, a single white light shone out from the top of our boat. A closer look revealed only a base and bare bulb, nothing else. One of the big waves must have taken away the casing. Whether the small white light was seen or not did not make much difference as the large Atlantic fishing boat passed our starboard side and slowly moved on into the night. This night-time meeting was long forgotten by the time my watch was finished.

"Is that porridge I smell?"

Whether Keith heard me or not he continued to put the breakfast kettle on.

A quick discussion on the weather and our progress over two mugs of coffee completes our breakfast. The clear sky prompts me to pick up my sunglasses in readiness for the glaring sun that is already slowly rising. 12.30pm cannot come a moment too soon. It takes only seconds to fit my mask and fins, flip over the side, and start scraping, providing our friends with their usual meal. All through lunch I look forward to my afternoon read. The difference today has to be credited to the sea-state, which has subsided even more, allowing us to open the rear hatch again. The cool breeze that blows through the rear cabin feels incredible. When I think of the hours spent pouring with sweat in the stifling heat of the aft cabin. Just as I begin to lose myself in one of Maurice's stories I'm covered in water. Right, time to lock the hatch.

Time for another small cross on our chart - 13° 54′ north and 46° 09′ west, overall our daily run not too bad. The most interesting thing is our slight northerly track. If we can keep this up over the next few days I'll feel much more confident. We'll have a much better approach to the north side of Barbados, providing the wind doesn't change. Back to the oars. 2½ hours should give me a good appetite, what am I thinking about? I am starving now!

28th November 1997

Rain squalls seem to be the main problem tonight. With so many discomforts brought with the sharp wind, getting wet adds to the overall feeling of misery. I find it hard to believe that in two weeks all this will be over. Well that is if the weather stays like this. As I come to the end of the morning row I can't remember whether I engaged in a body scrub yesterday, or, for that matter, the day before. Washing every couple of days should ensure that the soap lasts until we reach Barbados. Decision taken, I lather up as best as I can and roll over the side. A quick summersault underwater soon rinses off the soapsuds, then its back to writing.

1985 De-masted Outside of 'The Jolly Sailor': Sailing is another sport that I regretted not staring earlier in life. When I eventually did it was with a thirteen-ton boat. Obviously, it didn't take long for me to realise that learning to sail is somewhat better achieved in a smaller boat. This led me to my next purchase - a mayfly class sailing dinghy. Opportunities to go sailing at that time seemed to be far and few between until a holiday break came along. As Margaret's mother was now on her own we asked her to come to Southwold in Suffolk with us for a change of scenery. We were to stay at my aunt's cottage, a holiday retreat that she lets from week to week especially during the summer. Seaward or inland, depending on the weather, there were many places suitable for a novice sailor. The journey was not without its problems as one of the trailer tyres made a loud noise and promptly turned into shredded rubber. Not being able to find a spare the right size in our hurried departure, I had taken what I thought at the time was the next best thing. Two old mini tyres I had saved from of a long departed mini van, somewhat larger than the trailer tyres. They would be our option should a puncture occur. Changing two tyres with one jack on the fast flowing A45 can only be described as akin to working beside a race track. The last time I had been involved in a lengthy tyre change at the side of a busy road, I had left my jack at home holding two new, recently fitted hull planks on my sailing smack. A spade had been the most useful piece of kit I had with me and fortunately the ground underneath the prostrate vehicle was as soft as the tyre so forcing a piece of broken tree trunk under the back axle I had dug a neat hole under the wheel to allow space to change it.

The first day of our holiday was spent in a relaxed mood with me checking over the dinghy. On the day I bought her, which was at auction, my mind had tried to cover all eventualities. This resulted in the added purchase of a two horse power seagull outboard engine, which I now tested. No matter what I attempted to fiddle with it refused to start. Being of a practical nature, I thought why would I need an engine when I have sails? What kind of sailor would I be, depending on an engine? With that resounding breakthrough in logic I turned my attention to find a place for the maiden voyage. A quiet lake did not seem challenging enough. It has to be somewhere with tides to put my new found knowledge to the test - an interesting place, a place with a history. The River Ore in Orford would be the perfect place to acquire new skills I remember thinking to myself. On one of my earlier trips to Orford as a lands-man, a walk to the quay had stirred my imagination. I remember looking across the river at a few small boats tugging at their moorings and slowly turning with the fast flowing tide and thinking I'd be in the midst of the all action soon enough. Knowing the conditions at the time I knew our sailing trip had to be up the river away from the sea.

A leisurely stroll into the centre of Southwold gave me the chance to purchase one of Imray's Charts. Mapping the rivers of the Ore and the Alde my plan for tomorrow was complete. I would sail as far as possible using the incoming tides, the wind direction ENE, not too bad for a sail up the entire stretch of river to Snape. I remember the next day beginning very sunny. Leaving a chair in the garden for Margaret's mother to sit on if she felt inclined Margaret and I set off for Orford. It wasn't long before we were passing the Orford Castle which I'm told was built by Henry II in 1165. The castle took eight years to built and cost, at that time, £1400 9s 2d. This perfectly exact figure has always stuck in my mind. When was the last time I quoted for a loft conversion down to the last pence? The nearest ten pounds was exact enough for me.

Arriving at the quay I was amazed to see so many people, fishermen and sailors in all directions. Never having rigged the boat, the prospect of so many spectators was rather daunting. A plan of discretion soon materialised. I would drive back up the road a small way to the car park of 'The Jolly Sailor' Public House and there in comparative isolation I rigged the boat. On successfully completing this task I stood back to admire the stout 22' mast and then, without further ado, I began the drive back down to the quay. Five yards out of the car park there was aloud crash. 'Turning my head in startled anticipation I could see through the rear window that the mast was now lying along the boat, wire shrouds dangling down the sides. Leaping out I quickly gathered up the odd bits hanging over, backed up the car and drove back into the car park for examination of the cause. It was evident that the stem plate attached to the bow had parted releasing the fore stay. Why it had parted at that particular time was a mystery. Breathing a sigh of relief I raised the mast once more using the remaining eye on the stem plate to attach the fore stay. While this activity was taking place Margaret sat waiting patiently in the car.

"Don't worry Margaret, it's only a tiny setback. We'll soon be on the water."I said.

Driving out of the car park once more, at the exact spot where the mast had come down before, there was another mighty crack followed by the sound of splintering wood. Jumping out of the car I was met with an unforgettable sight. The mast lay across the boat in two pieces, not a clean break, but almost four feet of splits and shreds of wood coming back from the break. Raising my hopeless eyes to the heavens I found the culprit. A thick black cable was stretched across the road approximately 20' from the ground. Helpless frustration turned into a challenge.

"We will go up the river to Snape Maltings whatever the cost." I shouted to Margaret, oblivious of the gathering onlookers.

"How are you going to row?" she exclaimed in astonishment.

"'I am going to row the dinghy all they way there." I said.

"I think that this latest disaster has gone to your head."

"No, I'm determined to get there. The tide is still with us for another five hours."

Collecting all of the loose wire I unscrewed the shrouds, tying them and the broken mast to the top of the car before driving down to the quay. Another five minutes saw the boat launched and tied up at the quay. Loading on the sandwiches and flask we set off.

Our dinghy turned rowing boat entered Halfway Reach, leaving Reyden Reach behind and Margaret with a more relaxed look on her face. The only sound breaking the silence was the dip and slash of the oars.

"How do you feel now Margaret?" I asked, smiling.

"Much better. I could hardly stand all those people staring at us, it made me feel very stressed, but people are naturally curious."

"The worst thing for me was that I was made to look like a real idiot and novice. There I was trying to be discreet, taking the boat down to the sea without attracting any attention and what did I do, the opposite. Anyway, let's put it all behind us and enjoy the trip. You might like to know that we're just entering the River Alde."

"What's the difference?" she asked quizzically.

"History I suppose."

After passing Lower Dan's Hole, and Upper Dan's Hole, without the faintest idea who Dan was, the impressive looking Martello Tower came into view. Rounding the sharp bend in sight of Aldeburgh my stomach informed me that it was time for lunch. Leaving the dinghy to make it's own way I pulled out the flask and sandwiches. A cool breeze blew across the river while we tucked into cheese and ham sandwiches. For me it was a refreshing break after 2½ hours of rowing, a contrasting view from Margaret who hoped that the sun would shine again.

It is difficult to describe how certain memories can be more powerful than others making it hard to press on in years, the only way to purge the lingering thoughts with some success involved a pen and paper. Once trapped in this method the memory can relax and move on.

29th November 1997

"Is it my imagination or is the wind dropping?" I say as I change places with Keith.

"Yes probably only force three now." he replied.

I can feel the relaxed state of the sea through the oars. So overcome by this feeling of well being I completely forget the time, 6.00am suddenly becomes 7.00am.

"Keith, wake up, I've forgotten to watch the time and I've given you an extra hour."

Once inside the aft Cabin I felt the sheer luxury of a cool breeze blowing through the cabin. Realising that the sea had calmed down, Keith had opened the rear hatch fully. I lay back with my head on what has been my pillow for the last seven weeks, my sponsors Sub zero fleece jacket, gazing out of the wide open hatch at the star filled sky.

"Graham, breakfast. I've let you lie in because of the long watch you did, it's 9.50am."

The first thing I noticed on climbing out was the sea-state, now drastically reduced. Although the wind had dropped in the early hours of the morning the darkness had disguised the lowering in wave height. Midway through the morning my mind turned to the time, our watches were in need of correction. Since leaving Tenerife we had brought them forward an hour. Things were made slightly easier by the fact that the Canary Isles had the same time as Britain, GMT in winter and daylight saving time during the summer. Working things out in my head was probably not the best way. Taking the longitude 47° degrees west, roughly our present position, we should have altered the time passing 45° west to zone time plus three, but it is not a problem. I will wait until I get the afternoon fix and then change the longitude into time by the means of a small graph called Conversions of Arc to Time, flick the GPS on to GMT giving me the present time at Greenwich, and simply add them together.

The temperature has gradually risen, and the fact that I have agreed to do 50 minutes more has not helped. The swim under the boat comes at the perfect time. Although the sea is calmer now there are some mild discomforts in the form of strange stings. It's not the first time I've experienced this. Since we left Tenerife these stings seem to increase when the sea is calmer. Before long I see in front of me is what I assumed to be the cause of the stinging sensation, a small round body with long wispy tentacles about the size of a human hair. While drying myself I decide that I must get to the bottom of these strange mild-stinging creatures. Sitting back after lunch, a real pleasure in these much calmer seas, I thumb through a small book on sea life, stopping at a page on the Portuguese Man of War. Nobody really knows how these creatures reproduce. They have found baby Portuguese Men of War consisting of just a tiny float with a single tentacle hanging down. Whilst the stinging is rather discomforting I can't help but think these creatures are slightly worse off than us. They can't swim, their only means of propulsion is with the current or with the wind. The commune making up the Portuguese Men of War definitely have to hit it off together. When feeding, the tentacles part of this unfriendly group sting and raise their prey towards the eagerly waiting mouths and stomachs, of which there are an equal number. Sensing the captured prey they begin to twist about as the approaching food nears the mouth of this strong group of jelly creatures, their mouths increasing to 20 millimetres, shrinking back to one millimetre when resting. This reminds me of a certain tussle with a Monkfish, all gaping mouth and no body. I can just imagine an innocent fish swimming by without a care in the world when suddenly down come 20 tentacles, up goes the fish to be devoured by 20 hungry mouths. With that thought I retire to the air-conditioned cabin and pick up Maurice's book and see that the title of the next short story looks familiar, 'Rescue at Sea'.

30th November 1997

A shout brings me out of a deep sleep, and opening my eyes I could just make out an empty rowing seat. Fearing the worst I lunge forward, entwined in the lumpy sleeping bag, to find Keith's stretching body as he frantically hauls on the fishing line.

"What's all the drama Keith?"

"There's a long black thing hanging on to the end of the line, get the bucket ready."

"Okay." I say whilst scrambling around for the bucket. Over my shoulder the creature Keith is wrestling with looks like an eel. Pulling it out of the water the eel is around a metre long. It's ribbed body curls round into a big dorsal fin that runs down the whole length of it's slimy body. In the dark I can just about make out the eels piercing eyes. Agreeing to have a closer inspection when the sun rises we leave our new passenger quite happily in the bucket full of saltwater.

My first row of the day is punctuated by thoughts of this black monster from the deep. During breakfast we studied the vicious mouth, the teeth before casting it back into the Ocean after breakfast. The wind is now on the increase. Thank God it's blowing from the southeast again. That allows us to row further south. Climbing out of the water after my regular morning scrape under the boat I have a weird flashback in which I'm climbing out of a muddy river, not over the side of a boat, but a rubbish skip. I recalled more details during lunch and think it's time to put pen to paper again.

1984 River Journey: A telephone call from my good friend Rob, set in motion a rescue operation of a very unusual kind. The conversation went something like this, "Graham, how would you like to combine a bit of business with pleasure?"
The business side sounded interesting. As for pleasure, I was dubious to say the least.

"Go on then Rob, fill me in on the details."
Incidentally, Rob ran a waste skip business at that time.

"Well, I would like you and a few friends to search for a missing skip." asked Rob. Somewhat puzzled I asked why saying, "Surely it's just a matter of driving around until it's spotted?"
To which Rob replied, "Not that simple, it's under water." Now the realisation came to me. What Rob had meant when he had said 'and a few friends', was that the few friends would have to be divers from my local diving club.

"It's simply a matter of walking along the river bank and trying to spot any unusual water flow." Rob saved me from asking the next question, 'how'. Apparently, after the skip had been emptied at the rubbish tip that backed close to the river, it had been left over the weekend. Unfortunately it rained constantly over the two days and Monday morning saw the River Soar completely burst it's banks and flood all the low lying land. This included the tip. The skip must have floated off as the water level dropped and the floodwater rushed back to the river.

We discussed the rescue operation over a couple of drinks until a plan emerged. Firstly we would have to find the skip, re-float it and then row it down the river to a suitable place where it could be picked up with a lorry. This just happened to be 'The Hope and Anchor Inn' and if all went well business would then turn into pleasure in the shape of copious amounts of brown liquid.

The following week three of my diving pals turned up at my house. We decided to start at the tip and work down the river. After less that half a mile we arrived at a spot where the fast flowing river bubbled and swirled in a disturbed nature. We all came to the same conclusion that this had got to be the spot. Splitting into two pairs we donned our wet suits with the idea that two would descend the murky depths whilst being held by ropes worked by their partners. As I was the organiser I insisted on being first in, a decision I instantly regretted as the brown cold water pulled me along until checked by the rope. Once completely submerged I held my hand out approximately 12" in front of my face in case of contact with any solid objects. I was unable to see my hands or my arms for that matter. Edging further my hand touched a slimy substance, and approximately two inches from my diving mask a vague outline emerged through the dark brown haze of a muddy riverbed. The search would have to be by feel only. Suddenly I felt a bump, then the usual okay signal from Pete who was to be the second diver in, his thumb and forefinger staying pressed against my mask for a few seconds before disappearing into the dark brown soup. Working our way down what we could only assume to be the centre of the river, a solid object barred my way. Groping around I discovered what I could only assume to be the skip upside down. After surfacing and climbing out of the muddy water a short discussion is held on what would be the best approach to raising the skip.

Thirty minutes later my old Land Rover is driven across the fields to within towing distance of the submerged skip. Kev and Paul attach two chains to the lifting hooks, who to this day must regret missing the opportunity to dip themselves into the muddy brine. Once attached Rob put his foot down and the Land Rover sprayed both Pete and I from head to foot in dripping soft mud. The lack of traction is soon sorted by the offer of an increase in the liquid reward. Manpower was added to the drive and slowly the vehicle moved forward bit by bit. With our backs to the Land Rover we were able to see the steep rise of steel plating emerging from the murky depths. Luck was on our side and the skip turned upright at the side of the river. Two brown figures then jumped back into the river. Five long paddles were then produced from the rear of the Land Rover, which had been carefully whittled from two old planks the night before. Images of the 'White Horse' pub at Birstall faded into the distance as we paddled away having launched the skip and climbed inside. The buildings of Thurmaston soon came into view. We cautiously drew up to the locks before we realised no one had a key to the lock gates. Mooring the skip, Rob walked to Thurmaston boat yard to obtain a key. The key borrowed we were soon opening and closing the lock gates. In a sustained effort of paddling we arrived at Johnson's Bridge, one last stretch of the river, although a long one. It is hard to believe that one could get a regular riverboat service from Belgrave in Leicester to Loughborough, and beyond, every Thursday, Saturday and Sunday. Cossington Mill was 2s 6d, Mountsorrel 3s 5d, mind you, that was in 1920. Time to pull in for a rest. As we did a narrow boat came into view.

"Let's ask him for a tow." said Rob.

"Okay, you ask him Rob, you look more like the Captain of a floating skip."

The skipper of the narrow boat must have felt sorry for us, agreeing to tow us up to the 'Hope and Anchor' Inn, a traditional stop for the cargo narrow boats stabling their horses there as far back as 1846. A few evening drinkers gave us strange looks as we moored up.

1st December 1997
It has been necessary to close the rear hatch again. The wind is probably force five to six. No matter what the situation is, it never seems to get any easier. My two mugs of coffee at 4.30am came as an unimaginable pleasure along with of course, the delicious Peak oat bar. 6.00am releases me for another sleep.

Keith tells me over breakfast that he has been fishing again and has lost another lure. That was probably the last one. Strange considering that I have not seen a single fish under the boat.

My morning watch begins quite cloudless. The most amazing sight is the sky full of birds. For the last six weeks all we have seen is our two friendly storm petrels and three seagulls. Looking towards the largest group I can just make out their long tail feathers. They must be Tropic- Birds, well known for dive-bombing flying fish. Mingled in amongst them are brown coloured birds, larger beaks with slightly longer wingspan. They look more streamlined they're probably Brown Boobies. With the sky so full of birds perhaps the sea below the boat will similarly be filled with fish. The time finally comes and I am over the side. What a disappointment. The sea has never felt so empty.

After taking the daily fix, 13° 37′ north and 48° 56′ west, I climb into the aft cabin while Keith prepares his new secret weapon - a new hook. Pulling out my book I decide to empty all of my bags in a last effort to find the star chart. Going through my folder containing mainly rowing race papers I find, not exactly what I had expected, but at least something to point me in the right direction - a 60p booklet, 'Signpost to the Stars'.

I think progress is improving. During the afternoon row I cannot help but think about tonight now armed with information that hopefully will guide me through the night sky.

After delving into a steaming hot silver pouch, which when I opened, produced a mouth watering smell, Keith informs me that he has produced the ultimate in fish catching technology. Keith proudly shows me his work of art. It's a vicious looking instrument comprising of three large hooks turned back to back and held together by wire that extends to a spinner. The idea apparently is twofold. When the fish bite it will be impossible for them to free themselves. Secondly, they will be unable to bite through the line.

Sitting back in the aft cabin after dinner I begin reading the first page. Whether by coincidence or importance the first constellation is that of the 'Plough', the only one that I have been able to distinguish over the last 25 years. Not necessarily through ignorance, time has always been the greatest problem or the lack of it to be precise. There is always something that takes priority, now could be the time to rectify that. Having thumbed through quite a few publications concerning studies of the heavens I realise that there are other given names to this constellation. 'The Great Bear', 'The Dipper'. Probably many people have their own ideas regarding names, mine has always been the saucepan. The last two of the brightest stars that make the pan shape, I have learned over the years always point to the pole star. The next page depicts Cassiopeia, found, I gather, forming a line from the end of the plough through the pole star approximately half the distance. ' Continuing through the next few pages I list a few stars and constellations to search for, 'Aldebaran', 'Capella', 'Pleiades' and the 'Seven Sisters'. I think that is sufficient for the first night. ' Putting down the book I drop off to sleep immediately.

Keith wakes me at 9.30pm and I climb out staring at the night sky. Great! The sky is completely covered by cloud. As the minutes tick by, rowing under this dark sky, I try to picture the first pages of the star book, and finishing at midnight I'm still hopeful that the sky will clear.

2nd December 1997
3.00am brings a slightly brighter sky. I'll just take a quick glance at the book before climbing out of the aft cabin. Unfortunately there is only one torch left. My small one and Keith's re-chargeable have both failed which just leaves my old diving torch encasing the only remaining batteries. I guess there's the deck light but that should be kept for emergencies too, the main emergencies as the main batteries aren't really charging through the daylight. I guess it's just too dark to look at the star book. The clouds slowly disappear leaving a more star filled sky. Difficult at first I manage to distinguish 'Cassiopeia'. Turning my attention to the 'Seven Sisters' next, which I find without too much trouble, having read some background I gather that there are only six bright stars now as one is losing it's brightness in the distant past. Boosted by this small success at distinguishing the night sky I begin searching

for Aldebaran in the constellation of Taurus. I think I have found it, although it does not quite match the picture I have in my head.

My three hours soon pass, if only I had found the book at the beginning of the trip. Waking up to much commotion on deck I can only assume that Keith's new hook has been tried and tested. As I poke my head out of the cabin I see him smiling and, holding his catch, a rather healthy sized yellow and silver Dorado.

"The super hook works then Keith?"

"Of course, there should never have been any doubt."

It seemed very strange to me. When I was under yesterday there were only a few small fish, nothing else. Eager to look under the boat after my morning row I quickly fit my mask and fins. The first look, after splashing into the water, reveals a reasonably sized Dorado swimming along behind the boat. No sign of the small fish, frightened off or even eaten I suppose I climb out and Keith has already gutted the fish and is cutting it into small steaks.

"Pasta and fish steaks for dinner?" asks an excited Keith.

Feeling full for the first time in about five weeks I climb into the aft cabin with many thoughts running through my head. A few days ago I had suffered with small periods of depression. When this happened one of the ways I used to counter the negative thoughts was by bringing back memories of an old friend, sadly now deceased. Nigel's courage in facing death will always stay with me.

The last time I saw him some six years ago, seven or eight days before he died, I had thought he was definitely on the mend having been in and out of hospital for the past four months, and now, here he was in front of me looking much better. I knew he was fighting cancer over these last months. He was always the optimist and I truly believed he had won. His generous gesture of offering me his new 24′ Stanley tape measure, did not register until after his death. Of course when I said to him that he would need it himself he replied that he had two.

We had become reasonably close since that first meeting at the Diving Club. Those early days of diving together did not always go to plan, usually ending with me scolding him for something but I am sure he took it all in good taste. As a bricklayer he worked on and off with me over the years. Sometimes he asked me to do work for him, and I was only too happy to oblige. His passion was cycling being a club rider and racer. At the time I probably hadn't been on a bike for ten to fifteen years, but he soon put a stop to that by talking me into taking part in the London to Brighton cycle race. With just three weeks to go he fixed up my old bike and took me out after work, training.

Our most memorable stunt that we worked together was cycling as fast as we could under water. The venue was Stoney Cove and the route was worked out, a sloping gradient, finishing with a 10m drop. Nigel, preparing the bike with masses of lead fixed to the handle bars, I was to have the first go, doubling the lead weight by carrying more around my waist to make sure that the bike had plenty of traction. Almost everything went to plan. A day of rain before our stunt lowered the visibility and the intention was to start very early in the morning to avoid the mass of divers found regularly at Stoney Cove. Visibility on our planned route was down to just over two metres, not necessarily a problem for us because at the side of the route lay a complete roadway of railway sleepers to guide us. I positioned myself at the start line with lots of lead weight and small cylinders, taking off my fins I sat astride the bike while Nigel held it in place. Pressing on the pedals the bike moved off faster and faster leaving Nigel behind. It seemed much easier than I had expected. Although I cycled in a straight line, every now and again I would confront groups of divers forcing me to take evasive action. As the visibility was only two metres they would appear and disappear just as quickly. I cannot imagine what the diving enthusiasts thought, as suddenly out of the swirling sediment appeared a cyclist hurtling by them. As I approached the edge of the drop off I automatically gripped the brakes yet the bike went straight over the edge. This was something else now that the bike was off the ground. We began a series of somersaults clinging on to the seat and handlebars after the second I let go of the handlebars and slammed my hand on the inflation valve on my stab jacket. The effect was almost immediate as the jacket pulled the upper half of my body out of the next somersault, wrenching the heavy bike from in between my legs. I sorted myself out, found the bike and began to ascend. Greeted by Nigel from above I gave him the thumbs up as we dragged the bike back to the start line for his attempt. Borrowing Nigel's bike for further practice an opportunity presented itself the following weekend. Clearing the last job on the Friday of all scaffolding, the idea had been to actually unload it on the Saturday morning but things do not always go to plan. A phone call to solve a small problem turned out to be a bigger job than anticipated. Saturday afternoon saw me playing Rugby, and, before I knew it, Sunday had arrived. Once more the Diving Club were using their option to dive Swithland Quarry.

Earlier in the week I had watched Eddie Kidd trying one of his stunts on the television. With this in mind and the fact that I still had Nigel's bike and the van was loaded with scaffolding. My plan was to drive the van to Swithland Wood complete with the scaffold, diving kit and Nigel's bike. I'd then build a ramp stretching over the water, similar to the jib of a crane, from one of the high cliff faces that surround the quarry. Once the plan had formed I loaded the van with my diving kit and, of course, the bike, laying them on top of the scaffold. All was ready and an early start was essential, as I had to be in one of the six vehicles allowed through the wood.

Waiting outside the gate for the person nominated to collect the key from the Park Ranger, I discussed my plans with some of the other divers, most looking at me in astonishment. Finally the gate was unlocked, by this time I thought my one ton van would be full of diving kit belonging to the majority of divers, not amongst the privileged first six allowed to drive through the wood yet for some unexplained reason most of the club members have some kind of aversion to placing their kit along side the odd bag of plaster, cement, broken slabs, old drain pipes, soil and sand. Just as I was about to leave a latecomer whose name was also Graham knocked on the dusty window of my van. "Mind if I have a lift?"
After loading his gear in, Graham who quickly became known as 'Little Graham' as he was smaller in stature than myself jumped into the passenger seat. I wonder to this day how long it took Little Graham before he realised by jumping in the van he was opting to help me erect the ramp.

Thirty minutes after pulling up outside the fenced off quarry we had managed to carry and erect the base of this ambitious project. More poles and clips were fitted and slowly pushed out over the high cliff face. The entrance to the quarry was probably a third of the way round and when entering to dive a slow gradient led down to the water. It was now the time to slide the runway into place. It was just 2′ wide and made from an 18′ by 2′ wide walkway. Three of these were necessary along with a few ordinary planks. As I was getting *the bike ready a green Land Rover approached, it was the Park Ranger. Fortunately for me Little Graham happened to be near the entrance. To be honest I hadn't even considered what the Park Ranger might say, only too obvious now as I could hear him shouting from the distance. Finally he turned on his heels, climbed into the Land Rover and drove away. I watched Little Graham run towards me with, what I was sure to be an urgent message.*

"What's up?" I said.

Little Graham blurted out the main point in between gasping for breath. "The Ranger said that if this is not removed from the woods in 30 minutes we'll all be thrown out of the club and barred for life." Grabbing the bike I strode towards the ramp.

"What are you doing Graham?"

"We've got to take it down and I haven't gone to all this trouble for nothing. I'm riding up the ramp, no time to fit any diving kit." One thing that did occur to me was that when the bike plus rider hit the water they would be over Black Hole, 60 odd metres of blackness. There would be no chance of finding the bike if it went to the bottom. I quickly solved this problem my attaching one end of a long piece of rope to the bike and the other end to the tip of the ramp. It would be simply a matter of hauling it out of the water afterwards. Laying out the rope beside the ramp so that it wouldn't get in the way I mounted the bike. Looking round anticipating an audience I was disappointed to see that everybody was engaged in various stages of dress and undress either preparing or after having had their dives.

"Get going." said Little Graham.

"Okay, here we go then."

I stood on the peddles and propelled the bike forwards trying to obtain as much speed as possible, but it was not to be. The ramp was at too much of an angle rising up over the quarry. As much as I tried the speed stayed at an average pace. The back wheel hardly seemed to leave the ramp before I felt myself plummeting towards the waiting water. A slow summersault began. I was convinced that I would hit the water at any moment in this precarious position, head and shoulders facing straight down and the bike still firmly trapped in between my knees. Suddenly the bike was yanked from between my legs and I hit the water headfirst. The downward motion through the water seemed to go on forever. A feeling of relief came over me as I burst through the surface water. Looking up I was amazed to see the bike securely hanging on the end of the rope 6′ above the water. I had drastically miscalculated the length, probably at least by 20′. I had intended to abandon the bike in the water as soon as I felt the pull back to the surface. I climbed back up to the ramp and found Little Graham furiously unbolting the scaffold. Luckily the 30 minute deadline came as we cleared up, just leaving us enough time to close the van doors and tie the long scaffold poles to the roof rack.

A strange satisfaction filled my mind, as we stood covered in sweat and mud. As for the Diving Club, we were barred for the rest of the year from diving in the quarry, although, in all fairness, there were only two dives left anyway.

Scribbling the fix down as fast as I can, 13° 44′ north and 49° 55′ west, I scramble to the hatch slightly late for my watch. Keith was oblivious to the time, wielding a screwdriver handle across the head of some poor fish.

"No need to tell me Keith, fish for dinner."

While I row Keith continued gutting his latest catch.

3rd December 1997

Ready to row at 3.00am, I am delighted to see a clear sky again. I scan the sky picking out the stars and constellations that I recognised yesterday. At the moment I have difficulty making out 'Orion', another constellation I'm eager to see.

Maybe I'm not looking at it from the right angle. If I am not careful I can see me developing a problem with my neck.

Back to my chores, the daily fix 13° 38′ north and 50° 46′ west, not too bad, a run of 50 miles. I am convinced that our best daily runs are over, not that our rowing stints are difficult, due more to the direction that we are having to row is more northerly now. The wind is still blowing from the north east, our course is due west. When the time comes for the evening meal Keith chooses chilli con carne leaving me to finish the fish. Whether this was partly due to the long white worms found in it's stomach when I gutted it, I don't know. It is definitely not a problem for me as this extra helping of Keith's share manages to make me feel full up again. Time for 20 minutes of reading.

4th December 1997
The first row of the day comes with thoughts of rain. Querying the possibilities with Keith, who is adamant that I should stay dry, I begin rowing without wearing waterproofs. The large dark shapes of rain clouds sweep across the heavens leaving patches of a star filled sky. Without the full picture it seems impossible for me to pick out any constellations. The first of the larger black shapes approaches, there is no doubt about it, I am going to get wet. Before long big gusts of wind tug at the boat until finally the harsh weather dissipates. I think cloud dodging is my main interest from now on.

I'm sure that's a tanker ahead. The navigation lights are beginning to worry me. Where are they? Slowly the black outline grows bigger until, suddenly, red and green beam out at me. I have no choice but to strap the oars and rummage around for the white collision flares. I try to change the fuse from one circuit to another, as we are now one fuse short. Our navigation lights, normally quite bright, have been washed overboard by a large wave, to be precise, the outer casing. For some strange reason the base and the bulbs have stayed intact. The shape of the super-tanker is getting bigger and bigger. Before I can make any drastic avoiding action I'm relieved to see the green starboard light indicating that the tanker will pass our stern, maybe a little too close for comfort.

With my stint ended I climb into the aft cabin.

1983 Chairman's Misdemeanour: Two days of good diving in Anglesey had put everybody in a cheerful mood. The day before we had found what was left of the Wallasey Ferry, a paddle steamer lying in fairly shallow water towards the western end of Bull Bay. The diving club's brand new Avon rigid hull inflatable was behaving perfectly. For us this was somewhat of a breakthrough in advanced technology. For the last 15 years we had carried two inflatable boats in a van or on a trailer, unpacking, fitting and manhandling them to the sea where we finally fitted the engine. Now we were able to back our new trailer and boat down the slip way and into the sea with the help of two powerful hydraulic rams. All this new technology was not obtained without a financial struggle.

Having applied to our local Council for a sport grant, 12 months of constant correspondence between City and local Council finally came to fruition with a grant of £5,000. This we matched with our 10 years of constant saving and producing an equal amount towards the cost. The person nominated to carry the responsibility of transporting the club's new possessions was me. At the time I had the honour of being the Club's Chairman and this must have had a lot to do with entrusting me with the club's new boat. As for my vehicle, another in a long line of buy and scrap modes of transport, in this case, an old Austin Ambassador, fortunately bought with a tow bar. Leaving a bit late for Anglesey I had only one passenger, Mark. This was Mark's second year with the club and he was eager to dive again after his diving career was put on hold due to an enforced holiday in Her Majesty's Prison.

We made our beds in a campsite near Tregehe which proved to be an ideal spot. On the first day a strong north easterly wind had blown up so picking a sheltered diving spot on the Southwest coast of Anglesey was no trouble. The 855 ton Norman Court fitted the situation perfectly. She was wrecked on the Crigyll Rocks off the coast of Rhoscolyn, a sad death in 1883 for such a famous clipper, racing the Cutty Sark to be the first home with her cargo of tea, and setting a record time of 96 days.

The second day the wind dropped, allowing us to dive on the north coast. A similar plan had to be envisaged for the following day with the same launch site as the day before. This time we were going in search of a different wreck. 10.00am struck as I manoeuvred the trailer down to the slip at Bull Bay village. As a few of our party had not yet turned up we decided to launch the boat and anchor it a little way from the shore. The late arrivals would just have to wade out with their kit. Our small band of diving enthusiasts interest of the day concerned a shipwreck named 'The Dakota', a steamship of 4332 tons, stranded on the rocks of East Mouse on the 9th May 1877. Most of the information on the wreck came from the BSAC Wreck Register, and the most interesting fact related to the cargo, bottles of wine, still full, plates and cups, some found recently. The boat, now full of divers, we set off.

Slack water was at 11.05am, we hoped we could start diving before 11.00am as time was running out. We had read in the Wreck Register that there was a four-knot current, being spring tides, so missing slack water would be drastic. I arrange with Kev, the Dive Marshall at the time, to dive last, which would give me the benefit of information on the wreck before I went down. Before my dive I learnt the wreck was well broken and spread over a wide area. Apparently the only objects of any significance were a collection of toilet bowls. I remember thinking to myself 'Oh well, souvenirs come in all different shapes and sizes.'

Under the water the visibility was not too good and the first objects to come into view were the two boilers standing out above the wreck. Deeper, I could make out scattered winch gear laying around the boilers. Swimming around the wreck it appeared to be in three sections. I soon found the area of broken earthenware, strangely there was no sign of any other bathroom related objects, only the toilet bowls. Sorting through the broken pieces I eventually found almost half a bowl. My search hadn't yielded any wine bottles or plates, so this seemed the best souvenir. Back on dry land and loaded ready to return to the camping site I took a closer look at this strange object, rubbing off one hundred years of slime. There I was confronted with the large words 'Staffordshire Earthenware', below stood the lion and the unicorn holding the royal coat of arms, obviously a popular make for royalty.

It wasn't until half way down a fairly deserted A5025 a loud crashing noise followed by a wild lurching motion brought me to my senses. Staring out through the windscreen I was unable to make out what on earth was happening. Grass and stone appeared before the car, on my right hand side was a steep grassy slope. I turned the steering wheel away from the embankment, nothing. Slowly the car moved nearer the slope, I sat, hands locking the steering wheel over, but the car refused to respond. Still moving forwards, it began a sideways roll over and over as it rolled down the embankment. Dust, diving equipment and clothes all flew about the car and, because I wasn't wearing a seat belt at the time, I joined the diving kit going over and over. Finally it came to a standstill, on its side. I climbed up and out of the driver's door. As I did so I noticed petrol running out of the carburettor, over a reasonably hot engine. Unsure of what else to do, I stood in anticipation yet thankfully it did not burst into flames.

Sitting at the edge of this ploughed field a thought, like a black cloud, slowly crept across my mind, where was the club's new boat and trailer? Standing up, all I could see high above me was a slightly broken dry stone wall. Rushing up the bank I was eventually met by a horrifying sight. The boat stood on it's side, a slow hissing sound coming from the torn and grazed inflatable pontoons. The trailer, still attached, was bent and twisted and a tyre had burst. Three or four cars had stopped, their occupants now milling around the boat. A plan was soon hatched between the crowd of helpers and myself. Firstly we'd roll the boat over on to it's right side, thereby clearing the road to enable the traffic to pass.

One of the helpers offered to run me back to the campsite to fetch the other divers. On the way I decided that I would try not to alarm them by just saying that there had been a slight accident probably due to the suspension of the car failing. On arriving back at the scene a police car awaited me, so that while my diving friends looked over the boat in disbelief, I was made to complete an accident report form. I kept on repeating that I assumed that the suspension on the car had collapsed forcing it across the road. I was informed that a breakdown truck was on it's way to retrieve the smashed car. Much banging and hammering managed to straighten the trailer enough to be towed after fitting a new tyre. I collected my things from the car including my souvenir, now slightly smaller as the smash had caused a piece to break off.

After loading my possessions into one of the cars we re-created the crime committed against the club. Protesting my innocence we re-traced the route of the car. After crossing the road it mounted the drystone wall at a place where it was much lower to the ground and at this point the trailer, with boat, had broken free and turned over. The car continued along the top of the wall, which would account for the loss of steering, considering that the wheels would be dangling either side as the car's belly tore stones off of the top. Slithering along and finally unbalancing and rolling over, the consensus was that I should feel lucky escaping without injury. As we prepared to leave the scene the break down truck arrived, two drag-lines were placed around the car and without further ado it was hauled up the embankment. To my horror the car was dragged straight through the wall making a large hole. Looking back on the whole incident it was obvious that I had fallen into a deep sleep whilst driving, something that has never happened to me before. There had been instances where I had, when driving through the night, started to nod, I am sure many have experienced the same. Having said that there have been a few times when I have fallen asleep not long after driving. The whole episode was difficult to forget, as I was fined for driving without due care and attention. £100 and four points were added to my licence, the drystone wall was another matter. An unprecedented decision was made by the Diving Club Committee to ban me from towing the boat.

5th December 1997

Breakfast has become a constant debate on our arrival date

and time. We have discussed all manner of things. Will the bars be open? How long will the Customs clearance take? Will it be dark? Lingering thoughts on our latest discussion occupies my mind for at least an hour into the morning row. Thank God I have reasonable eyebrows. They at least deflect streams of salty droplets from running straight into my eyes. My morning swim, can't come soon enough. In no time I'm scraping the bottom of the boat. I think this is becoming somewhat of a ritual. There are still no fish under the boat. I hope that it has nothing to do with the fact that I keep scraping their food off. Lunch brings me to the surface. There is only enough pasta for a further four days - hallelujah! A relaxing read this afternoon while I am off watch should maintain my good mood.

Time to write the daily fix has arrived, 13° 28′ north and 52° 38′ west, a very encouraging day's run of 60 miles. The downside is that we have dropped eleven miles south. The afternoon row, cooler now than the heat of the morning, goes quickly. he first treat of the week awaits us tonight after dinner - tinned pears with the added bonus of tinned cream. It is soon over but not forgotten.

6th December 1997

"What's the situation with the weather Graham?" said Keith looking at my dripping T-shirt.

"You may get away without getting wet, but I wouldn't guarantee it."

The weather forecast over, I dry myself and climb into my sleeping bag. The next thing I know after a particularly wet night's sleep is Keith shouting his usual breakfast wake up call.

The first row of the day starts off pretty well with a reasonably cloudless sky. The wind has moved round, only slightly, but it helps to maintain our latitude, as it is now east south east, force five to six. Every now and again a wave rises above the others a harsh reminder of the weather we had a couple of weeks ago.

Out comes the writing pad as soon as I have settled in the aft cabin.

1980 Roots: This particular trip was to The Gambia on the West Coast of Africa, not exactly a hazardous expedition, but a package tour. Landing on a hot and humid tarmac myself and Margaret had high expectations of a pleasant and luxurious break in this interesting country. The hotel where we were staying was at the centre of the waterfront port in the capital Banjul. The hotel was a relic from the old colonial days - its age was obvious from patches of peeling paint and decaying cement walls.

Compensating the drab appearance was the sound of hundreds of brightly dressed excited inhabitants rushing to and fro. Once inside our room we decided to wash and freshen up after the journey but to our amazement none of the taps worked. At the reception desk a smiling face assured us that there is no problem at all, the water is turned off while workmen fix a leak. Having also noticed that the air conditioning wasn't working either I thought I had better mention that too. Again, a straightforward answer, "At the moment the power station is undergoing major reconstruction."
Not thinking anything of it we decided to go for a walk through a

door at the back of the hotel, which opened directly onto the street. The street was filled with colourfully clothed women shouting and laughing and carrying bags bulging with strange looking vegetables. The full length of the street was one great big open market, vegetables, herbs and spices were spread out over the ground along with strange pots, pans and rolls of brightly cloth. As we walked back in the fading light a low thudding noise could be heard from the generator somewhere on the outskirts of town, and as if by some magical spell everywhere lit up as the lights came on again.

Back at our room Margaret was overjoyed by the latest development, we had running water coming from all taps. Unfortunately the cold water and the hot, were both at the same temperature, warm. The air conditioning was also working along with the lights. I am positive when I say, that neither Margaret nor myself were disillusioned by these small setbacks. Arriving at the dining room we were met by our friendly receptionist, who had now changed into what can only be described as a waitress' outfit. I remember how the dining room was empty apart from two African businessmen seated in a far corner. Studying the menu I looked at the two starters, soup of the day or egg mayonnaise. After settling for egg mayonnaise we were told that there is only soup available, "That's okay, the soup will do fine. We'll both have the lamb for the main course." I said politely. The waitress then disappeared briefly only to return looking glum.

"I am sorry Sir, Madam, there is no lamb."

We then choose steak, medium rare for Margaret and rare for me. Off goes our obliging waiter only to return with the same glum expression on her face. I helped her out, "It's not available?"

"That is correct Sir." she said timidly.

So with only one thing left on the menu we choose chicken. When the waitress returned she smiled continuously, I remember thinking to myself that John Cleese must have stayed in this hotel at some time.

The following day we decided we would take a walk along the sea front, heading south, our route would hopefully lead us to the newly built beachfront hotel where we could have lunch. There were mysteries to be found in this country, one of which I had read about, a series of ancient stone circles, which bear a striking resemblance, though much smaller, to those of Stonehenge. The Gambian circles are set at a much later date, each one enclosing a Chief buried with pottery, spears and copper bracelets. Everyone I asked, before going in search of the circles myself denied any knowledge of them.

Feeling in a relaxed mood after a day of eating, swimming and reading, we took a taxi back to our hotel. A refreshing bath in lukewarm water prepared us for dinner. Back in the dinner hall we found the menu had changed. We tried to order fish yet even that was unavailable, which was surprising considering that the fishermen had a makeshift stall filled with local fish outside the door of the hotel. It was then plainly obvious that chicken was the only dish that was cooked.

An after dinner walk seemed like the perfect way to end the day and I was surprised to see the streets still full of small groups eagerly engaging in conversation. Then, again, that dull thudding noise came back.

We decided to walk to the outskirts of the town subconsciously walking towards the constant dull thudding noise, now growing louder. As we approached the area where the noise originated all was revealed, four giant diesel generators belched black smoke, shaking and vibrating. I should have realised before how impractical the city's power supply was.

Bright sunlight burst upon us as we left the dark interior of our peaceful hotel the next day. A short walk took us to a rickety wooden pier where we would take a boat to St Andrews Island. Before long, a rust covered, flat bottomed boat, chugged into view, expelling thick clouds of black smoke from her one small funnel.

When the boat arrived I was surprised to find substantial stonework still standing despite being covered by vines. Walking round the old fort I could just imagine the anxiety of the poor slaves that were kept here years ago. Still fastened to the wall were large steel rings, used, I am sure, to hold the chains that shackled the poor creatures. Looking out over the clear waters I could just make out shapes that I took to be old cannons. Here and there lay small pieces of broken green glass, no doubt from some long since drunk and discarded rum bottles.

Leaving the ruins behind we headed up river to visit the village where supposedly Kunta Kinte was born, the hero of 'Roots', the fictional television programme. Our riverboat moored up to an ancient timber jetty, which was made of large logs tied together. Once we had disembarked a guide directed us to a circle of mud and straw huts. Groups of young children playfully joined our small gathering, pulling our hands as if personally guiding us to a round hut. An old woman emerged and ushered a few of us in. The guide informed us that she was a distant relative, and this, we are told, is the hut where Kunta Kinte was born. Receiving this information with some scepticism we glanced around the old hut, photographs hang from the walls together with a few blankets and assorted clothes, the earth floor is simple dried mud.

The weather the following day decided to change, whipping up the sea with a strong wind. I was keen to try windsurfing, a sport that had long eluded me. With breakers rolling up the white beach, mounting the board, let alone standing up was extremely problematic. I have always struggled in grasping the basic principles of windsurfing. As there were no other customers that day the instructors left me alone with the board, allowing me to persevere for well over two hours, by which time I was able to lift the sail and travel for a few yards before falling off. Up again I sailed for a few yards further until suddenly the base of the mast came out of the board hitting me straight in the mouth and knocking me into the water. Surfacing slightly stunned, I climbed back on the board before being immediately knocked off my feet by an incoming wave. After rolling over a number of times I managed to stagger to my feet again. Enough was enough. I dragged the sail and board, which luckily landed only yards away, along the beach towards the windsurfing shack. As the smiling owner of this small beach business was about to take my burden a look of horror spread across his face, catching the word 'hospital' immediately indicated all was not well. It wasn't until Margaret appeared and asked what on earth I had done to my face I realised that I had done some damage to my mouth. She handed me a mirror, blood was pouring out of my mouth. Our friendly entrepreneur immediately insisted that we go with him to the hospital. Up to this point of our holiday a tour of the old British hospital had not been on our itinerary. Dust rose from the dry pot holed road as we bounced along in a Land Rover even I would think twice about buying. Rust and black oil stains mixed to form a natural camouflage. Margaret had decided to stay behind and take refuge in a beach bar, I think, without doubt, the right option. A wave of the driver's hand permitted us a quick entry past a sleeping man who sat watching the gate. Pulling up outside the nearest building with a squeal of abused brakes we disembarked in front of a somewhat aged building, long past it's prime. Rounding a corner I was confronted by a long queue of people, some with bandaged arms and legs, others in wheelchairs. It didn't take long before it dawned on me that this endless queue was for the casualty out patients. Undeterred, my personal ambulance driver insisted that we pass this long line of people, my protests were completely ignored as I was ushered close to the front. To my amazement, instead of angry pointing fingers, I was met with greetings from more than one language.

"Jambagam."

"Samolay."

"Salaam A Leikum."

All I could do was nodded in response with a typically British, "Good morning".

When I was taken into a wooden cabin the sight took me by surprise, the floor, which I suppose was made of wooden planking, was completely covered in bloody dressings giving a gruesome impression that I was now to become part of the after effects of some terrible carnage. The doctor, looking more like a disco dancer in a large checked cap with matching trousers asked me a few questions while he cleaned my cut lips and gums. With a quick check around the inside of my mouth and a few dabs of thick purple antiseptic we were on our way back. By the time I found Margaret my top lip had swelled to twice it's normal size. The second she saw me, instead of concern she burst into hysterical laughter. Through the odd bout of hilarity I distinctly heard the name of Mick Jagger mentioned.

Looking up from my scribbling I can see Keith tying up the oars, it has already passed the change over time.

"Sorry Keith, I just get carried away with this doodling. I'll write down the fix after my watch."

The afternoon row always seems much easier than it does at night, I am sure it is all to do with the visual surroundings.

The small cloud formations are always different. Today cirrus streaks lightly fill the sky. These whiffs of smoky cloud appear to move across the sky at high speed. No great towering monsters today, only the odd few larger waves sometimes crossing at different angles. Time for the fix as my watch comes to an end. I start the GPS and take the first position, 13° 32′ north and 53° 36′ west. We've dropped another four miles on our latitude - must try to creep back up during the night.

7th December 1997

My nose wakes me up this morning as the smell of baked beans drifts through the cabin. I had completely forgotten the Sunday morning ritual! We worked out that there are enough tins of beans to keep us going until the end of the trip, one every Sunday that is.

"Come and get it while it's hot." said Keith, his smiling face appearing above the steaming saucepan. Although we had been eating baked beans every Sunday morning for the last six weeks, today seemed to be different. It isn't until I looked at the plate I realise why, there, mixed in between the beans were pieces of bacon. "Why didn't you tell me Keith?"

"I thought I'd surprise you."

"You know Keith, I've forgotten what bacon tastes like." Each piece was carefully picked out from the beans, chewed, eaten, and then commented on.

"A little bit salty, I'm sure that was a piece of smoked."

What a relief to dive over the side after my morning row. This is then followed by some medical attention to my backside, a squirt of toothpaste and a good scrub with my moulting toothbrush.

This is going to be no ordinary lunch today - it's the last of the pasta. Something I'm sure I'll never eat again. As much as I would like to put some fine rich sauce with it, gravy browning was the only thing left.

A slight sense of achievement prevailed as I climbed once more into our small covered world. Back to my book and Maurice has volunteered to crew on his wife's boat for a trip to Holland, and from his own words, it is, 'Not a happy thought.' I can now sympathise, having been at sea for some 56 days. Reading the last few lines of the second story brings back vivid memories of my own trip across the North Sea, leaving Ostend to be battered by a relentless gale.

I sailed with difficulty in a friend's 26' boat. I'm not usually prone to seasickness, only the normal bouts of nausea. On this occasion I had eaten a few roll mop herrings, which were quickly deposited back into the sea. Hanging on in this state of misery as the cockpit gyrated underneath me, I glanced over my shoulder for a second, and there, some distance away high in the sky was what must have been a red parachute flare. Shouting to my companion, who turned around just in time to catch the last sight before being lost in the black swirling cloud a quick decision had to be made. At this moment the boat was hard pressed, the main sail was reefed as small as possible, but even this area of canvas was too much for the lightweight boat. By turning back we would, without doubt, put ourselves in danger.

A call was made to Ostend Radio on Channel 27, the response garbled and inaudible. Switching back to Channel 16, a rough position and time explaining the sighting was given in case any other boats in the vicinity were listening. Shortly afterwards the wind dropped slightly bringing us more worries as this allowed the fog to descend on us just as we entered the shipping lane. Over the next two hours ships foghorns blew out of the murky night becoming louder then slowly growing quiet.

Once back home all was forgotten until two days later, glancing through the daily paper an article loomed out at me. 'Still no trace of fishing boat lost off the coast at Ramsgate, it's last position in the main shipping lane.' This wasn't far from our course and within hours of seeing the flare. I could not believe that there was any connection, mere coincidence. The story faded from memory until three weeks later I noticed an article in the newspaper, 'Wreck of fishing boat found, some bodies recovered.' From the damage and latest time of sinking, the article suggested that the unfortunate boat had been hit and had capsized trapping some of the poor crew inside, who, one would imagine, had waited hoping to be rescued. Tragedy as the upturned boat drifted helplessly until hit again by another large boat sending it to the bottom. This, of course, was only my theory.

Closing the book I realised that it was time for the fix, 13° 38′ north and 54° 33′ west. At last our efforts have paid off over the last 24 hours and we have actually gained six miles in latitude. Rowing north west is rather soul destroying, knowing it slows down our passage. Climbing out I pledge to carry on rowing north west.

8th December 1997

A vague voice rouses my dreamy mind. I open my eyes just as a burst of seawater tears through the open hatch and soaks the bottom half of me together with the sleeping bag. Keith explains that a medium sized wave had suddenly changed it's direction and curled over the bulwarks. This was the first time during the trip that a wave had found it's way through the main cabin hatch. The sea-state at the time could not have more than force four, which wasn't half as bad as it had been. After discarding the sleeping bag and bailing out the foot well, which was half full of water, it seems pointless to try and sleep as there are only ten minutes left before we change watch. Feeling a little cheated out of ten minutes sleep I begin rowing, the wind has come round slightly to east south east, which allowed me to row a more westerly course. It would have been a great advantage to row a straight course with the wind directly behind the boat, but from the very first day I knew this was not going to be possible.

How I envy the other competitors, some having had as much as a year to test their boats on the open water. It would not have taken them long to realise the importance of weight displacement reacting on the boat in a following wind. We were the only ones in the entire race to launch for the very first time only 24 hours before the official start. In retrospect I don't suppose that anybody could seriously alter their boat, the main criteria for the race was that the boats were to be exactly the same. The small relaxation on the rules could hardly change the way the boat travelled with the wind behind it. Although it would be good to talk to the few who altered their keels before the race, just to compare performance.

Rising for breakfast bleary eyed, I sip at the freshly poured coffee and initiate our, now regular, topic of conversation, our arrival.

"At least we haven't been blown south Keith. I think that there's a 99% chance that we'll make the north end of the island."

"Let's have a look at the sketch you were given of the north. I can only agree with you Graham, most of the boats are expected to head for the north."

"This drawing gives us a good idea of what to expect, and another thing Keith, it shows two turning places with a latitude and longitude. We can put them into the GPS as way points." I said. "The first one is a mile off Archer's Bay and the second one is North Point Lighthouse."

"What does it say for the characteristics of the lighthouse?"

"Flashing two over fifteen seconds with a range of 22 miles, 198 metres high. The only trouble with that, looking at it, I think that it will be blanketed by land. Strange though Keith, when I look at the chart, the lights of Harrison Point and the Tower, which I assume to be the lighthouse, flashed red once every 25 seconds. At least on the chart it shows the arc of visibility."

The discussion continues for some time. I wonder what light we'll see first.

"What about Ragged Point, Graham?"

"That's got to be the one flashing once every 15 seconds. I'd better start rowing or we'll never get there."

The morning flies by as I try to imagine our landfall. During my morning swim I catch sight of a group of small brown fish, unfortunately once I get in the water they all swim away. Drying myself, thoughts of food give me a roaring appetite. Today's lunch was to be the first without the obligatory pasta. Two pouches of chilli con carne later I retire to the aft cabin for a session of pen pushing.

1988 An Explosive Situation:
The first day of working on my boat, 'The Albion', at West Mercia, went strangely to plan. My helper during this working holiday was my diving friend Little Graham, whose motive for giving me a helping hand was not exactly out of enthusiasm for wooden boats. It was the usual promise made with the shake of hands over a considerable quantity of alcoholic beverages.

Our first days labour involved removing the diesel tank from underneath the counter stern - not an easy task considering the small space below the narrow deck. By the end of the first day the tank lay on the cockpit floor cleaned of all the loose rust. As the small pinholes did not necessarily warrant a major welding job we decided to solder.

Rising early we began by flushing the tank in readiness for the arranged soldering work. All went well and by the end of the day there stood the 'Albion's' diesel tank soldered and painted with two coats of car body under-seal. Apart from a few other minor jobs, the only distraction during the last two days was the inshore lifeboat. With the blustery weather, a few unfortunate sailors had found themselves in dangerous situations.

The first indication of a problem usually began with the alarm on the side of the newly built lifeboat shed bursting into life, followed by the screeching brakes of vehicles pulling up outside. Rushing feet on shingle, whoosh, and the inevitable bang of the flare to call the lifeboat crew. The third day dawned with a clear sky, thinking it to be a good omen we began work early, me, carrying on replacing a few small frames while Little Graham fitted the diesel tank. Engrossed in the difficulties involved in replacing a small frame I missed Little Graham's first shout and the second made me jump.

"What's up?" I asked.

"I've just tested the tank with two gallons of diesel and it's still leaking from one part."

"Fibreglass," I said, "It's too much trouble to start soldering now."

But Little Graham insisted that he could solder the tank pulled slightly out from under the deck. At the same time my stomach began to rumble starting a chain reaction, which always ends with a rush to the toilet, thankfully the public convenience was only a short walk away. Seated in the appropriate manner contemplating the difficulties that had arisen over the last few days I was shaken by an almighty thump accompanied by a loud bang. I could feel the ground trembling beneath my feet. My immediate thought, the lifeboat, maroons exploding in the sky having been called out yet again. Pictures of a speeding craft arriving at some stricken boat just in time as it slowly slides beneath the surface. These thoughts soon fade as I finish my morning ablutions and walk out of the front door of these recently built toilets. Little Graham rushed into view, at first lost for words, then in a kind of muted speech said, "I've blown myself up."

Pushing past him I shouted, "The boat, what have you done to the boat?"

I dashed through the dinghy park expecting to find a burned out hulk, but everything looked normal except for the still smoking diesel tank that was lying on the loose shingle, peeled like a giant banana.

"Thanks for your sympathetic words."

"Sorry Little Graham, for a minute I thought you'd blown up the boat.'

Dropping his trousers to show me his legs I realised that he must have been in considerable pain, they were black, purple and blue. Not wanting to hurt his feelings I had to ask, "How's your wedding tackle?"

"Very painful but looks okay."

"Come on, we'll go for a coffee and you can tell me all about it."
While drinking the hot beverage Little Graham unfolded the story.

"Forgetting that we hadn't flushed the tank since testing it with diesel I began to heat the area ready for soldering. I was about to put down the soldering iron when suddenly there was a huge explosion and I felt myself being hurled into the air. Fortunately for me I landed back onto the aft deck rather than 10′ below onto the shingle, so did the burning diesel tank. The boat, having survived the explosion was now in danger of burning so I grabbed the tank and threw it over the deck burning my hands in the process."
Having made the point of how he had sacrificed himself to save the boat from catching fire I knew that my limit on pints of beer tonight in the pub would have to go by the wayside.

Time to take the fix, 13° 27′ north and 55° 32′ west, another eleven miles further south, this means we must continue rowing north west.

9th December 1997
The light goes on and I know it's 3.00am already.

"Right Keith, be there in a minute." I said.
Wind north easterly, force four to five, no ships sighted. The sky is almost clear. I gaze up after the first few strokes, finding the largest signpost in the sky almost immediately - Orion. I am positive that there is a lot more to Orion than described in this small paperback of only 32 pages. I'll have to read up on it when I get back. If only the binoculars hadn't got water logged.

Morning brings the familiar clanking of the stove being fitted to the bracket, a very welcoming sound. The morning row is well under way by the time the clouds have cleared, leaving us at the mercy of the hot sun once more. Throughout the row I have been looking out for the large fish we saw yesterday.

At last my watch comes to an end and I am over the side in a flash. I begin my usual morning task of scraping the bottom with the old sweet tin when a feeling that someone is watching comes over me, turning my head I see another pair of eyes slowly gliding by approximately six feet away. They belong to a five feet long Dorado. It's yellow body turns turquoise green towards the top with silver underneath. As it swims by I notice a white line dangling from it's mouth. Is that Keith's fishing line? He did say that he had lost the hook and lure. After circling me a few times it swims away and I reluctantly climbed back onto the boat. During lunch I tell Keith of my chance meeting under the boat.

"Are you sure it was a fishing line?" he asked.

"Yes. I tried to communicate by eye contact to inform that I was the innocent party."

"You make me sound like some careless hunter. If he was up here and not under there you'd be the first to get your chops round him."

"He's like good omen."

"That's it Graham, I think you've finally gone mad."

"I think he's like Moby Dick. I can just see you rattling your bones to see what the future holds. What was his name, Queequeg? Fortunately we have nothing on board to make a coffin. Do you remember the tale Keith? As soon as the bones were thrown, Queequeg saw death and had the ship's carpenter make a coffin."

"I think that all this writing is going to your head

Graham."

"In that case I think I'll do a bit of reading."

10th December 1997

I am awake before Keith turns on the light, a quick glance at my small paperback before emerging under an overcast sky.

"Some rain showers about but we've escaped so far." With that exchange of information, Keith climbs into the aft cabin. An hour into my row the sky begins to clear leaving a small cloud formation I scan the sky. I search for the Square of Pegasus. That's got to be it.

Keith, looking at yesterday's fix of 13° 21′ north we can't go further south than 13° 20′, only another half mile."

"Yes, I know. As long as we're still 13° 21′ north at today's fix I'll be happy."

"You know Keith, if the wind goes round to the north and starts to blow we'll have to gain a few miles north before attempting to go round the north end of the island. It would be a horrible end to the trip to be blown onto those reefs."

This morning's row seems lasts forever, the only consolation is that the water supply has lasted well since rationing, we can now drink more without worrying.

The seawater feels even better today, looking around I am pleased to see a few friendly fish. Two Blue Fin Tuna, approximately 16" long, swim around followed by two slightly smaller silvery yellow fish. I think they're Horse Mackerel. As I scrape they dart here and there picking up the crustaceans that drift by then suddenly they dart off. Swimming back to the stern I can just make out a shape approaching. It's our friendly Dorado complete with white string still dangling from it's mouth. Just as I am about to turn my head another shape emerges, a second Dorado, slightly smaller, as I swim under the boat they both keep circling, always keeping their distance until finally swimming away. During lunch I tell Keith that our friend with the mouth string had brought his mate along to see us. I think he thinks I'm going mad. Maybe I am going mad.

It is now a pleasure to climb into the aft cabin out of the hot sun, with the rear hatch open the cool breeze that blows through is great, perfect for scribbling.

1973 Al Capone's Henchman: I had been working hard all week on a loft conversion just outside Bath. My part-time helper, a Bathonian Postman and I were happy to accept an invitation from some of his friends to a fancy dress party on the Saturday night. Being a bit on the conventional side I went as one of Al Capone's henchmen. Where I got my double breasted pin stripe suit I'll never remember. The grey fedora I borrowed from grandfather. I wasn't sure at the time, and I'm still not sure to this day if I looked like a hardened gangster or an overdressed saxophonist.

Finding a parking space for my battered Morris Minor outside a local pub, the Postman had suggest I ventured inside feeling slightly self-conscious but I need not have worried, there standing at the bar was Robin Hood in close conversation with Count Dracula. Beside them stood Captain Bligh, the mutiny had obviously not set him back much looking at the large round he was buying. I was relieved to see the familiar face of the postman, even though the only clothes around his body were rough animal skins.

He was holding a large plastic club covered in rubber nails ordering a couple of pints of the local beer, gleefully swinging the weapon around his head. The night drew on and it was time to set off to the party. The Postman agreed. Waiting at the bar I remember seeing him disappear briefly before returning with a Belly Dancer, who was arm in arm with Cleopatra.

Having driven approximately half a mile, who should I see thumbing a lift but a full sized gorilla complete with head and as I have never had a gorilla as a passenger this seemed to be the ideal time. We had only gone a hundred yards when a uniformed Policeman stepped out onto the road, holding his hand up for us to stop, this was when I remembered that I had drunk three or four pints of beer and became a little nervous. We weren't exactly the most inconspicuous group. Pulling to a stop the Police Constable approached, "Going to a fancy dress party?' he asked.

"Yes officer." I replied hoping he didn't hear the fear in my voice.

"Good, move over so that I can get in."

And that is how we arrived, three somewhat squashed individuals, a Police Officer, a gorilla and an excuse for Al Capone's batman.

It's time for another cross, 13° 21′ north and 57° 13′ west. It could have been better but forty-five miles will have to do. Looking at how tantalisingly close Barbados seems to be on the chart I can almost imagine the island. The afternoon row passes without any problems, dinner is chicken casserole followed by a late read.

11th December 1997

The bright light of the cabin slowly lights up my dark sleepy world. Pulling on my T-shirt and waterproofs I climb out.

"I don't think you'll need those, the rain squalls have been way over to the south."

"We'll see how it goes Keith."

After about an hour I begin to think that I was inciting the weather to do it's worst by wearing my waterproofs as black rain clouds headed straight for us. I could feel the wind building and there was a light downpour that becomes heavier as the massive black clouds block out last the few visible stars, as if the hard physical drain of rowing is not enough.

At last my wet and cold body slowly warms as the rain clouds pass, a cold trickle of water runs down past my waist until there is a small pool nicely trapped in my underpants, a wet backside, again. I suppose there is one thing about this squally weather - it gives me something to think about. Which rain clouds will pass overhead? Most pass either side, giving only a hint of wind and light rain as the outer edges of the cloud pass above. Two hours pass and I eagerly put on the kettle for my early morning mug of coffee in the hope that the rain keeps away while I relax for five minutes whilst drinking it.

The sunshine always seems to perk me up if I am feeling a bit down. 12.30pm brings another refreshing swim and, in no time, our friend turns up, this time without his buddy. Today he swims around the boat for a much longer period darting by me every now and again. Lunch is a far more relaxing affair knowing we are only two days away from land and that the food is not going to run out. Afterwards, while Keith rows, I finish reading my book, a bit reluctantly. 'The Magic of the Swatchways' has got to be one of the best books I have ever read. I am tempted to start from the beginning again but instead I dig out one of the last books from under the floor, hoping that it hasn't gone the same way as the binoculars, fortunately it is stored at the opposite end of the main under floor locker and dry. 'Redburn', by Herman Melville, a story I read a few years ago, quite a few years when I think about it. After getting reacquainted with the beginning the time has rolled on and it is time for the daily fix, 13° 19′ north and 57° 58′ west, another 45 miles nearer.

12th December 1997

Whack! I have only been rowing five minutes into my three-hour watch when suddenly I receive a cold slap across the face and, from the sound of vigorous flapping, we must have taken on board approximately eight or nine Flying fish. It is the first sign that there is a shoal of Dorado hunting their prey. The poor old Flying fish, a shoal will leap out of the water when chased and glide anything up to one hundred feet. Trying to catch these flapping slippery creatures is another thing. Most of the time they get washed into all kinds of places on the boat, with buckets, bottles and oars strapped around the deck there are loads of places for them to become jammed in, unseen by the eye until a tell tale smell of rotting fish wafts past your nostrils.

At the moment the sky is clear giving me an opportunity to do a little stargazing. After the first hour I can see my stargazing coming to an end as black clouds head this way, I decide to have my coffee now. The last hour of my stint is a constant downpour. The wind is blowing at what must be gale force conditions. I brief Keith on what to expect and dive into the dry aft cabin.

During breakfast, and before the conversation gets round to our impending landfall, I ask Keith how he had coped with the weather. To my amazement he informs me that the wind was blowing north east and there hadn't been a drop of rain. I can't believe it.

Two thirds of the way into my watch a giant splash attracts my attention, it is our friend the Dorado. He must have leaped out of the water about four times last night. He really does jump an amazing height, at least seven to eight feet and right beside the boat, it is almost as if he is trying to communicate with us. My morning swim can't come soon enough.

Almost immediately our Dorado appears, swimming around the boat, and each time that he turns, his eyes seem to be staring straight at me. Today he swims slowly up alongside of me and hovers a mere 12" away, his mouth clearly visible. I think it's time to give you a name. 'Nigel', you seem like a Nigel. The idea then occurs to me to try and remove the hook. Slowly I edge my hand towards his mouth, still he remains in the same position, my thumb and forefinger close on the line hanging from his mouth and as I touch it he moves his head away and swims off into the distance after circling one last time. I knew, sadly, that that was to be our final meeting.

Climbing back onto the boat I told Keith that I had attempted to remove the hook and he agrees that it was a kind gesture to this unfortunate fish.

Lunch is a larger affair today, meatballs in pasta sauce, beans and bacon, followed by fruit dumplings in butterscotch sauce, we have assumed this to be our last on board 'The George

Geary'. Keith rows while I go through the same routine and retire to the aft cabin. I was expecting to be in an excited state being so close, but my mood hasn't changed in the slightest. So I do what I have every other day, reach for pen and paper and write down a day's thoughts. Most of my thoughts and memories occur during the long rowing hours of darkness, probably due to the lack of visual contact with my surroundings.

1993 Stormy Memories: Looking through the quarterly magazine from my local Night School produced by the New Parks Cruising Association, a few lines caught my eye, 'Crew wanted for Atlantic delivery, Antigua to Falmouth, sailing a Moody Forty Seven, contact Ron Barratt'. This I did and was pleased to find that one of the crew was someone that I had got to know through the Yacht Masters courses at night school, Hugh Butler. At the time Hugh was teaching others his skills. he skipper for the trip was Mike Baines, who was already in Antigua. Two more crew who had already agreed to go were friends of the skipper, Dave and John, I was to be the last. after a brief meeting halfway between our homes at a café on the M6 we decide to leave on the 26th April.

The first setback happened on the air trip to Antigua, flying via Barbados. Our charter tickets for Barbados did include a return although we would not be using it, whereas the second part of our flight, Barbados to Antigua had been bought as single tickets, which we duly presented at the customs.

"Sorry sir you cannot fly one way to Antigua without a return ticket."

"But we're sailing back to England from Antigua." I said with a rather confused look on my face.

"Sorry sir, you will have to buy a return ticket and obtain a

refund from the Airline office in Antigua."
Although it seemed like a strange and pointless procedure, I agreed.

Landing in Antigua we made our way to Falmouth Harbour for a meet with Mike, who unfortunately was waiting at the bar next door rather than the one we found ourselves in. A few beers later we decided to have a look around and fortunately bumped into him. He wasn't too pleased, but I'm sure to this day it was his mistake, not ours. The first day was spent partly on business and part sightseeing at English Harbour, Nelson's House, Dry-docks and the Officers Quarters built on the top of a four hundred and fifty ton water cistern. Two trips to the Customs saw us on the crew list, and our first full day finished with a few drinks in the local bars in English Harbour. This gave us the chance to talk to boat crews who had come specifically to race. It was Antigua Race Week and boats from all over the world were there to take part in the race.

Our second day was spent on a trip to the capital, St John's, and emergency dental treatment for John. Rather him than me, considering that he had to be careful with what pain killing injections he could have because he has had a triple bypass operation. I now knew where his 'Dickey Ticker Club' T- Shirts came from. While his painful treatment took place the rest of us went on to the airport to claim our money back on the return tickets. Another blow, we had to be paid in Eastern Caribbean Dollars that would not much good to us on our way back. We return to St John's to collect John who was relieved to be free of the dentist.

It was time for a drink before attacking the Ministry of Finance in order to obtain a permit that would allow us to change our Caribbean Dollars into Sterling. That evening was also spent in the relaxing atmosphere of a few local taverns, but with a purpose. Quite a large group of boats were leaving to sail to England at the end of the week and a radio network had been fixed for a daily call from all of the boats involved.

Day three and at last the anchor came up with a sail to St Martin, which gave us the opportunity to practise sail handling and reefing. Specific areas of responsibility were dished out, safety, engine, and deck equipment. As I am far from mechanically minded, mine was the engine! Mooring in Philipsburg in the early hours of the morning on the fourth day we hoped to fill the boat for our Atlantic crossing with cheap fruit and supermarket bargains. A sail to this island was not complete without a visit to the local carnival and calypso competition. Five EC Dollars bought an entry ticket including a free condom and appropriate health warnings.

Up came the anchor and we set off for England. 25 of wind brought a lumpy sea, an east south east wind just allows us to clear the islands. Two days of snacks due to odd bouts of nausea left me with an enormous appetite on the third day. Radio chats with nearest boats 'Viva', 'Dana' and 'Castaway' became a daily routine at midday. A welcome radio station, Herb, transmitting from Barbados, kept all the boats up to date with the latest weather. Our watch system seemed to work smoothly, Hugh and I starboard, John and Dave port watch. Each watch took turns at being galley slaves, cooking and washing up, while the others, boat skivvies, checked the engine, water and oil and cleaned the toilets - Mike oversaw all of this.

Halfway through our journey home the genoa roller reefing snapped in 35 knots of wind. Time appeared to stand still as we tried to bring it under control. Aboard a deck that rose out of the sea one minute then plunged under the next this was not easy. I remember hearing

Herb transmitting warnings of deepening depressions, hearing this we checked the routing chart and discovered that this part of the Atlantic, for the month of May, had virtually not experienced any serious storms for the past twenty years. The barometer was steady at one thousand and twenty millibars. Gradually, through the night, our confident mood dissolved, and by dawn the wind was up to 50 knots - force 10. All of the cabin lights began to leak, cushions, shelves, books, even the radio was wet through. We heaved to and dropped the mainsail. I was wrestling with the sail as the wind endeavoured to wrench it from my hands.

The next afternoon we decided to reduce the reefed genoa to almost nothing considering that we would still be sailing at ten knots. The repaired reefing line jammed virtually putting an end to our idea of sailing under bare poles. The thought of trying to repair it had to be dispelled as the foredeck was under the water fifty per cent of the time. We sailed on leaving what was left of the genoa behind.

High on adrenaline I wanted to stay on deck as long as possible. Two hours of driving rain sent everybody down below, apart from me, this was my watch. Most of the steering was by the wind vane, steering gear adjustments had to be made every now and again. The skipper gave me a course change that headed away from the depression. Realising that it was too late the instruction to heave to was delivered. One of jobs I had been given before setting sail was to lash 10, 5 gallon, plastic cans full of diesel somewhere on the deck where they would be out of the way. The only place I found that was suitable was within the confines of the safety bars attached to the deck that kept us supported whilst working at the mast. Fortunately for me I had spent a considerable amount of time ensuring that they were lashed solid. Every time a wave rolled up the deck, the cans impeded its progress. Despite the circumstances a good evening meal was served. As I had the last watch before the evening meal I was given a break of nine hours until I had to return to my watch.

Sleep was much easier than I had imagined, being on the top bunk a few adjustments had to be made to prevent me from hitting the roof of the fore-cabin every time that the boat lurched. My kit bag full of clothes made a perfect wedge between me, and the ceiling. 3.00am on that wild, storm tossed night was not as pleasant as I had hoped, watching the wind indicator flicking up to 60 knots did not help.

As daylight emerged through the storm laden skies the wind started to drop. The barometer, now on 1000 millibars, exactly the same as when I came on watch, a few sharp taps with my finger made no difference.

The boat was sailing again by the time that I was back in my bunk. Climbing out at 9.00am, the first thing I did was glance at the barometer, still 1000 millibars. Everyone assumed that the storm had past, the wind then was only approximately 30 miles per hour. With the sun shining down we dried the boat by opening the hatches. In a relieved mood we managed to untangle the reefing line that enabled us to set more foresail with the main still lashed. We gathered from the radio broadcast that the storm centre was approximately 31° north, 53° degrees west. Our midday position was 32° 09′ north, 52° 04′ west. All indications led us to believe that it had passed south of our position. During the course of the afternoon, as yesterday, the wind began to increase, by 6.30pm we had 40 knots and above, the genoa is reefed again. The barometer was then showing 997 millibars and falling, a decision was made to heave to.

With the experience of the night before we knew that she lies well in the water, presenting her port bow to the wind and waves. Earlier in the day while sorting out the genoa I had inspected the lashings on the diesel cans, which to my amazement stood firm. With the boat's increasingly erratic movements dinner was a much more basic affair. The barometer, by this time, was at 993 millibars, if only I could stick something against the needle to prevent it from falling any more.

I made a definite effort to climb into my bunk at 10.30pm, 20 minutes of hard labour was rewarded as I hoisted up the lee cloth. Being too slow to wedge myself between the ceiling of the cabin resulted in a heavy thud as my head made contact with the fibreglass. Sleep did not come too easily, laying there with the booming noise as consecutive waves pounded the side of the boat, although, eventually, I did doze off. I woke to a hand shaking me, I feared the worst, "What's the matter?"

My tormentor was Dave. "The skipper's asked me to wake you, he thinks we ought to be dressed in waterproofs and life jackets just in case."

I looked at my watch. It was 11.00pm, four hours before my turn out in the windswept nightmare. Trying to dress in my wet weather gear, life jacket and harness was difficult as the boat lurched about like a wild beast. Once in the main cabin I could see that John had a serious expression on his face.

"How are we doing?" I asked.

"Mike and Hugh are out in the cockpit watching for the first signs of damage to the boat. The wind's over 60 knots and going off of the clock at 70."

John did not have to spell it out - hurricane. I checked the barometer, 985, then the hatch opened and the voice of the skipper, "Graham, get out the sheet of ply and handsaw, we may lose windows." Just the thing I wanted to hear after being woken up. As I rummaged around for the pieces of ply I noticed that the life raft was now lashed to the bottom of the companionway.

My watch came along, the first hour the skipper sat with me shouting out odd observations about the storm over the roar of the wind. Fortunately for us the diesel cans were preventing the force of the waves as they rushed along the deck. By the time they reached the spray dodger, their force was spent and the seawater just cascaded off the sides. To lose the spray dodger would have been a real blow as it provided good protection from the elements. Every now and again a wave would race in from a different angle, break over the cockpit and flood the foot-well, but soon drained. I couldn't help but sit mesmerised by towering waves, some 35 to 40' high. By the third hour of my watch the wind wasn't rising above 60 knots, the worst was over. Thinking back on that night I am disappointed not to have any photographs of the people or the situations on the boat, only memories.

Over the radio the next day we hear that 'Aurora', our nearest yacht, was knocked down twice sustaining some damage. Of the 12 yachts that left around the same time as us, two were lost, but as far as we could make out over the radio, there was no loss of life.

The following day the wind had dropped to 40 knots, control lines on the wind vane steering gear finally gave way under the strain. Then that night when I was on watch, the inner fore-stay parts gave way too. I then had the unfortunate task of informing the skipper, who was asleep at the time. We rigged a temporary one with the spare halyard as soon as daylight appeared.

I learnt when we made port at Horta Harbour, Faial, in the Azores that two boats were lost in the storm, one, 'The Ocean Vagabond', on passage to England with a crew of six. Luckily all aboard were picked up by another boat. The other boat lost was less fortunate, she was on a passage to France. A large cargo boat picked up the crew of three after they abandoned their life raft. Sadly the skipper, being the last to leave, slipped from the ladders hanging down the side and fell back into the sea, nothing was ever seen of him again.

The break on Horta, talking with the 100 or so yacht crews sailing the Atlantic one way or the other was a very interesting experience.

Two days later we were sailing for England only to be met by two more storms. One on 25th of May when the barometer dropped to 995 millibars, with 40 knots of wind, then on the 28th and 29th similar wind strengths, finally arriving at Falmouth on the 1st June.

I put away my writing pad because that was the last story, and, by a strange coincidence, there are no clean pages left. Is this going to be the last fix? I hope so. 13° 22′ north and 58° 56′ west, only 43 miles to Archers Bay, that is according to the drawing we were given of the north coast of Barbados. Looking at the chart there is no Archers Bay, only North Point.

"Just 43 miles to go Keith."

Immediately after dinner the sky clouds over and the wind rises, though still in our favour, east north east. I put the stove away and glance up, there, before my eyes, is Barbados - a grey distant headland. I turn towards Keith, strangely unemotional.

"I've just seen Barbados."

Keith turned to me and a broad grin crossed his face.

"We've made it. What an incredible sight."

It is now 7.00pm and Keith rows with added passion while I prepare to cut my hair and beard, although we have no mirror. I know that I must resemble Robinson Crusoe without hair, well most of it. I find the little pair of scissors that I bought before leaving, now rusted with the blades seized together. An extensive search under the seat locker finally reveals a tin of easing oil, which, after liberal doses, eventually does the trick. This is another first in my life, cutting my hair and beard by touch alone.

Eating dinner later this evening the watches are changed I climb into the aft cabin for an hours sleep before my watch at 10.00pm. Switching the cabin light on at 9.55pm I peer out at Keith and am amazed to see him still dry.

"You must live a charmed life Keith, how come those rain clouds didn't get you?"

"You always think the worst Graham, has anyone ever told you that?"

"I can see that you got the light at Ragged Point."

"Yes, it's been in view for about an hour, not long after you turned in. Anyway, it's all yours."

I climb out wearing only a weatherproof top and T-shirt anticipating the best. 30 minutes later the skies open. By the time I have put my hood up, half a pint of rain water has already gone down my neck. How does he always get away with it?

The sky clears about 15 minutes before Keith's watch.

"How did you get on?" he said looking with a smirk at the water now collected in the foot well. "I see you've not bothered to bail out the foot well."

"I can't see the point Keith, it's going to piss it down any minute." I say.

Water in the foot well has been a constant problem, the wale gusher pump works fine when the open end of the hose is permanently under water, with the side to side motion of the boat air is soon sucked in cancelling the drawing action. I had intended to build duck boards for the floor, which would have kept our feet out of the swilling water, but I never got round to it.

13th December 1997

The cabin light awakens me. I look at the clock, 2.55am.

"How's the weather?" I say trying to speak through a giant yawn.

"It's been okay, I've bailed out the foot well."

"Well I hope it stays dry now you've gone to the trouble."

"The course is about 280 magnetic.' said Keith.

"Sounds like that north easterly wind has pushed us too far south."

"It looks that way, we'll just have to keep plodding on."

I put on my weatherproof bottoms, a wise decision as 10 minutes later the rain starts lashing down. The only consolation in this misery is that we are drawing nearer the north of the island, probably now only six to eight miles away.

At 5.00am I decide to take another look ahead, there in the distance I can see navigation lights and can tell from the way that the port and starboard lights are keeping the same configuration that a vessel is heading straight for us. The white steering light indicates that it could be *3 Com* motoring out to meet us. I shout to Keith to tell him. We should turn on the battery light to help them see us.

I row on and eventually the black silhouette of a large sailing boat motors around us. Keith got on the VHF and it was confirmed that they have come to guide us in. With the wind strength increasing rowing becomes more difficult. The nearer we get to the north end of the island the steeper the waves become. We are thrown about as these short breaking waves batter the boat, shouting to Keith over the roar of the wind, "I can't believe that we've faced severe storms out in the ocean and here we are nearly at journey's end and the weather does this to us."
We continue with Keith steering and me rowing, for the next hour. Looking across at *3 Com* I can see that they are fairing no better as the large boat is thrown about like a toy in the short waves. Keith shouts above the noise of the relentless wind that he is going to clear the forward seat and row too. I agree that more speed would give us better steerage way.

Dawn sees us both striving to clear the headland. Finally the sea becomes calmer as we round the north side of the island. Three hours have passed since we began rowing as a pair, not only is it brightening, but the ugly grey clouds have almost vacated the sky. A red burning sun now rises over the land. People start to appear on the deck of *3 Com* taking photographs of us, their silhouettes against the sunrise. Slowly we draw level with Harrison Lighthouse, the time about 10.15am. I have been rowing non-stop for seven hours, time to put on the kettle.

We both stop rowing and look back at *3 Com* where people are sitting on the deck, two of whom have been on deck for some time now come into focus. I cannot believe it, Brett and John,

Brett, who had spent so much time helping me build the boat, and John, my old business partner, who had come to see me off, there they were, both staring over.

"I'm glad to see you two have come over to row the boat back." I shout.

That particular drink of coffee tasted incredible along with, of course, my half a Peak bar, which I cut into two halves, and feeling generous mood, gave one to Keith.

Feeling refreshed we begin rowing again past the Cement Works jetty where we are joined by a flat bottomed sight-seeing boat. Eyeing the passengers shouting encouragement, I recognise Mark and Steve from *Toc H Phoenix*, John Searson from *Commodore Shipping*, and a few others. We pass the Cement Works and the wind now decided that we were having things too easy and turned, more or less dead against us.

At first we're unable to see the harbour entrance, only a mass of rock and steel piles. The tourist boat stayed with us, those on board shouting directions as we struggle against the wind;

"Hard a port, hard a starboard."

I glance round and could see that the rocks on both sides enclosed the entrance. Suddenly the sound of a loud hooter burst out. We've made it!

Wobbling on unsteady legs I lost my balance, reached for an oar and fell overboard still wearing my lucky working cap. Submerged in the cool water I swam to the ladders and climbed up to the quay. Up until that moment I had no idea how thin our legs had become. Shuffling along I wondered if I would ever walk properly again.

Out of the remaining competitors we have come tenth, a position neither Keith nor I had envisaged in our wildest dreams.

Soon seated in a crowd of well-wishers, food and beer was placed in front of us. This moment will hopefully live in my memory for many years to come.

Little Things

Little drops of water, little grains of sand
make the mighty ocean and the pleasant land.
So the little minutes, humble though they be,
make the mighty ages of eternity.

Julia Carney (1823-1908)

Glossary of Nautical Terms

Abaft the beam	Further aft than the beam: a relative bearing of greater than 90 degrees from the bow: "two points abaft the port beam". That would describe "an object lying 22.5 degrees toward the rear of the ship, as measured clockwise from a perpendicular line from the right side, center, of the ship, toward the horizon.
Alee	1. On the lee side of a ship. 2. To leeward.
Astern	1. Toward the stern (rear) of a vessel. 2. Behind a vessel
Beam	The width of a vessel at the widest point, or a point alongside the ship at the midpoint of its length.
Belay	1. To make fast a line around a fitting, usually a cleat or belaying pin. 2. To secure a climbing person in a similar manner. 3. An order to halt a current activity or countermand an order prior to execution.
Bilge	The compartment at the bottom of the hull of a ship or boat where water collects and must be pumped out of the vessel.
Block	A pulley or set of pulleys.
Bobstay	A stay which holds the bowsprit downwards, counteracting the effect of the forestay. Usually made of wire or chain to eliminate stretch.
Bowline	A type of knot, producing a strong loop of a fixed size, topologically similar to a sheet bend. Also a rope attached to the side of a sail to pull it towards the bow (for keeping the windward edge of the sail steady).
Bowsprit	A spar projecting from the bow used as an anchor for the forestay and other rigging.
Broach	When a sailing vessel loses control of its motion and is forced into a sudden sharp turn, often heeling heavily and in smaller vessels sometimes leading to a capsize. The change in direction is called *broaching-to*. Occurs when

too much sail is set for a strong gust of wind, or in circumstances where the sails are unstable.

Bulwark or Bulward (/ˈbʊlək/ in nautical use)	
	The extension of the ship's side above the level of the weather deck.
Capsize	When a ship or boat lists too far and rolls over, exposing the keel. On large vessels, this often results in the sinking of the ship.
Cats paws	Light variable winds on calm waters producing scattered areas of small waves.
Cockpit	The seating area (not to be confused with Deck). The area towards the stern of a small decked vessel that houses the rudder controls.
Cuddy	A small cabin in a boat.
Displacement	The weight of water displaced by the immersed volume of a ship's hull, exactly equivalent to the weight of the whole ship.
Draft or draught (both /ˈdrɑːft/)	
	The depth of a ship's keel below the waterline.
Drogue /ˈdroʊg/	A device to slow a boat down in a storm so that it does not speed excessively down the slope of a wave and crash into the next one. It is generally constructed of heavy flexible material in the shape of a cone.
Fender	An air or foam filled bumper used in boating to keep boats from banging into docks or each other.
Fluke	The wedge-shaped part of an anchor's arms that digs into the bottom.
Freeboard	The height of a ship's hull (excluding superstructure) above the waterline. The vertical distance from the current waterline to the lowest point on the highest continuous watertight deck. This usually varies from one part to another.
Gaff rigged	A boat rigged with a four-sided fore-and-aft sail with its upper edge supported by a spar or *gaff* which extends aft from the mast.
Gunwale /ˈgʌnəl/	Upper edge of the hull.

Jib	A triangular staysail at the front of a ship.
Lanyard	A rope that ties something off.
Lee shore	A shore downwind of a ship. A ship which cannot sail well to windward risks being blown onto a lee shore and grounded.
Leeway	The amount that a ship is blown leeward by the wind.
Magnetic north	The direction towards the North Magnetic Pole. Varies slowly over time.
Nautical mile	A unit of length corresponding approximately to one minute of arc of latitude along any meridian arc. By international agreement it is exactly 1,852 metres (approximately 6,076 feet).
Overfalls	Dangerously steep and breaking seas due to opposing currents and wind in a shallow area, or strong currents over a shallow rocky bottom.
Pintle	The pin or bolt on which a ships rudder pivots. The pintle rests in the gudgeon.
Pitchpole	To capsize a boat stern over bow, rather than by rolling over.
Point	A unit of bearing equal to one thirty-second of a circle, i.e., 11.25°. A turn of 32 points is a complete turn through 360°.
Port	The left side of the boat. Towards the left-hand side of the ship facing forward (formerly Larboard). Denoted with a red light at night.
Reef	1. Reefing: To temporarily reduce the area of a sail exposed to the wind, usually to guard against adverse effects of strong wind or to slow the vessel. 2. Reef: Rock or coral, possibly only revealed at low tide, shallow enough that the vessel will at least touch if not go aground.
Rowlock /ˈrɒlək/	A bracket providing the fulcrum for an oar. Also see *thole*.
Rudder	A steering device which can be placed aft, externally relative to the keel or compounded into the keel either independently or as part of the bulb/centerboard.
Sampson post	A strong vertical post used to support a ship's windlass and the heel of a ship's bowsprit.
Sculling	A method of using oars to propel watercraft in which the oar or oars touch the water on both the port and starboard sides of the craft, or over the stern. On sailboats with